Doctoring the Novel

Doctoring the Novel

Medicine and Quackery from Shelley to Doyle

SYLVIA A. PAMBOUKIAN

Ohio University Press
Athens

Ohio University Press, Athens, Ohio 45701
ohioswallow.com
© 2012 by Ohio University Press
All rights reserved

To obtain permission to quote, reprint, or otherwise reproduce
or distribute material from Ohio University Press publications, please
contact our rights and permissions department at (740) 593-1154 or
(740) 593-4536 (fax).

Cover art from istockphoto.com

Printed in the United States of America
Ohio University Press books are printed on acid-free paper ⊗ ™

20 19 18 17 16 15 14 13 12   5 4 3 2 1

Library of Congress Cataloging-in-Publication Data
Pamboukian, Sylvia A.
 Doctoring the novel : medicine and quackery from Shelley to Doyle /
Sylvia A. Pamboukian.
    p. cm.
 Includes bibliographical references and index.
 ISBN 978-0-8214-1990-8 (hc : acid-free paper) — ISBN 978-0-8214-
4406-1 (electronic)
 1. English fiction—19th century—History and criticism. 2. Literature
and medicine—Great Britain—History—19th century. 3. Quacks and
quackery in literature. 4. Physicians in literature. I. Title.
 PR890.M42P36 2012
 823'.92093561—dc23
                    2011053206

This book is dedicated to my mother, Mary, and to my father, Ben, who many years ago walked with me to the library during the summer holidays and told me the most fantastic stories. It is also dedicated to my husband, Jon, and to my daughter, Alina, to whom we tell stories now. May she remember her childhood stories as fondly as I remember mine.

Contents

Preface

How do we know whether a literary representation of a medical practitioner signifies authority or foolishness, science or irrationality, compassion or self-interest, orthodoxy or quackery? Scenes involving medical practitioners are common in nineteenth-century novels and are frequently addressed in criticism about this period, often taken as signs of medicine's social power and science's dominant epistemology. Do these representations celebrate medicine as the symbol of emerging professionalism or satirize it as the sign of human overreaching, vanity, and folly? During the nineteenth century, British medicine was a vast and complicated marketplace that included devices such as the stethoscope, pharmaceuticals such as ether, and practices such as antisepsis that would become recognized as breakthroughs. At the same time, other practices such as hydropathy (water cures) and teetotaling and products such as patent medicines and arsenic were widespread and popular, prescribed by trained and untrained, licensed and unlicensed practitioners alike. It is tempting to celebrate the breakthroughs and deride the rest as quackery, but without the benefit of hindsight or the now-familiar procedures of training and licensure, defining quackery is a tricky task. What words indicated medical orthodoxy or quackery to nineteenth-century readers? What tropes did medical institutions and practitioners deploy to generate an aura of respectability and trust, what I call orthodoxy? Which words resisted categorization as either orthodox or quack, and which shifted from orthodox to quack or vice versa? How did notions of orthodoxy and quackery alter in relation to emerging medical subfields such as pharmacy and to cultural currents such as nationalism, gender, and class?

The first chapter examines the meaning of the word *anatomy* in Mary Shelley's *Frankenstein* (1831) and in early nineteenth-century culture. Since Ruth Richardson's groundbreaking *Death, Dissection and the Destitute,* critics have viewed the Anatomy Act of 1832, which mandated the donation of bodies of workhouse paupers to medical schools for dissection, as a sign of the medical profession's increasing prestige, a symbol of bourgeois medicine's exploitation of the poor, and evidence of modern medicine's

x   union with science. In contrast, this chapter argues that *Frankenstein* displays the complex significations of the word *anatomy* during the early nineteenth century, when it sometimes connoted scientific proficiency and competence and sometimes connoted incivility, ignorance, and misconduct. In matters of burking, especially, anatomists were openly called quacks because they were seen as either complicit with murderers or pretenders to knowledge they did not in fact possess. In place of Richardson's repressive hypothesis, this chapter discovers the limitations of medico-legal forces to define either orthodoxy or quackery because of the unruly nature of language, which allows the same term to connote both.

Chapter 2 examines the double meaning of "doctoring" in two novels by Charles Dickens, *Little Dorrit* (1857) and *Bleak House* (1853). The word *doctor* means both to falsify and to heal, and thus this word yokes orthodoxy and quackery together by hinting that within orthodox doctoring lies always the potential for fraud. Dickens's novels appeared at a time when professional medicine was attempting to distance itself from quackery through measures such as the Medical Act of 1858. What is remarkable about this pairing of novels is Dickens's displacement of fraud onto other professions and the shared language of Christian heroics, language also deployed in contemporary medical and public accounts of medicine. Although critics (and even contemporary commentators) often link medicine's increasing prestige to scientific breakthroughs, this chapter challenges the fallacies that distinguishing between quackery and orthodoxy depended largely on science and that bourgeois professionals were a united group, since medicine in these novels benefited from Dickens's critique of other professions.

We explore next the relationship between professionalism, masculinity, and nationalism in Charlotte Brontë's *Villette* (1853). Dr. John Graham Bretton appears at first glance to embody professionalism, bourgeois values, and Englishness. However, chapter 3 views John in the context of midcentury concerns about "professional quackery," or quack practices by orthodox practitioners, and argues that John signals to readers the permeable nature of boundaries between quackery and orthodoxy, Englishness and foreignness, and masculinity and femininity. The novel appeared at a time when reformers were calling for ever-more-stringent boundaries on the behavior of orthodox practitioners in an effort to contain perceived rampant quackery, but Brontë suggests that considerable linguistic and narrative trickery was required to maintain such boundaries. John's professional quackery may signal the failure not only of the boundary between orthodoxy and quackery but also of those very important categories Lucy claims he defends: Englishness, masculinity, and truth.

From practitioners, we turn to Wilkie Collins's 1866 novel, *Armadale*, and the contemporary debates about poisons in chapter 4. Critics claim that this novel borrowed from the sensational newspaper and periodical coverage of female domestic poisoners; although this is true to an extent, the chapter argues that notorious poisoning trials constituted only a small part of Collins's engagement with the long-standing, high-stakes, medico-legal debate over the very nature of drugs. In the Select Committee reports on the 1857 Poisons Act and the 1865 Chemists and Druggists Bill, various substances—including arsenic (which was used for treating cholera), opium, and alcohol—were simultaneously considered medicines, poisons, industrial chemicals, and pesticides. The novel depicts the dangers of such substances because they challenge official control through their multiple identities. Far from merely exploiting poisoning for sensation, *Armadale* displays the complex manner in which the word *poison* came to be defined by Victorian culture.

Chapter 5 explores quackery in two works by Victorian physician Arthur Conan Doyle: the Sherlock Holmes story "The Adventure of the Speckled Band" (1892) and the medical novel *The Stark Munro Letters* (1895). Whereas earlier chapters depict struggles against quackery, this chapter explores quackery as a necessary part of everyday medical practice. Although Holmes famously champions science and reason, Doyle depicts Holmes and Munro as deeply invested in deception and pretense, struggling to distinguish between the laudable deception of polite practice and the improper deception of quackery. In both texts, a little quackery might be necessary for successful practice, but its deceptions may all too easily slide down a slippery slope toward manipulation, exploitation, fraud, and even murder. In this way, Doyle offers a unique view of quackery as integral to orthodox practice because of medicine's inherent uncertainty and ambiguity.

The conclusion, "The In-Laws: Orthodoxy and Quackery in *Vernon Galbray*," examines a narrative of quackery unmasked, identifies the repetitive features of this genre, and suggests alternate configurations of the quackery/orthodoxy binary.

Acknowledgments

Research for this book began several years ago at the Historical Library of the College of Physicians of Philadelphia with the generous support of an F. C. Wood Fellowship, for which I was and am very grateful. My research continued in Pittsburgh because of two invaluable Faculty Fellowships from Robert Morris University. In my archival research, I have enjoyed the assistance of wonderful library staff, including Ed Morman at the Wood Institute and Jonathan Erlen at the History of Medicine collection of the Falk Library of the Health Sciences at the University of Pittsburgh. Without the expertise of these and other librarians, the nineteenth-century voices in this project might have been lost.

Many of my colleagues have been instrumental in the development of this project, especially the always-supportive Victorian studies faculty at Indiana University, including Patrick Brantlinger, Ivan Kreilkamp, and Joss Marsh. For their generous assistance during the seemingly interminable publication process, I must thank Sara Newman, Matthew Ramsey, and Michael A. Flannery. For their help during the final phase of revision, including an eleventh-hour retooling of the title, I thank Paul Robichaud, Allen Salerno, and Steven McLean, as well as David Jamison, wizard of the Bluebook. Finally, the two anonymous readers at Ohio University Press provided me with very detailed and thought-provoking responses, and I am grateful to them for encouraging me in the homestretch.

Over the past few years, I have presented sections of several chapters at conferences, and I must thank the organizers and attendees of these panels who encouraged me to develop short papers into full chapters. I presented a section of the *Armadale* chapter in 2007 at the British Society for the History of Science conference in Manchester on the "Poisonous Perspectives" panel, which was held very early on a Sunday morning, and I would like to thank the members of that doughty panel: Amanda Caleb, Andrew Mangham, Ian Burney, and Bettina Wahrig. I also presented a section of this chapter at the 2008 North American Victorian Studies Associations conference at Yale, and I must thank the respondent on the "Poisoning" panel, George Robb, for his insightful comments. I would like to thank Jack Truten for organizing the panel xiv "Exploring the Text" at the 2010 Pennsylvania Medical History Consortium conference in Philadelphia, where I presented a section from my then-developing Doyle chapter.

I am very fortunate to have had the support of my family and friends during this long process. I would not have been able to complete this project without the encouragement of my friends Andrea and Shannon; my sister, Salpy; my nieces Emily and Ava; my brother, Paul; and my parents, Mary and Ben, whose enthusiasm has been unflagging. This project has taken too much time away from my partner, Jon, and my daughter, Alina, but I hope that they know how much joy they daily bring into my life. This book is about deception, confusion, and insincerity, but in my family and friends, I know I have the genuine article.

Introduction

False Professions
Defining Orthodoxy and Quackery

> A quack is someone else. The sentence "I am a quack" is
> one that has rarely, if ever, been spoken or written.
>
> —William H. Helfand, *Quack, Quack, Quack*, 2002

> Now we have no desire to draw down condemnation
> upon ourselves for letting the guilty escape, simply be-
> cause the delinquent may belong to our own order. We,
> who fearlessly, in the discharge of our public duty, mete
> out no measured castigation to those beyond our pale
> for their vulgar and unbecoming practices, must not be
> less fastidious and less sensitive to derelictions against
> propriety, when the latter are committed within our own
> professional circuit.
>
> —From "The Profession and Its Dignity," *Lancet*, 1858

In one dramatic scene in Charlotte Brontë's *Jane Eyre*, Mr.
Rochester leaves Jane to nurse his guest, the bleeding,
traumatized Mr. Mason, on the third floor of Thornfield Hall after a
mysterious midnight incident in which Mason is stabbed and bitten.
After a long, dark night sponging Mason's bloody wounds, Jane is re-
lieved when Rochester returns with the surgeon, Carter, who dresses
Mason's wounds, then prepares to accompany Mason from the house.
As he dresses Mason for this journey, Rochester sends Jane to his own

1

2   bedroom to fetch a cordial, which he administers to Mason under Carter's nose: "Now, doctor, I shall take the liberty of administering a dose myself; on my own responsibility. I got this cordial at Rome, of an Italian charlatan—a fellow you would have kicked, Carter. It is not a thing to be used indiscriminately, but it is good upon occasion: as now, for instance. Jane, a little water."¹

In Rochester's pithy statement, Brontë illuminates the dynamic relationship between Victorian medicine and quackery. At first, Rochester's description of the Italian charlatan seems to draw a clear boundary between proper English medicine, as embodied by Carter, and foreign quackery, as represented by the Italian. That Rochester expects Carter to *kick* the Italian charlatan clarifies which pole of this binary Rochester considers prestigious and privileged, although whether this privilege derives from Carter's expertise, from his nationality, or from his religion is unclear (the cordial comes specifically from Rome, the center of Roman Catholicism). At the same time, Carter is not so prestigious that he can object to Rochester's conduct; on the contrary, Carter submits silently to being cast aside by this amateur physician in favor of an admitted quack remedy. In this, Carter parallels the obedient Jane, who unquestioningly provides Rochester with the required water. Both governess and surgeon are addressed fairly courteously by this member of the landed gentry but are expected to obey—and they do. However, Rochester's clear boundary between foreign quackery and English orthodoxy is somewhat muddied by his simultaneous distrust of the cordial (it is not to be used indiscriminately, and he takes responsibility for misadventure) and valuing of it (it is good upon this occasion). Indeed, Mason perks up following administration of the cordial, and thus we must assume, as Rochester does, that this foreign, Catholic, quack, possibly dangerous remedy is as effective as, or more effective than, Carter's orthodox, English, presumably Protestant treatments. Finally, Brontë emphasizes the murky nature of medical reliability by putting this speech in Rochester's mouth: can we trust Rochester's evaluation of quackery at all, given Rochester's love of questionable shenanigans, as readers have already discovered during his charade as a gypsy fortune-teller and as we will discover again at his wedding?

Although brief, this incident raises questions that perplexed the medical profession and Victorian society generally throughout the nineteenth century. What is the medical practitioner's place in the social hierarchy? What is the appropriate role of amateurs in medicine? What is the relationship between amateurism, quackery, and orthodoxy? How can orthodox practitioners assert professional standards of care? How can one discriminate between a quack remedy and an orthodox remedy, if not, as in the case of the Italian cordial, on the basis of efficacy alone? What limitations should be placed on quack (or home?) remedies without infringing upon patients' freedom of choice and the free market? From what viewpoint may one judge such matters fairly? In October 1885, Richard Quain, M.D., F.R.C.P., and F.R.S., addressed similar issues in the annual Royal College of Physicians' Harveian Oration. The Harveian Oration embodies tradition through its very name, which honors the discoverer of the circulation of the blood, William Harvey; through its nature as a prestigious, annual event; and through its genre, since oratory is associated with classical, gentlemanly education. Quain acknowledges this tradition by praising the "long roll" of previous speakers who, since 1656, "have been highly distinguished, not only in the annals of our College, but also in the still wider annals of English science and literature."[2] After admiring recent speakers for their "patient research," "philosophic spirit," and "eloquent and impressive manner," Quain proposes to address the state of medicine in 1885: "Why is Medicine depreciated? . . . Why is it that, amongst a vast number of persons, alike in ancient and in modern times, medicine has not enjoyed that high estimate of its value, as an art and as a science, to which it is justly entitled? . . . Why then is it that, both in ancient and modern times, medicine has been so often regarded with skepticism and want of confidence, and so often treated with satire and even with contempt?"[3] Quain's description of medicine's public image seems at odds with the ceremonial nature of his oration, because the former associates the audience members with a lowbrow activity while the latter implies the opposite. The description of physicians' professional woes echoes the surgeon Carter's situation in *Jane Eyre* as both an orthodox practitioner who embodies Englishness and respectability and a lackey who is caught between a Catholic, Italian charlatan and an amateur practitioner-gentlemen. Although Quain implies that the Harveian Oration is a part of a great tradition practiced by great physicians in the name of a particularly great man, he states openly that medicine is, and has always been, the subject of ridicule and skepticism: "Evidence of the existence of such doubt, both in the past and in the present, is to be found in the judgments of men of science, not excluding indeed members of our own profession; in the sarcasms of dramatists and satirists; and still more in the daily action and behaviour

4   of the sick, who by submitting themselves to the treatment and by accepting the nostrums of charlatans and quacks, in the same spirit in which they would have recourse to our own aid, manifest the equal esteem in which they hold us all."[4] Like Rochester, Quain unhesitatingly applies the label *charlatan*, but, like Rochester, he cannot maintain this binary. In this passage, Quain uses quackery as a foil for his own profession, an opposing pole to set against a single, great, medical tradition descending from Harvey through the Harveian orators to himself (presumably). Yet the next section of Quain's speech complicates this binary by introducing another, incompatible model of medical orthodoxy. Where he began with a model physician as a gentleman-orator, Quain concludes with the model physician as a man of science. In *Jane Eyre*, the gentleman trumps the trained physician, but in Quain's speech the gentlemanly physician emerges as the less-desirable model.

The latter portion of this speech defines the modern medical profession almost entirely according to scientific criteria, and this definition seems to suppress the earlier, more literary and gentlemanly, model. Quain describes medicine's "path of uninterrupted progress" from the superstition and ignorance of the ancients through the emergence of great men of science such as the Hunters, Sydenham, and, of course, Harvey to the contemporary state of practice, which is rich with new scientific devices (he mentions the microscope, thermometer, stethoscope, ophthalmoscope, laryngoscope, and cardiograph) and new drugs (he includes morphine, nitrous oxide, nitroglycerine, chloral hydrate, quinine, and salicin). Quain concludes that "we must not only claim to have replaced blind groping along the pathways of knowledge by a method based on reason and observation, in which we recognize the nature of our ignorance as well as the extent of our acquirements; but, as exponents of a practical science, we are bound to show that our progress has been real."[5] If science is "real" progress, then what of the earlier model of gentlemanly medicine, which is now apparently lumped in with the superstitious and ignorant past? Are gentlemanly physicians now quacks, despite their social dominance and public prestige? Are all modern technologies and drugs evidence of progress and professionalism, regardless of who wields them or how they function?

As members of a culture that likewise places great weight on scientific epistemologies, we may similarly approach medicine through binaries such as quack and orthodox, literary and scientific, historical and progressive. But these binaries limit our ability to analyze nineteenth-century models of quackery, to account for quackery's persistence, and to recognize permutations within medical orthodoxy that verge on or are quackery, giving us a false notion of the medical profession's status, unity, and power. As Peter Stallybrass and Allon White assert, high and low are only mistaken for opposites: "The top attempts to reject and eliminate the bottom for reasons of prestige and status, only to discover, not only that it is in some way frequently dependant upon that low-Other . . . but also that the top includes that low symbolically."[6] Indeed, the low may serve the interests of the high in unexpected and necessary ways, since the top derives "imaginative sustenance from precisely those groups, practices, and activities which it was earnestly and relentlessly working to marginalize and destroy."[7] Similarly, Roger Cooter identifies the interrelationship between orthodoxy and quackery in nineteenth-century medicine in the support of so-called fringe practices by orthodox practitioners and in the highly respected and lucrative nature of many fringe practices.[8] This is not to disregard the considerable scientific activity of the nineteenth century, which has been amply canvassed by earlier historians of medicine. For example, Erwin H. Ackerknecht's *Short History of Medicine* devotes eight out of twenty chapters to the discoveries of nineteenth-century medical science, including areas such as abdominal surgery, antisepsis, microbiology, public health, pharmacology, pathology, and physiology. Similarly, Lilian R. Furst devotes a chapter entitled "From Speculation to Science" in her reader *Medical Progress and Social Reality* to describing medical legislation and scientific breakthroughs of this period, although Furst qualifies her narrative of progress with the contentions that breakthroughs were slow to reach patients and that many physicians were suspicious of science.[9] Even Quain himself admits that unscientific attitudes and practices persisted in the nineteenth century because there is an "inherent tendency of the human mind to accept the marvelous and supernatural, [and] to court deception" and because science, "whilst lighting up a path for the few, left the masses untouched."[10] Although there were indeed great discoveries in nineteenth-century medical science, we should not, as Quain does, dismiss the complexities of medical orthodoxy and quackery during a century in which, as Brontë shows, medicine was practiced daily in very complicated and certainly unscientific circumstances.

Moving beyond the commonplaces that medicine is an art and that quackery is notoriously difficult to define, this study examines specific configurations of quackery in literature beyond the knee-jerk definitions

6   of quackery as a lack of scientific knowledge or as bizarre practices by strange practitioners. Instead, it explores the ways in which cultural formations in the public sphere generate notions of orthodoxy and quackery and what is at stake in these processes. Despite science's emergence as a dominant epistemology during the nineteenth century, analyzing literature offers an avenue into a professional field that was simultaneously high and low, liberal and scientific, and professional and tradesman-like. If multiple configurations of medical orthodoxy and quackery coexisted and interacted with each other, then the boundaries of quackery and orthodoxy cannot be reduced to simple breaches of scientific theory. Instead, the very notions of regular, acceptable, progressive, what I call orthodox, practice and of quack practices must be determined by a variety of cultural codes, despite Quain's assertion that science alone defines modern medicine. In this ongoing and dynamic game of definition, medicine and quackery are not preformed categories developed in the laboratory and implemented in the wider culture but are woven using a variety of threads: medical, scientific, legislative, sociological, economic, and literary.

Words, Words, Words

Where Quain uses words such as *profession, medicine,* and *science* to delineate his own practices (and those of which he approves), he uses terms such as *charlatan, quack,* and *nostrum* to describe his opposition and its treatments. As William H. Helfand's epigraph to this chapter aptly states, the word *quack* is always a pejorative, an epithet to be thrown at the opposition, a word of undesirable connotation. Yet, as the second epigraph shows, medical reformers realized that conduct and practices that could be identified as improper, inappropriate, and even quack originated from within the College itself, as Roger Cooter's work confirms.[11] In the second epigraph, the word *delinquent* describes those trained and professional men who follow the "vulgar" and "unbecoming" conduct of those "beyond our pale." The issue of language here is not trivial. We cannot take for granted terms such as *professional, quack, unbecoming, propriety,* and *vulgar,* because these terms imply fixed, generally acknowledged boundaries between proper practitioners and improper charlatans and between effective, safe treatments and ineffective or dangerous products. That is not the case. If a well-trained, socially prominent College member, one who seems to be, in my term, *orthodox,* behaves unbecomingly or vulgarly, he can become like those (or indeed one of those?) beyond the pale. The term *quack*, although always pejorative in connotation, requires additional explanation in practice since quackery seems to derive not from technical incompetence, weak social position, or lack of professional registration but from some other criteria, which seem to be assumed rather than explicitly stated. Thus, we should accept the terms *orthodoxy* and *quackery* as only the beginning of this process of analysis, not the ending, since both terms derive from a continual negotiation between various discourses rather than from set definitions or checklists. The following chapters examine the mechanisms through which orthodoxy and quackery are defined as cultural and linguistic categories and describe the consequences of labeling certain groups, individuals, and practices as proper or improper, authentic or fraudulent, appropriate or inappropriate.[12]

It could be argued that words such as *quackery* and *orthodoxy* (and their various synonyms: *charlatan, fraud, irregular, fringe* and *professional, regular, scientific, progressive*, respectively) ought to be defined by scientists alone. After all, isn't the heart of quackery scientific ignorance or at least misrepresentation? According to Edward Schiappa, the definition of a scientific word (*orthodoxy? quackery?*) should not be limited in this way, because even so-called scientific language is as much cultural as scientific. Schiappa critiques the "belief that the objects of our world (including language) are simply 'there' and can be taken for granted."[13] Instead, Schiappa asserts that "it is more productive and ethical to see definitional disputes as a matter of competing interests, while insisting that some interests are better than others. Accordingly, the questions we ask are 'Whose interests are being served by a particular definition?' and 'Do we want to identify with those interests?'"[14] In his study of the word *wetlands* (as opposed to *swamp, bog, marsh*, and so forth), Schiappa finds that arguments over scientific definitions are often expressed as binaries with scientists on one side and nonscientists on the other, but this binary is false, because of the interested nature of all parties and the lack of uniformity in either the scientific or the public position. From Schiappa's work one may infer that even scientific definitions are not merely conflicts between the "right" definition (that is, the one proposed by the scientists) and the "wrong" definitions (those proposed by nonscientific groups such as business people, government agencies, and public groups). On the contrary, there are conflicts between various scientific fields (for example, biologists and physicists), between government

8   agencies, and between various social groups (for example, manufacturers and conservationists). Schiappa's work reveals the importance of the wider culture in supposedly scientific debates, the self-interested and conflicted nature of all parties, and the stakes behind apparently trivial matters of naming.

Similarly, Thomas F. Gieryn recognizes the complexities of definitional disputes over so-called scientific words and concepts. Gieryn calls these "credibility contests" and describes them using the metaphor of a map, arguing that all parties locate themselves within the boundaries of science and banish their opponents to the fringe.[15] The benefits of winning a boundary dispute, according to Gieryn, include the "authority to make truth provisionally sustained" as well as "esteem," "influence," and "material resources."[16] In this model, scientific definitions are negotiated entities: "When considered as a cultural space constructed in boundary-work, science becomes local and episodic rather than universal; pragmatic and strategic rather than analytic or legislative; contingent rather than principled; constructed rather than essential."[17] Gieryn reveals the interrelated nature of these opposing territories, since both rely on the boundary between them and both have an interest in generating, maintaining, or shifting the boundary. Moreover, science's prestige is only enhanced by credibility contests, since claims of scientific legitimacy come from all sides.[18] In this, Gieryn emphasizes science as a dominant epistemology but recognizes that despite science's powerful cultural position, it is not a simple or self-evident term.

Neither Gieryn nor Schiappa examines literature, although both draw attention to issues of language. In "Plato's Pharmacy," Jacques Derrida examines the meaning of the word *pharmakon* in a text by Plato. Denoting at once drug, poison, and remedy, *pharmakon* is a tricky word, and translating *pharmakon* is no easy task because the term's many meanings are all active and relevant at any moment: "The translation by 'remedy' can thus be neither accepted nor simply rejected. Even if one intended thereby to save the 'rational' pole and the laudatory intention, the idea of the *correct* use of the *science* or *art* of medicine, one would still run every risk of being deceived by language."[19] In its attention to language, Derrida's work diminishes the false boundary between literary and nonliterary work, reminding us that language's play cannot be constrained by genre. Moreover, Derrida points to the chain of signification always at work, which destabilizes even the most apparently self-evident language. However, Derrida does not explore the consequences of his deconstruction of *pharmakon* for material practices, medical professionals, or legislation regarding medicine and pharmacy. Raymond Williams, in contrast, asserts that linguistic play has very high stakes because language is the stuff of hegemony. Williams reminds readers, "Language, then, is not a medium; it is a constitutive element of material social practice."[20] For Williams, language produces meaning as a "socially shared and reciprocal activity, already embedded in active relationships, within which every move is an activation of what is already shared and reciprocal or may become so." Accordingly, this study attempts to go, as Williams says, not "beyond" the literary work but "more thoroughly into its full (and not arbitrarily protected) expressive significance."[21] The very word *medicine* denotes simultaneously a profession and a chemical entity. A given compound is called a *medicine* if useful, a *poison* if harmful, or a *nostrum* if useless; however, in different doses the same compound may qualify for all three descriptions. Sold by a druggist, a given chemical (for example, arsenic) may be called a medicine, but sold in a dry goods store, the same chemical may be labeled a poison or, as in the case of oil of bitter almonds, perhaps even a flavoring or foodstuff. What words signified medical orthodoxy or quackery in Victorian culture? What linguistic strategies were deployed by various parties in boundary disputes? What slippages or play of language complicated or frustrated efforts at defining medical quackery or orthodoxy?

Defining Quackery

Despite the Victorian emphasis on regulation through professional associations, journals, and legislation, quackery remained a vexed topic. Within the medical professions, there was a drive throughout the nineteenth century to define orthodoxy expressly for the purpose of identifying and combating quackery. For example, this period witnessed the founding of the British Medical Association (1832), Pharmaceutical Society of Great Britain (later Royal Pharmaceutical Society) (1841), and British Dental Association (1880). At the same time, Parliament undertook lengthy debates over several pieces of legislation aimed at defining, tabulating, and regulating the medical professions and at setting standards for the handling, sales, and labeling of pharmaceuticals. The former include the Apothecaries Act of 1815, the Medical Act of 1858, and the Pharmacy Act of 1868, and the latter include the Arsenic Act of 1851 and the Poisons Act of 1857, along with other, unsuccessful bills.

10   W. F. Bynum and Roy Porter credit the Medical Act of 1858 with bringing about an end to the quack practices that thrived in the unregulated eighteenth- and early nineteenth-century medical marketplace, because it created a register of licensed physicians, a list that allowed the public to discriminate for the first time between the trained and untrained, between those registered with an official establishment and those not registered.[22] As we will see in later chapters, this legislation was touted at the time as the death knell of quackery in Britain. However, legislation alone cannot eradicate quackery, because it may come from high as well as low social stations and from within the ranks of the establishment itself. In later chapters, we will see that even the medical witnesses before these legislative committees did not maintain a uniform point of view about what constituted either sound or poor practice. Porter accounts for the Medical Act's failure to stem quackery: "To the chagrin of GPs however, the practice of healing by non-registered doctors was in no way made illegal. Parliament knew that any such ban would have been exceedingly unpopular with the public and anyway utterly impossible to enforce."[23]

The importance of lay (quack?) practitioners (such as Mr. Rochester) cannot be overemphasized in this era of "self-help," a term popularized by Samuel Smiles's best-selling account of great men who rose to prominence through individual effort.[24] If this period was the heyday of scientific breakthroughs, as Quain asserts, it was also the heyday of self-help, and these practices, particularly by high-status individuals, complicate our understanding of quackery. Michael Neve provocatively labels patient self-help a species of quackery.[25] Conversely, an article in the *Westminster Review* complains about physicians who "longingly anticipate the time when mothers shall be forbidden to administer Caster Oil and Godfrey's Cordial to their children without their sanction."[26] Where Rochester's cordial appears to be quackery provided by a charlatan (an Italian charlatan, no less), the mothers' patent medicines appear perfectly respectable (orthodox?) to the writer of the *Westminster Review*, if not to physicians who wished to curtail the number of patent medicines sold by druggists to the public. Is this an interprofessional gripe in which mothers stand in for the real competition, druggists? Or is this fear of amateurism's (specifically, female amateurism?) usurping professional authority or genuinely endangering patients? Is this a sentimental view of motherhood? As we will see in later chapters, patent medicines remained in a contentious borderland throughout much of the century. Michael Flannery asserts that professional power was limited because

the public could draw medicines and practices into the realm of orthodoxy by deeming them respectable, appropriate, and effective.[27] Flannery
identifies this "populist impulse in medicine" as dating from the early
modern period and deriving in some measure from Evangelicalism, and
he points to the repeated printings of Nicholas Culpeper's seventeenth-
century pharmacopeia for laypeople as proof of patients' desire to treat
themselves and each other.[28] The influence of religion on Victorian amateurism (and quackery?) can hardly be overemphasized, but, as we will
see in later chapters, it is also a key component in medical orthodoxy's
struggle for prestige and power. Is self-treatment quackery or empower-
ment? How does amateurism in nineteenth-century medicine complicate the role of official, medical, and scientific discourses in delineating
orthodoxy and quackery? How does religious belief impact both quackery and orthodoxy?

If neither legislation nor professional groups define quackery, surely
we might have recourse to classification of medicines based on efficacy,
usage, and safety. On the contrary, P. S. Brown examines nineteenth-century
patent medicines and finds that they differed from regular prescriptions
"more in the context of their supply than in their composition."[29] Com-
monly dismissed as quackery, patent medicines, according to Brown,
employed ingredients found in orthodox prescriptions but were cheaper
and available without a prescription.[30] Thus, Brown concludes that the
"fringe" was "a matter both of medical theory and of social boundaries."[31] Similarly, K. Codell Carter finds that quacks and orthodox physicians employed similar medicines and expected similar results except
that only quacks were associated with secrecy and with advertising,
despite the common practice of both advertising and secrecy by members of the various colleges.[32] William H. Helfand recognizes the relative nature of quackery in his epigraph to this chapter and the passage
beyond: "A quack is someone else. The sentence 'I am a quack' is one
that has rarely, if ever, been spoken or written. One accuses others of
practicing quackery when their methods are not considered proper, are
not sufficiently scientific, or possibly might be considered deceitful or
dishonest. It is thus effortlessly applied to rivals whose competitive systems might encroach on the activities of the accuser."[33] Helfand clarifies
later that "quack is a pejorative term, disparagingly, albeit sometimes
defensively, applied by a member of the establishment, the orthodox,
regular, professional, credentialed and accepted class to describe the
unorthodox, unlicensed, disapproved member of the fringe or irregular

12   group."[34] Similarly, Irvine Loudon claims, "At every level the individual shouts 'Quack!' to all below him," yet Loudon asserts that well-trained practitioners and even clergymen sometimes "adopted the manners and appearances of the quack," which implies that quackery is identified through social behaviors, not efficacy or safety of treatment.[35] Credentials, social class, advertising, secrecy, cost of goods, and vulgarity all conspire to create a sense of the quack and the quack product as inauthentic medicine, yet quackery cannot be reduced to a laundry list.[36] Bynum and Porter's introduction to *Medical Fringe and Medical Orthodoxy* argues that quackery and orthodoxy are deeply interdependent, and in *Quacks: Fakers and Charlatans in Medicine*, Porter asserts that the history of quackery requires an understanding of the history of orthodoxy, particularly "the place of the doctor, and the resonances of the healing arts, in society."[37] In some measure, this study aims at fulfilling this gap by exploring representations of orthodoxy and quackery in fiction as interdependent, negotiated entities highly dependent on linguistic and cultural categories.

False Professions

In George Eliot's *Middlemarch*, Lady Chettam disparages medical men as "more on a footing with the servants."[38] Like Mr. Rochester, Lady Chettam asserts the power of social rank over scientific accomplishment and medical training in determining the status of a medical practitioner. While social status seems unrelated to professional status, we must question what weight Lady Chettam might place on the directions of a practitioner who is a mere servant to her and wonder about her probability of seeking alternative (quack?) or amateur therapies. The professional consequences of such attitudes are bewailed by Richard Quain in his Harveian Oration, since he views them as fostering quackery and damaging his profession. However, tempering readers' sense of Lady Chettam's assertion as trustworthy is her status in the novel as an unsympathetic character, particularly next to medical practitioner Tertius Lydgate. Far from advocating Lady Chettam's opinion, Eliot may be undermining the privileging of rank over medical training by association. That Eliot is intervening in a cultural dispute over the place of medical practitioners is clear not only from Quain's complaint about patients who conflate quacks with professionals but also from similar material in the medical press. For example, a letter in the *Lancet* asserts that "a physician's wife was spoken of as 'not visitable.'"[39] Being "not visitable" might seem trivial and hardly worth mention in a professional journal, but it might also reveal the profession's concern about social status and its relationship to professional power. In Lady Chettam's brief aside, Eliot seems to be both drawing upon and shaping the terms of this debate, as surely as the physician writing to the *Lancet* or Richard Quain, since her widely circulating novel not only presents the issue but also seems to advocate increasing the status of medical professionals who, like Lydgate, are gentlemanly, well educated, and technically proficient.

In its broad canvass, *Middlemarch* unites social concerns, professional development, political conflict, and domestic life. Like *Jane Eyre*, it weaves together a variety of points of view and disparate cultural formations. Because of this ability, novels offer an avenue into the mechanisms that determine the readers' sense of the authentic or inauthentic in medicine, because this sense itself derives from many seemingly disparate venues: scientific institutions, such as laboratories, universities, and scientific societies; official bodies, such as legislatures and professional associations; trade and public discourse, including advertising, manufacturers, and shop owners; and private relationships including families and friends, whose anecdotes may be more persuasive than any official registration. As in the examples of Rochester and Lady Chettam, novels allow us to explore the ambiguities of day-to-day medical encounters in specific circumstances. In his impressive work on eighteenth- and early nineteenth-century smallpox, David E. Shuttleton calls for more literary analysis of medical themes, since lack of it leaves criticism as a whole "impoverished, in so far as they [critics] have both tended to down-play the role of the literary imagination in the cultural framing of disease."[40] In contrast, Shuttleton's work displays the benefits of attending to the interplay between scientific, medical, artistic, and literary discourses when he uncovers the power of the literary imagination in both public and medical views of smallpox's nature, origin, prognosis, and consequences. While our focus is on quackery and orthodoxy in fiction, this cannot be an exhaustive survey of literature involving medical themes because (as will become clear) of the prominence of such themes in nineteenth-century literature, nor does it include American or continental texts, although such work would be a valuable addition to this topic. Instead, I examine the specific medical encounters in novels almost as case studies that in their specific circumstances, test, dispute, or reimagine the boundaries of proper or improper medical care.

14   Literary and cultural critics influenced by Michel Foucault have traditionally emphasized medical orthodoxy's power, in some measure downplaying the issue of quackery.[41] For example, Mary Poovey's landmark *Uneven Developments* aligns medicine with patriarchy and views medical practitioners as authoritative and oppressive figures, particularly toward women. Her discussion of anesthetic in childbirth during the mid-Victorian period positions medicine as a discourse of power because of scientific advances in anesthesia, although Poovey shows that the use of chloroform was deeply impacted by religious and ontological views about the nature of women. Despite this reservation, Poovey asserts that the orthodox medical establishment waged a "territorial campaign" against women.[42] Poovey's depiction of Florence Nightingale similarly positions orthodox medicine as a hegemonic discourse that, even as it admits women into nursing, supports a constricting model of domesticity.[43] Several studies of fin-de-siècle culture also position orthodox medicine as a disciplinary power. For example, in *Vampires, Mummies, and Liberals: Bram Stoker and the Politics of Popular Fictions*, David Glover places Bram Stoker's works "at the center of a number of conflicted and conflicting currents," including sexology, phrenology, and criminal anthropology.[44] While Glover produces brilliant readings, what of Richard Quain's concern about medicine's lack of power, weak social position, and vulnerability before patients' whims? What of the failure of the Medical Act to stem quackery, as described by Porter, because of amateurism and free market economics? Where are the amateurs, gentlemen, Lady Bountifuls, and foreign and establishment quacks that even Parliament shrank from offending in the relatively toothless Medical Act of 1858?

Recent criticism on the subject of professionalism foregrounds struggles within the bourgeois professions themselves. For example, George Weisz's *Divide and Conquer: A Comparative History of Medical Specialization* argues that social currents favoring professionalization were responsible for the development of specialties in Victorian medicine, not, as asserted by several scholars, scientific developments.[45] Weisz identifies the unscientific nature of English medicine in particular: "Where continental hospitals prided themselves on the advancement of knowledge, [medical] elites in London prided themselves on their gentlemanliness, literacy, and morality."[46] As in Quain's address, there seems to be a division between gentlemanly and scientific models of medical orthodoxy, and Weisz notes that medical specialists, unwelcome in the hospital system, developed an outsider status and "could be easily dismissed as opportunistic interlopers, if not charlatans and quacks."[47] In this discussion, Weisz complicates the orthodoxy-quackery binary by showing that various models of professionalism (and unprofessionalism) circulated within medical culture itself. Critics examining Victorian professionalism in general similarly foreground the work of generating and maintaining the sense of authenticity that is the hallmark of the appropriate, the proper, what I call the orthodox. In addition, these studies foreground literature's role in shaping professional boundaries.[48] Perhaps because of their focus on professions other than medicine, these studies say little about quackery, fraud, or unprofessionalism in general.[49] For example, Amanda Anderson's excellent study complicates the concept of professionalism by examining various meanings of *detachment* in Victorian culture, a word that means "science, critical reason, disinterestedness, and realism, but also a set of practices of the self, ranging from stoicism to cosmopolitanism to dandyism."[50] Anderson argues that novels reflect Victorian ambivalence about the emergent professions and their ideal of detachment: "The dandy, the Jew, and the fallen woman, for example, respectively focused anxieties about ironic distance, rootlessness, and heightened exile, while the doctor, the writer, and the professional tended to represent the distinct promises of modernity: progressive knowledge, full comprehension of the social totality, and the possibilities of transformative self-understanding."[51] Anderson's approach seems fruitful; however, Anderson locates the doctor as a symbol of progressive modernity, where we will examine medicine as a more ambiguous field. Monica F. Cohen in *Professional Domesticity in the Victorian Novel: Women, Work and Home* examines the complexities of professionalism in literature about domesticity, arguing that for Victorians, amateurs who worked for vocation trumped professionals who worked for pay. Cohen offers a way to approach the nineteenth-century cult of amateurism and the power of Evangelicalism, although Cohen engages only minimally with medicine. The state of criticism is such that quackery has been addressed by historians of medicine, although without much attention to literature, and that professionalism has been addressed by literary critics, although without much attention to quackery. This study hopes to cross these boundaries.

This is not to downplay the serious consequences of disease, to claim that all medical practices are equal, or to argue that efforts to reduce medical misconduct are unimportant. On the contrary, the ways in which a culture frames illness prove vital in understanding its concept of

16   suffering. As Elaine Scarry asserts, suffering worsens if met with doubt or skepticism.[52] The purpose of this study is not to undervalue or disregard the material practices of medicine and their impact upon patients; quite the contrary, it acknowledges that attitudes, words, and behaviors can materially worsen or ameliorate suffering. Is this physician *really* knowledgeable? Will compounding by a druggist rather than a shopkeeper *really* prevent accidental poisonings and improve outcomes? Will this patent medicine *really* do what the bottle says it will? The answers to these questions are not unimportant to people whose health and lives are at stake, or to people living in the midst of a family or of a community struggling with the serious and very real consequences of disease. In some sense, the sick are already deeply aware of the definitional complexities surrounding quackery and orthodoxy, since these definitions guide (or frustrate) them as they search for legitimate, proper, effective, authentic (what I call orthodox) care, especially if they perceive that such care appears to others as quackery. Physicians, druggists, pharmacists, apothecaries, surgeons, and specialists are defined as orthodox against those called quacks. A practitioner within one of these orthodox disciplines who trespasses onto another's turf is also called a quack. Those within each discipline who act in ways deemed inappropriate are labeled quacks, too. Quackery is not just between the orthodox and the fringe but also between and within the orthodox professions themselves. In turning to novels, we hope to discover the ways in which questions about orthodoxy and quackery are framed and answered by nineteenth-century authors, who were themselves, of course, patients and sometimes practitioners of medicine.

Chapter One

Orthodoxy or Quackery?
Anatomy in *Frankenstein*

> [T]he degree of perfection with which anatomy has been studied at any successive periods, may be safely taken as the rule, by which the progress of all the other branches of the science may be ascertained.
>
> —"Regulation of Anatomy," *Westminster Review*, 1832

> [Resurrection Men are] the lowest dregs of degradation; I do not know that I can describe them better; there is no crime they would not commit, and as to myself, if they would imagine that I should make a good subject, they really would not have the smallest scruple, if they could do the thing undiscovered, to make a subject of me.
>
> —Sir Astley Cooper before the Select Committee on Anatomy, 1828

In 1828, the president of the Royal College of Surgeons, Sir Astley Cooper, testified before the Select Committee on Anatomy. Charged with inquiring into the state of anatomical research, the committee's report consists of questions by the legislators to various witnesses including surgeons, physicians, hospital authorities, magistrates, and resurrection men. Cooper, the first witness, begins by asserting anatomy's importance: "[I]t ought to be earnestly cultivated by those who really wish to understand their profession [surgery] and to become respectable in it."[1] Asked if a surgeon ought to perform a new

18   procedure without practicing first on a corpse, Cooper replies, "[H]e must be a blockhead if he made the attempt" (15). According to Cooper, anatomy benefits more than surgeons: "[T]he cause [anatomy] which you gentlemen are now supporting is not our cause, but your's [sic]; you must employ medical men, whether they be ignorant or informed; but if you have none but ignorant medical men, it is you who suffer from it" (16). To Cooper, anatomy connotes surgical competence, social respectability, and public benefit. However, Cooper laments the gap between his view and that of the general public, and he blames this gap in perception on the methods of procuring anatomical specimens: execution (legal) and exhumation (illegal), informally called resurrection, grave robbing, or body snatching.[2] He complains that "the anatomists of London were completely at the feet of the resurrection men," who obtained bodies from churchyards by clandestine exhumation or by bribery (17). In the epigraph to this chapter, Cooper calls resurrection men "the lowest dregs of degradation" and states, "I do not know that I can describe them better; there is no crime they would not commit, and as to myself, if they would imagine that I should make a good subject, they really would not have the smallest scruple, if they could do the thing undiscovered, to make a subject of me" (18). To Cooper, resurrection men are not only thieves but also potential murderers (they would *make* a "subject," or corpse, of him). On the whole, Cooper seems to view anatomy as the basis of progressive, scientific medicine, which connotes, to him, surgical competence and social benefit. He attaches anatomy's positive connotations to anatomy itself and offloads its negative connotations (criminality, degradation) to the mode of procuring specimens: hanging and body snatching. In doing so, Cooper minimizes his own criminality, since possession of a snatched body was a misdemeanor, and exaggerates the resurrection men's criminality (from thievery to murder).[3] Of course, Cooper was in the midst of asking Parliament to provide new avenues for obtaining specimens, so it is perhaps unsurprising that he credited Parliament with the ability to purge anatomy of its negative connotations, which, he argues, could be fairly easily jettisoned along with the practices of resurrection and of dissecting felons. For Cooper, *anatomy* connoted science, progress, professionalism, and beneficence because medico-legal discourse had determined its meaning, a meaning that he advocates as the standard for the public as a whole. Cooper's testimony exemplifies this often unspoken assumption that official discourses (legal, scientific, medical) determine the meaning of medical practices such as anatomy.

In her reading of *Frankenstein*, Ludmilla Jordanova contends that Mary Shelley's novel explores conflicts within science itself: "Far from being a simple moralistic tale of masculinist, scientific overreaching, drawing on simple definitions of 'science,' 'medicine' or 'surgery,' *Frankenstein* is a remarkably precise exploration of the internal conflicts felt by practitioners in a variety of fields."[4] The novel is not, Jordanova explains, a "direct critique of science" but an exploration of the "instability, uncertainty, ambiguity" of the emerging fields of "natural knowledge."[5] Jordanova's persuasive analysis stops short of addressing quackery, although she mentions "violent contests over definitions of 'quackery'" and identifies contemporary clichés about quacks.[6] For example, Jordanova cites contrasts between Hippocrates, the "good progenitor," and Galen, the "bad father," and between the "Benevolent Physician, who gives to his patients" and the "Rapacious Quack, who robs them."[7] Here, quackery seems easily recognizable by its "desire as greed for money, possessions and sexual domination."[8] This chapter builds upon Jordanova's contention that *Frankenstein* explores the instability of emergent scientific fields by reading the novel through the contemporary discourse of anatomy. However, anatomy complicates Jordanova's model of orthodoxy and quackery, because anatomy was a field considered simultaneously the foundation of the medical sciences and the site of gross misconduct and crime. Through rich description, this chapter recovers *anatomy*'s many meanings, both in the novel and in cultural documents, and discovers that *anatomy* is able to connote both orthodoxy and quackery simultaneously. In doing so, anatomy displays the slippery boundaries of quackery and the limitations of medico-legal discourse to determine the meaning of apparently simple, clear-cut medical concepts.

Often, *anatomy* and *dissection* are considered synonyms. The *Oxford English Dictionary* defines *anatomy* as "the process, subjects, and products of dissection of the body . . . ; dissection" and "the science of bodily structure."[9] In this definition, *anatomy* and *dissection* are more than mere synonyms because they share the same connotations, which is not the case for all synonyms.[10] For example, synonyms for *fat* include the cute *plump* or *chubby* and the pejorative *porcine* or *gross*, words with very different connotations despite their similar denotations. In contrast, the *OED*'s definitions of both *anatomy* and *dissection* partake in a constellation of prestigious connotations, such as science, biology, logic, reason, study, progress, education, knowledge, and enlightenment. That this constellation should appear in an official definition is perhaps unsurprising;

20   after all, Astley Cooper bestows similar connotations upon *anatomy*. However, this chapter uncovers another constellation in which *anatomy* signifies misconduct, greed, exploitation, ignorance, and crime. Despite Cooper's belief in the power of the medico-legal establishment to control language and hence meaning, the word *anatomy* displays the artificiality and fragility of the boundary between orthodoxy and quackery, since the very same term signifies both constellations of meaning at once. In arguing that multiple connotations function at all times, this chapter is drawing upon linguistics. For example, J. L. Austin asserts that words communicate more than facts (locutionary acts) and more than simple denotation. For example, the statement "This is a cup of tea" means just that fact based on the definitions of *tea* and *cup*, but it may also mean, for example, disputation (that is, I didn't order this!), emotion (I love tea!), or desire (How about some biscuits?). Illocutionary acts generate perlocutionary acts, for example, inspiring the waitress to take back the tea or a companion to get biscuits. While some of these acts are under the control of the speaker, not all of them are controllable or even foreseeable by the speaker. On the contrary, Austin points to the difficulty of grasping the intended meaning amidst the many available meanings in play. This chapter asserts that *anatomy* and other medico-scientific terms function in a similar manner and communicate multiple layers of meaning. Familiar from Saussurean linguistics, this approach to language is often applied to literary texts, but scientific works should not be excluded. Edward Schiappa describes a tendency to defer to scientists for the "real" meaning of scientific terms, but Schiappa points out that this deference is unjustifiable because it glosses over the lack of uniformity within the scientific community and the overlap between scientists and nonscientists. As this reading of *Frankenstein* will show, *anatomy* connotes contradictory concepts such as justice and cruelty, progress and barbarism, and orthodoxy and quackery in the novel because it carried these meanings in nineteenth-century culture. In this sense, *anatomy* is not a battleground between public and scientific or between orthodoxy and quackery, but an example of the difficulties of defining orthodoxy and quackery because of the complexities of meaning within medical language itself.

    Since the publication of Ruth Richardson's *Death, Dissection and the Destitute*, anatomy has attracted attention from historians, literary scholars, and cultural critics. Richardson argues persuasively that the dead body had many meanings during the early nineteenth century but that proponents of anatomy ruthlessly quashed many of them. For example, Richardson describes rituals that honored, comforted, and perhaps even saved the departed person's soul and attributes the public's strong, sometimes violent, opposition to anatomy to its interference with these rituals.[11] She asserts that the Anatomy Act of 1832, which allowed dissection of all unclaimed paupers, was the vanguard of a new, harsher Poor Law: "Only incidentally did it [the Anatomy Act] endorse the respectability of scientific medicine. Above all, it served as a class reprisal against the poor."[12] Richardson considers Parliament's *Report on Anatomy* a cover-up for exploitation of the poor and asserts that Cooper may have been called as the first witness as part of a concerted effort to exploit the poor.[13] Richardson mentions the Parliamentary committee's exclusion of G. J. Guthrie, a prominent surgeon who openly considered dissection an indignity, as another sign of the report's class bias and concludes that "no part of the Bill lacked a double meaning."[14] Although Richardson's reading of class and anatomy remains a landmark, this chapter examines more fully the report's multiple meanings. By pursuing carefully the implications of witness testimony as testimony (a first-person narrative with partial knowledge and layered, uncontrollable language), readers discover that *anatomy*'s connotations are unruly, even in this official document. Far from negating *anatomy*'s many meanings, this report, like the novel itself, may unconsciously highlight the very tensions it consciously seeks to repress. Nevertheless, Richardson's work has influenced other critics to view anatomy as a tool in a larger clash between science and culture, at the expense of the poor.[15] In these studies, the Anatomy Act of 1832 represents the triumph of the medico-legal establishment and alters anatomy's meaning, resonances, and connotations in the cultural imagination. For example, Brian Bailey concludes that "the new Bill successfully dissociated the study of anatomy from crime."[16] Similarly, Hugh Douglas asserts that after the Anatomy Act, "[s]urgery became respectable, and those who had passed through anatomy schools in the days before the Act were left with tales to tell their children."[17] Here, the legislature seems able to jettison anatomy's association with cruelty, crime, and greed along with the practices of exhumation and execution (just as Cooper suggests).[18] In this reading, legislation successfully limits the word *anatomy*'s connotations to scientific progress and surgical orthodoxy (its former connotations relegated to mere children's stories).

In contrast, W. F. Bynum and Roy Porter assert that the laboratory dictates *anatomy*'s meaning, which is only reinforced by legislation.[19]

22   They argue that William Hunter's anatomy school "helped to transform
the medico-scientific standing of the surgical profession" and helped
to create "the figure of physician as guardian of culture."[20] In a separate essay, Porter claims, "Hunter used his private anatomy school as
his base, physical and symbolic."[21] Here, Hunter's anatomy school symbolizes scientific progress and social prestige even before the Anatomy
Act, and Bynum calls anatomy "the queen of the medical sciences" during this period, despite its general unpopularity.[22] This implies that the
medical establishment, not the legislature, was able to control and to
direct anatomy's meaning during this period, although in both Bynum
and Porter's version and in Richardson's version of events the medical
establishment and the legal establishment were in cahoots. This chapter
concurs that the hegemonic view of anatomy may be as the queen of
the medical sciences, but it does not accept anatomy as *only* the symbol
of the hegemonic power of the bourgeoisie, the medical establishment,
and the government. Instead, this chapter argues that the term *anatomy*
has multiple connotations: beneficence, progress, and knowledge as
well as immorality, exploitation, and crime. It argues that slippages between these meanings are apparent in contemporary documents, both
fictional, such as *Frankenstein*, and nonfictional, including the *Report on
Anatomy* itself, because these documents emerged from the same cultural
milieu. These slippages demonstrate the difficulty of identifying, defining, and containing quackery because language itself communicates
both orthodoxy and quackery simultaneously and is able to slip, to resist, and to frustrate control.

Anatomy, the Corpse, and the Anatomist's Corpse in *Frankenstein*

In his university lecture, Mary Shelley's Professor Waldman
echoes Cooper's claim that science is the foundation of knowledge and
benefits society as a whole: "The labours of men of genius, however er-
roneously directed, scarcely ever fail in ultimately turning to the solid
advantage of mankind."[23] Like Cooper, Waldman connects anatomy
(presumably through Harvey, Lavoisier, and others) to science and discovery: "[T]hese philosophers, whose hands seem only made to dabble
in dirt, and their eyes to pore over the microscope or crucible, have indeed performed miracles. They penetrate into the recesses of nature, and
show how she works in her hiding places. They ascend into the heavens:
they have discovered how the blood circulates, and the nature of the air

we breathe" (53).[24] For Waldman, as for Cooper, anatomy and the other sciences connote knowledge, progress, and beneficence.[25] In *Frankenstein's* 1831 edition, Captain Walton similarly explains, "I would sacrifice my fortune, my existence, my every hope, to the furtherance of my enterprise. One man's life or death were but a small price to pay for the acquirement of the knowledge which I sought; for the dominion I should acquire and transmit over the elemental foes of our race" (38). Walton echoes Waldman both in the shared first syllable of his name and in his philosophy, for Walton, who has studied medicine and other sciences, likewise advocates scientific study as a means to discovery and to public good. Victor Frankenstein himself echoes this sentiment when he urges Walton's mutinous crew to continue their voyage to the North Pole because it is an "honourable undertaking" and will make the crew "benefactors to your species" (182). The words *race, species,* and *mankind* appear in speeches by Waldman, Walton, and Victor and imply that each speaker, like Cooper, connects scientific enterprise with universal human good. But Shelley presents Cooper's point of view in both sympathetic and unsympathetic circumstances: Waldman's beneficence seems genuine, especially because he takes lonely student Victor under his wing after Victor is ridiculed by Professor Krempe. Walton's beneficence seems questionable at first, but Walton in the end sacrifices his scientific ambition to protect his crew, a gesture reminiscent of Waldman's paternalism. In contrast, Victor often seems self-serving and cruel. His deployment of language about species seems self-aggrandizing when he wishes for a new "species" that would call him "creator" (58) and seems evasive when he argues that he is not to blame for abandoning his creature because of his duty to his "own species" (184). In placing similar language in Waldman's, Walton's, and Victor's mouths, Shelley invites readers to question the relationship between science and humanity and between discovery and beneficence. Anatomy is a unique field through which to explore Shelley's questions because it examines structures common to all humankind and thus shared by both anatomist and subject. In this sense, anatomy simultaneously differentiates Victor from his creature (Victor is normal, the creature is large; Victor is handsome, the creature is ugly; Victor grew, the creature is made) and joins them together (they share human anatomy). Anatomy's very object of study muddies boundaries between science, society, and self, and Shelley's deployment of anatomy in her novel is perhaps less a sweeping condemnation of scientific enterprise than an invitation to consider carefully the nature of such relations.

24   Astley Cooper was only one of many witnesses before the Select Committee on Anatomy for whom anatomy signified scientific discovery and social benefit. The report's opening page describes the "the importance of the Science [anatomy] to the well-being of mankind" (3). Surgeon Benjamin Collins Brodie claims, "There can be no knowledge of surgery without it [anatomy], and very little knowledge of medicine" (23). Surgeon John Abernethy argues that "it would be little less than the commission of murder not to do [anatomy]; it would be a cause of the greatest aggravation of human sufferings" (28). Surgeon William Lawrence asserts that "a man cannot understand, and he certainly ought not to practice, the medical profession, without the diligent study of Anatomy by actual dissection" (34). When asked whether restrictions on anatomy form "a degradation of the profession," Lawrence replies, "[I]t places a stigma on what ought to be encouraged, and to be considered as a ground of respect" (34). The president of the Royal College of Physicians, Henry Halford, expands upon anatomy's usefulness: "I think it is impossible to practice physic rationally, without such knowledge as is acquired by dissection itself" (76). Lecturer Southwood Smith concurs: "Now that knowledge of Anatomy which is essential to every practitioner, can be acquired only by dissection. I feel that no language at my command can adequately express my conviction of this truth" (85). Magistrate Samuel Twyford agrees that "nobody can deny it is absolutely necessary" (98). But anatomy is not the cornerstone of surgery only: Smith alludes to the "danger of an opinion which I have heard expressed, namely, that dissection is not necessary to the general practitioner, who occupies the lowest rank in the profession, and to the physician who occupies the highest" (85). For these witnesses, anatomy is vital to surgery and medicine as a whole because anatomy is the basis of scientific discovery and its associated virtues: beneficence, reason, and respect.

In many ways, Shelley's novel shares the conviction that medical science is based on anatomy: Victor's anatomical research is strongly associated with the successful creation of his "monster" and thus leads him, as its proponents claimed it would, to knowledge about the nature of human life. When anatomy is viewed in this light, Shelley does not challenge anatomy's status as a science so much as revise the way in which this science might be deployed. If Shelley maintains anatomy as the queen of the medical sciences, she questions Cooper's double standard regarding anatomical specimens, and it is here that Shelley reimagines a more sympathetic configuration of an apparently necessary and effective science. Cooper views his body, which conducts anatomies, as fundamentally different from those bodies used in anatomies, and thus he is outraged at the idea that body snatchers might view *his* body as potential fodder for anatomical research. This outrage seriously undermines Cooper's contention that it is body snatching, not anatomy itself, which is objectionable. Cooper states that the mode of obtaining specimens is responsible for anatomy's public odium, but his outrage at the thought of being anatomized implies that the mode is less significant than the objectification of the body inherent in anatomy itself. Like Cooper, readers of the novel may focus on the creature's body and erase the anatomist's body, but reading *Frankenstein* in light of the anatomy debate focuses our attention on the many ways that Shelley foregrounds bodies, including the creature's body, Victor's, Elizabeth's, William's, Justine's, and Henry's.[26] In the context of anatomy, Shelley's depiction of bodies, particularly Victor's body, deserves close attention because it intervenes in a contemporary debate about the nature of science and its interaction with humanity.

Like Astley Cooper, Victor both asserts and resists the view of the dead body as sacred. To Victor, the grave is a repository of raw materials that will be wasted by natural decay if not salvaged for public good, but, like Cooper, Victor is inconsistent. Upon his brother's death, Victor says, "Poor little fellow! one only consolation have we; his friends mourn and weep, but he is at rest. The pang is over, his sufferings are at an end forever. A sod covers his gentle form, and he knows no pain" (73). The sod in this passage recalls elegies, such as Ben Jonson's "On My First Daughter," which asks the grave to "cover lightly, gentle earth." Victor views his brother's grave as a place of rest, not a site of work or of chemical and biological processes. Victor also repeatedly articulates views in which the buried dead are subjects who retain identity, not objects for study. For example, he begs, "Wandering spirits, if indeed ye wander, and do not rest in your narrow beds, allow me this faint happiness, or take me, as your companion, away from the joys of life" (92). Here the "narrow beds," presumably graves, hold beings possibly capable of communication and desire. These entities are not mere raw materials. When Victor goes to the graveyard where his father, William, and Elizabeth are buried, he describes it as "solemn and affecting even to an uninterested observer" (172). He swears his oath of revenge: "By the sacred earth on which I kneel, by the shades that wander near me" (173). In the midst of his account of his trip to England, Victor recalls

26   Henry Clerval's body and exclaims, "No, it is not thus; your form so divinely wrought, and beaming with beauty, has decayed, but your spirit still visits and consoles your unhappy friend" (138). What sanctifies the grave? What is significant about the narrow beds that Victor both reveres and violates? Is Henry's decayed body fodder for anatomy, even though his spirit is apparently still alert and aware? Victor views Henry's and William's bodies as different than those from which he fashions his creature. That Victor should view the corpse in this manner testifies to Shelley's careful delineation of anatomy's ambivalence toward the dead body. The clash here is not a simple one between scientific and public views or between materialist and spiritualist forces, but a complex interplay of competing strands of belief that exist simultaneously in a single anatomist. Neither Victor nor Cooper rejects fully the notion of the dead body as sacred and aware, although both are inconsistent in their application of this idea.

It may appear obvious that anatomists might wish to exempt their own bodies and the bodies of their loved ones from anatomical study, despite their claims of anatomy's importance and beneficence. However, despite almost universal advocacy for increased anatomical research, both surgeons and nonsurgeons before the Select Committee on Anatomy advocated for funeral rites and interment for all dissected bodies. This idea appears in testimony by Cooper, Brodie, Abernathy, Lawrence, Green, Mayo, Grainger, Somerville, Barry, Halford, Rose, Fernandez, Pattison, and Smith. The idea complicates the surgeons' position regarding body snatching because it implies that anatomy itself is the issue, not the means of obtaining the body. Whether executed or donated, the body deserves the rituals of burial with which anatomy necessarily interferes. The report's introduction describes "that natural feeling which leads men to treat with reverence the remains of the Dead; and the same feeling has prompted them, in almost all times and countries, to regard with repugnance, and to persecute, Anatomy" (3). Cooper claims, "It would be very proper; and it is my strong desire that the funeral rites should be performed over each body" (21). On being asked whether surgeons should give "Christian and decent burial" to subjects after dissection, Green, Grainger, Fernandez, and Smith agree that surgeons should undertake such rites (38, 47, 80, 86). Henry Halford asserts, "I think that as great importance is attached to the ceremony of burial, it would as much tend to mitigate the prejudices against dissection, if you were to obtain that security" (77). Peregrine Fernandez claims that "the poor are fond of having a 'comfortable funeral', and if it was known that they would not be disturbed, but they should be taken only according to the taste of the poor people, I have no doubt there would be no objection," except, Fernandez claims, for the Irish, for whom a wake "would not lessen their objection to dissections" (81). This issue of burial generates questions from the committee members about the ways in which anatomy is conducted throughout Europe. David Barry notes that in Portugal the dissected are buried in consecrated ground (61), and Gaetano Negri asserts that in Parma funeral rites are performed prior to dissection (67). There is a contradiction in the position of several of these witnesses, just as there is in Victor's attitude and conduct. Several argue that anatomy is not objectionable in itself but is tainted by exhumation and execution, but at the same time, they argue that anatomy is objectionable because it interferes with cultural rites that signify respect to the recently dead. While Victor's inconsistency might seem based on personal feelings alone, the testimony before the Select Committee on Anatomy suggests that such contradictions were a feature of anatomical discourse during this period.

If Victor occasionally articulates a view of the buried corpse as sacred, he also famously describes the corpse as mere raw material. Victor violates graves as a body snatcher in his own right in some of the novel's least sympathetic incidents:

> To examine the causes of life, we must first have recourse to death. I became acquainted with the science of anatomy: but this was not sufficient; I must also observe the natural decay and corruption of the human body. . . . Darkness had no effect upon my fancy; and a churchyard was to me merely the receptacle of bodies deprived of life, which, from being the seat of beauty and strength, had become food for the worm. Now I was led to examine the cause and progress of this decay, and forced to spend days and nights in vaults and charnel-houses . . . I beheld the corruption of death succeed to the blooming cheek of life; I saw how the worm inherited the wonders of the eye and brain. I paused, examining and analysing all the minutiæ of causation, as exemplified in the change from life to death, and death to life. (56)

Victor's description of churchyards, vaults, and charnel houses implies that he is a body snatcher, since he is using buried corpses, not legally supplied hanged ones. Whereas William's grave is sacred earth, these graves are receptacles, and the awe that impresses Victor in the churchyard where Elizabeth, Alphonse, and William are buried is here dismissed as fancy. In this passage, the body is inert "food," associated repeatedly with worms, decay, and corruption. In another passage, Victor downplays the corpse's identity:

> I collected bones from charnel-houses; and disturbed, with pro-
> fane fingers, the tremendous secrets of the human frame. . . . I
> kept my workshop of filthy creation: my eye-balls were starting
> from their sockets in attending to the details of my employment.
> The dissecting room and the slaughter-house furnished many of
> my materials; and often did my human nature turn with loathing
> from my occupation, whilst, still urged on by an eagerness which
> perpetually increased. (58)

Although the "human frame" appears to Victor to be sacred (hence the profanity of touching it), it is also merely "materials" for him to use in his experiment. He both loathes his task and engages enthusiastically with it. Victor's duality might be easily understood as the difference between the graves of known and loved people and the graves of strangers, or it might be the echo of a contradiction common in this discourse. However, in these passages Shelley refocuses the reader's attention from the corpse to Victor's own body in powerful descriptions of his living and breathing anatomy. Even as Victor describes his anatomical specimens as food or as raw materials, Shelley represents Victor's body as bloody, breathing matter, akin to that of the corpses he sees as food for the worm. Victor's eyeballs start from his sockets in a description more vividly anatomical than the vague language of filth that describes his anatomical subjects. Where Cooper draws a strict boundary between his body and those of his subjects, Shelley focuses on Victor's body and, in doing so, complicates significantly the discourse with which she is engaged.

Shelley's juxtaposition of the anatomist's body and the anatomical specimen's body attacks directly the boundary created by Cooper and others in this discourse. This boundary is worth exploring fully since it is a key feature of anatomists' argument in favor of new sources of bodies for dissection. Many witnesses before the Select Committee on Anatomy blamed anatomy's disrepute on the methods of obtaining bodies, both execution and exhumation, not on any barbarity or disrespect intrinsic to

anatomy itself. Almost every witness, including Cooper, Brodie, Abernathy, Lawrence, Green, Hawkins, Mayo, Grainger, Somerville, Pattison,
Arnott, Halford, Rose, Fernandez, Smith, Ballantine, and Wakley, mentioned exhumation and execution as responsible for anatomy's negative
connotations. Cooper claims that "it is distressing to our feelings that
we are obliged to employ very very faulty agents [resurrection men]
to obtain a desirable end" (18). Thomas Wakley argues that "the great
prejudice which exists in this country against the practice of dissections,
appears to arise from that enactment of the legislature which consigns
the bodies of murderers to dissection; also from the disgusting and filthy
practice of exhumation" (116). Cesar Hawkins argues that the British
dislike of dissection "must greatly depend on dissection being made a
part of the punishment for murder, and likewise, by exhumation" (43).
William Lawrence strongly criticizes the dissection of murderers: "I
deem it highly objectionable, as being directly calculated to maintain
and increase the existing prejudices on the subject; it gives the most
powerful sanctions, those of the legislature and judicature, to the horror
and aversion which mankind are perhaps naturally disposed to entertain
against what they deem a profanation of the dead" (33). Asked about
the use of murderers in anatomy, Benjamin Collins Brodie replies, "[T]he
effect is injurious; at the same time it appears to me, that some of my
friends regard it as being more injurious than it really is; on the whole, it
would be better, as far as Anatomy is concerned, that the practice were
abolished" (24). Brodie also asserts that "the dead body of course does
not feel either injury or disgrace, and where there are no friends to feel it,
the mischief to society can be none at all" (24). Surgeon Herbert Mayo
blames execution and exhumation for the public dislike of anatomy, not
anatomy itself: "I suppose it [anti-anatomy feeling] must greatly depend
on dissection being made a part of the punishment for murder, and likewise owing to the mode in which the bodies are procured by us in this
country, namely, by exhumation; I never observed any feeling expressed
among the poor in reference to examination or dissection in their own
case; I do not therefore believe that the anticipation of dissection . . .
would be a source of distress or apprehension to patients dangerously ill
in work-houses [who would be dissected if unclaimed after death]" (43).
Anatomy professor Richard Dugard Grainger, surgeon David Gale Arnott, surgeon Thomas Rose, and surgeon Peregrine Fernandez argue that
repeal of the Murder Act would mitigate the public dislike of anatomy
(47, 76, 79, 81). Magistrate Samuel Twyford concurs that public feeling

30   is "more against exhumation than dissection" (100). Vestryman Richard
Spike claims that people "would want very little reconciling to the thing
[anatomy] itself" (121). When asked whether parishioners would mind dissection of unclaimed bodies, Spike argues, "I do not think the parishioners
would give themselves any trouble to think about it at all; I think it
would be a matter of perfect indifference to them" (121). Anatomist
James Somerville argues very strenuously: "I wish to observe, that the
prejudice created by giving up murderers is infinitely stronger, according to my own experience, than has been stated by any witness" (47).
In this testimony, the Murder Act and resurrection men are blamed for
anatomy's negative connotations, and many witnesses suggest the repeal
of the Murder Act and the abolition of resurrection. Such suggestions
imply that once these methods disappear, public dislike of anatomy will
also dissipate. The position takes for granted that the objection is not to
anatomy itself but to the means of procuring specimens.

At the same time, several of the above-mentioned testimonies can
be read rather differently. In this against-the-grain reading, the testimony
implies that anatomy itself has negative connotations. Although Ruth
Richardson and other critics view these witnesses as a united front joined
in bourgeois contempt for the poor, a range of positions can be seen
even within this small sample. For example, Brodie's assistant, Somerville,
strongly blames the Murder Act for anatomy's odium, but Brodie claims
that the effect of execution is perhaps overstated, although he supports
the Murder Act's repeal (24). If the effect of execution is overstated,
what then generated public repugnance for anatomy, if not anatomy
itself? Lawrence states that people are "naturally disposed" to think of
anatomy as "profanation," which also implies a dislike of anatomy regardless of the means of obtaining bodies (33). John Abernathy openly
denies that the means are the issue at all: "I do not think such stigma
affects the public mind; yet we gain so little by obtaining the bodies of
murderers, that we should have no objection to its being removed" (31).
Like Brodie, Abernathy doubts that execution and exhumation are to
blame, although he supports the repeal of the Murder Act. The treasurer
of Guy's Hospital, Benjamin Harrison, argues, "I do not consider it is
on account of murderers being dissected that they [the public] abhor
it [anatomy] themselves" (91). Upon being asked the cause of public
dislike, Harrison responds, "I believe it is the national character, and I
believe it to be a very general feeling of abhorrence, which we all feel
more or less, and if it could be banished from the minds of the poor,

much of their best feelings would be banished with it" (91). Police magistrate Thomas Halls argues similarly, "I think it a natural feeling, and such a feeling as must exist in a high state of civilization" (95). When asked whether repeal of the Murder Act might affect public opinion, Halls replies, "I know such a notion has been entertained by many persons, but it is one of which I am exceedingly doubtful" (95). Officers of Union Hall James Glennon and Richard Pople admit that feeling is more against resurrection men than surgeons, but they claim that people would oppose the dissection of complete strangers as strenuously as they would their own because people dislike dissection and body snatching equally (105). In these accounts, dissection itself conjures negative connotations, the removal of which, several witness claim, is undesirable or impossible. Here, anatomy connotes not enlightenment but barbarity, such that civilized people cherish a laudable dislike of it. To remove this dislike is undesirable because this dislike derives from good feelings such as fellowship and civility. As a result, these witnesses acknowledge the unpopularity of exhumation and execution but place much less emphasis on the Murder Act and on body snatching.

Shelley's representation of Victor's body as a biological entity most strongly reveals anatomy's ambivalence. Whereas Victor, like many anatomists, draws boundaries between himself and his specimens, and between his family's graves and those of strangers, Shelley breaks down barriers. This implies, as several witnesses above also imply, that shared anatomy creates shared fellowship. The emphasis on physicality is a feature of the Gothic genre, but Shelley deploys it to enter powerfully into the anatomy debate and to question the ways in which anatomy itself may create or destroy fellowship and civility.[27] Rather than wholeheartedly condemn anatomy or shift blame onto resurrection (although she depicts Victor's graveyard adventures as thoroughly repulsive), Shelley critiques the simplistic views of anatomy as either purely scientific or purely objectionable. For example, Victor says of Justine after her death, "Justine died; she rested; and I was alive. The blood flowed freely in my veins, but a weight of despair and remorse pressed on my heart" (86). Victor views himself as different from Justine because he is alive and she is dead; however, Shelley's description of blood, veins, and heart recalls Harvey's studies on the circulation of the blood, the very same that Waldman mentions as a scientific landmark. Here, it is Victor's body, not Justine's, that furnishes the example of Harvey's discovery. Similarly, when Victor sees Henry's body, Victor "gasped for breath; and, throwing

32   myself on the body, I exclaimed, 'have my murderous machinations deprived you also, my dearest Henry, of life?'" (153). He ruminates, "Death snatches away many blooming children, the only hopes of their doting parents: how many brides and youthful lovers have been one day in the bloom of health and hope, and the next a prey for worms and the decay of the tomb! Of what materials was I made, that I could thus resist so many shocks, which, like the turning of a wheel, continually renewed the torture?" (153). It is Henry's body that lies in the coffin, but Shelley focuses on Victor's "materials" and on his "gasping" lungs, which recall Waldman's mention of the composition of air as a landmark discovery. Similar boundaries are crossed in Victor's dream just prior to the creature's birth. Victor sees Elizabeth in the "bloom of health," but then her lips turn "livid" and she morphs into Victor's dead mother, "a shroud enveloped her form, and I saw the graveworms crawling in the folds of the flannel" (61). Worms are repeatedly associated with the dead bodies that Victor finds in the charnel houses and graveyards from which the creature originates.[28] This dream collapses the bodies of the still-living Elizabeth, Victor's mother's corpse, and by implication, the creature's newly living body. It reminds readers, and Victor, on an unconscious level, that, anatomically speaking, no body can be viewed as different from any other. His creature becomes a member of Victor's own family and of the human family in a fellowship shared with Elizabeth, Victor's mother, and Victor himself.

    If some anatomists, such as Cooper, would draw a line between anatomist and corpse, Mary Shelley would erase this line. Nowhere is this erasure as significant as in the case of the creature himself. Judith Pike argues that in the creature Shelley "debunks this conventionalized portrayal of the death and the cult of mourning" by showing us an "unsublimated dead body."[29] Victor and the creature have also been described as doubles, a common Gothic trope.[30] However, in the context of anatomy, this trope deserves particular attention. The creature's ugly body is viewed as a mark of inhumanity, but Victor's descriptions of himself as a decaying or revivified corpse undermine these claims of difference. Walton describes Victor as a revivified corpse; "From this time a new spirit of life animated the decaying frame of the stranger" (37). Victor often describes himself as a decaying corpse, "a shattered wreck,—the shadow of a human being. . . . I was a mere skeleton; and fever night and day preyed upon my wasted frame" (158). Suffering from fever in Ireland, Victor describes his features "livid like those in death" (154). As a student, Victor claims to be a "wreck" with "incipient disease" (60) even as he calls the creature a "demonical corpse" (61) and describes the creature's "black lips," "watery eyes," and "muscles and arteries" (61). While describing the creature's arteries, Victor becomes aware of the "palpitation of every artery" in his own body (61). Anatomy, which seems to demarcate one from the other, also binds them through common structures. Victor says of the female creation, "I now also began to collect the materials necessary for my new creation, and this was to me like the torture of single drops of water continually falling on the head. . . . [E]very word that I spoke in allusion to it caused my lips to quiver, and my heart to palpitate" (139). The body of the female creature renders Victor aware of his own lips and heart, his own quivering and palpitations. The novel's end collapses differences between Victor and creature, since it ends with Walton and the creature viewing Victor's corpse just as Victor viewed the creature's corpse earlier. Walton notes Victor's "apparent lifelessness" (182), then describes Victor's "remains" (185) and "lifeless form" (187). The monster describes Victor's body "white and cold in death" (188). The creature "hung over the coffin" (185), just as Victor hung over his coffin, Henry's coffin, and Elizabeth's corpse. Whereas Victor views the anatomical specimen as fundamentally different than the anatomist, Shelley links corpse and anatomist through their shared structures, whose discovery is, after all, the aim of anatomy. Shelley's view of the anatomist's body as kin to the specimen's body suggests a way of conceptualizing anatomy that is materialist and scientific but also compassionate and egalitarian, a way that several witnesses before the Parliamentary committee also endorse.

Several witnesses before the Select Committee on Anatomy suggest ways of reconceptualizing anatomy by collapsing boundaries between medicine and public, just as Shelley suggests collapsing boundaries between anatomist and specimen. For example, witnesses claim that including the public in anatomy will overcome anatomy's odium.[31] Herbert Mayo points out that in Holland there is "no prejudice at all; for in the principal towns in Holland there are lectures on dissection publicly and dissected subjects are exhibited" (43). Granville Pattison argues, "I have found the prejudice which existed in the minds of the lower orders, was at once removed; that they were not aware what dissection was, till they saw it performed; and when they saw it performed, they no longer looked upon it with the detestation which before existed" (84). Southwood Smith argues that "secrecy and mystery" is not productive;

34 "they [the lower classes] are quite able to perceive the reasonableness of the measure if it were properly represented, and that their feeling is so good, that they would ultimately acquiesce in it" (86). In contrast, David Barry argues that in Portugal, dissection is conducted with "decency and secrecy, so as not to outrage the feelings of individuals" (60). Somerville notes that despite open dissection, "the priests in France have always beheld with great jealousy the progress made by medical students, the priests are rather anxious to check the study of medicine, or to lower it" (52). These suggestions repeatedly use the word *prejudice* to describe anti-anatomy feeling. The word implies that the public is merely mistaken in its belief that anatomy is profane, disgusting, or barbaric, but the suggestions about public education and openness by the medical faculty imply some overlap between public and professional, a commonality evident in Shelley's novel. Where these witnesses suggest crossing boundaries between medical faculty and public, Shelley depicts a crossing between anatomist and corpse. Witnesses still claim that discretion is required in conducting public anatomies but these suggestions, like Shelley's, point to a more holistic view of anatomy as neither scientific nor public, neither sacred nor profane.[32] While Victor's activities in charnel houses and churchyards are rightly viewed as horrifying moments in the text, Shelley's novel as a whole does not condemn anatomy; on the contrary, Shelley positions anatomy as the basis of medical knowledge, just as witnesses before the Select Committee on Anatomy do. In the novel, as in the testimony, bodies are both sacred and material. Shelley also depicts the widespread unhappiness with body snatching, shared by the public and by medical practitioners themselves. Yet in her depiction of Victor Frankenstein's own body, Shelley voices support for that faction of the medico-scientific community that tries to reimagine anatomy in more holistic terms, giving it connotations of progress and humanity, medical science and publicity.

To Sport with Life: Murder, Quackery, and Anatomy

On one hand, Shelley represents anatomy as an orthodox procedure and supports that faction of the scientific community trying to reconfigure anatomy into a more open and humane practice. On the other hand, Victor is hardly an orthodox anatomist. If Victor Frankenstein might be viewed as an immoral but successful anatomist, he might also be viewed as a quack. After all, Alphonse Frankenstein and

Professor Krempe dismiss alchemy, Victor's passion, as "sad trash" and "nonsense," respectively (46, 51).[33] Alan Rauch points to Paracelsus, Agrippa, and Albertus Magnus as mistaken in method, a form of science that is "product-oriented" instead of "process-oriented."[34] Coupled with Victor's social isolation, alchemical study renders Victor unable to understand science's social context, and as a result, Victor is unable to contribute meaningfully to knowledge.[35] Using the context of contemporary galvanic research aimed at reviving unconscious individuals, Rauch contends that Victor's failures to restore life to the monster's victims and to his own mother are quite remarkable given that many others in the novel revive the dying: Caroline Frankenstein saves Elizabeth, the creature revives a drowned girl, the Irish revive Victor and try to revive Henry, and Walton revives Victor on the deck of the ship.[36] Rauch claims that "Frankenstein does not lack for knowledge, the monster is proof of that; but he is clearly unable to see how the application of that knowledge can be used in a way that is proper and judicious as well as humane and rational."[37] Rauch's persuasive argument points to a configuration of quackery similar to Ludmilla Jordanova's in which quackery arises from vice, not necessarily incompetence or ignorance.[38] But readers must also wonder about Victor's competence. Ought one to assume, as Rauch does, that the creature is proof of Victor's competence? Can scientific competence be based on only one instance of success (reviving the creature)? What if Victor cannot replicate his experiment but exaggerates his abilities to impress Walton, his listener?

The question of Victor's skill also strikes Marilyn Butler, who writes that Victor is "not so much a mythical Prometheus, more a humble Sorcerer's Apprentice" and points out, "Frankenstein as first devised seems to know too little science rather than too much."[39] Viewed in this light, Victor's refusal to tell Walton about how the creature was made becomes suspect. Is it indicative of Victor's desire to spare Walton, as he claims, or a cover for his ignorance? Shelley famously omits mentioning specific scientific processes during this conversation with Walton and during the initial creation scene, although, as many critics have shown, she was familiar with galvanism, anatomy, and other scientific issues of her day (179, 60).[40] This section explores the ways in which anatomy signifies quackery, both in the sense of immorality and in the sense of incompetence. It is difficult today to imagine anatomists as quacks, but texts from this period that describe burking, the murder of persons for the purpose of sale to anatomy schools, often position

36   anatomists as charlatans, either because of their participation in criminal activities themselves or because of their inability to distinguish between a snatched body and a murdered one. Burking placed supporters of anatomy in the awkward position of praising the science for adding to the store of human knowledge while simultaneously claiming ignorance of burking, a process that surely leaves marks on the victim's body that a skilled anatomist might identify. In Victor Frankenstein, Shelley explores this thread of early nineteenth-century culture and positions anatomy as a signifier not of science, progress, and reason but of crime, immorality, and even incompetence.

Marilyn Butler credits (or blames) the Burke and Hare murders for Shelley's "damage-limitation" in the 1831 edition of Frankenstein.[41] Similarly, Anne K. Mellor suggests that Shelley's 1831 preface views anatomy in a sinister light because of the recent Burke and Hare murders.[42] In this preface, Shelley claims that the dream that inspired her novel centered on "the pale student of unhallowed arts kneeling beside the thing he had put together" (24). Here, the body is a "thing," and the student kneels by the corpse, an attitude that evokes the graveside activities of a body-snatching medical student rather than a formal dissecting room or surgical theatre in which bodies are raised upon tables. A few lines later, the student hopes that the newly alive creation might "subside into dead matter" and "the silence of the grave would quench for ever the transient existence of the hideous corpse which he had looked upon as the cradle of life" (24). Here the creature's body is "dead matter," a "corpse," yet also the "cradle of life," terms with contradictory implications. In light of the Burke and Hare scandal, Victor's desire to quench the creature's new life and to *make* dead matter might be understood as an allusion to burking. Is Victor about to make a corpse the way Sir Astley Cooper worried that resurrection men might make a corpse of him?

Shelley does not use the terms *anatomy* or *burking* in this passage; however, Shelley taints Victor with criminality through the word *unhallowed*, a term that recurs throughout the novel. Victor says that Justine and William are "the first hapless victims of my unhallowed arts" (85). He says, "I pursued nature to her hiding-places. Who shall conceive the horrors of my secret toil, as I dabbled among the unhallowed damps of the grave, or tortured the living animal to animate the lifeless clay?" (58). After Henry's death, he worries, "[D]id they [the public] know my unhallowed acts, and the crimes which had their source in me!" (159). The creature says that he will destroy by fire "this miserable frame, that

its remains may afford no light to any curious and unhallowed wretch,   37
who would create such another as I have been" (188). The *Oxford English Dictionary* defines *unhallowed* as "not formally hallowed or consecrated; left secular or profane" but also as "not having a hallowed or sacred character; unholy, impious, wicked."[43] Shelley's repeated use of this word might suggest simply that Shelley condemns anatomy as a practice; however, in the preceding section, Shelley seems to support anatomical research as effective and tries to imagine a way of viewing anatomical specimens humanely. In contrast, the 1831 preface seems to draw upon another cultural thread in which anatomy is not a necessary scientific activity at all but a sign of criminality and wickedness.

Despite the Select Committee on Anatomy's praise of anatomy as the foundation of surgery and medicine, witnesses before this committee frequently allude to crime. Crime provides the only legal means of obtaining specimens (hanged felons), it provides the illegal means of obtaining specimens (body snatching), and it taints anatomists themselves. The report includes numerous instances in which anatomists are viewed as culpable in some way by mobs bent on rescuing victims from the dissecting rooms. Joshua Brookes recounts several instances when neighborhood mobs attacked his dissecting theatre and adds, "I should state my premises would have been laid waste, and I suppose I should have been immolated, but for my contiguity to the police office; . . . by which means I was protected" (82). Similarly, Scottish surgeon Granville Sharp Pattison recalls, "[I]nvariably if a body was taken from the place of execution to the class room of the teacher, it was followed by a mob, and the individuals who carried it off, were pelted with stones" (83). Irish surgeon James Maccartney claims that rumors about kidnapping children for dissection resulted in the need for police protection of an anatomy school (107). Maccartney also describes assaults on resurrection men and on anatomists and medical students (107). Maccartney's testimony implies that anatomists and medical students, like resurrection men, were engaged in illegal exhumation, and his testimony also shows fear of anatomists as criminals in the accusations of kidnapping (and presumably burking) of children. In "The Tyburn Riot against the Surgeons," Peter Linebaugh argues that class identity is at the heart of such incidents, noting that Irish mobs rescued Irish corpses and demobilized soldiers and sailors rescued their fellow servicemen's bodies from the gallows.[44] Somerville's testimony supports this interpretation, but Brookes, Maccartney, and Pattison imply that the mob defended

38   corpses on a broader principle, since these mobs apparently would defend any body regardless of social class or individual identity. In these incidents, the anatomists are viewed as criminals by the mob, but the mob is viewed as criminal by the anatomists; the anatomists viewed themselves as victims of the mob, while the mob viewed the corpses as victims of the anatomists.

Several witnesses attempt to clarify the surgeons' position by displacing criminality onto resurrection men alone, who quickly slide down a slippery slope from body snatching to thievery, informing, and fraud. Somerville asserts that resurrection men are all criminals: "[T]hey are in the lowest grade in the community, thieves, pickpockets; and the better class are [sic] receivers of stolen goods" (48).[45] Hawkins says that "their faith is certainly very badly kept; their practice is occasionally to steal bodies, and then to inform against the professors . . . and against their brother resurrection men still more" (41). The Select Committee on Anatomy's report includes testimony by several resurrection men who confirm the surgeons' claims. A resurrection man identified only as C.D. admits to criminal acts beyond simply digging up corpses, including impersonating family members to get bodies from workhouses and hospitals (119). Newspapers confirm this sort of impersonation: "When the 'snatchers' hear of an inquest, they immediately repair to the neighbourhood in which it is held, [and] pretend to be friends of the deceased, . . . [T]hey almost in every instance succeed in carrying away the prize."[46] Similarly, a news report describes a young woman who appeared at St. Giles's workhouse to claim an unidentified corpse: "[O]n beholding the countenance, she gave a shriek, and exclaimed, 'My uncle, my dear uncle': she was recognized as an accomplice of resurrection men and arrested."[47] When asked what crimes most resurrection men commit, C.D. replies, "[T]hieving, thieving, most unquestionably" (118 [original italics]). C.D. also hints at competition among resurrection men so fierce as to approach murder: he confirms that resurrection men left graves open purposely to create trouble for their rivals; "[I]t was not fair in a case where life was at stake; life was at stake, you know; if I went into the ground after a body was gone, a watch might be set, and I not know it" (119). C.D.'s repetition of "life at stake" implies considerable danger of violence at the hands of watchmen. Resurrection man A.B. also admits to criminal behavior, including using the excuse of resurrection to avoid authorities (71). Yet A.B. claims that "a man may make a good living at it; if he is a sober man, and acts with judgment" (71).

He discriminates between business-like old-style trade and the new cutthroats: "I think thieving by the greatest part of the men that have lately got into the business" (71). At first glance, the resurrection men confirmed surgeons' claims of criminality, yet they also showed that resurrection men may have been quite professional ("sober") in their trade, which was one of considerable hazard. Were these men chosen to testify because they would confirm surgeons' claims? Did they provide a false "lower-class" view of anatomy that would support the dissection of paupers? Or were class lines not as distinct in this matter as modern researchers have presumed? Glennon and Pople, officers of Union Hall, agree that resurrection men live by "thieving, more or less" (104). But Glennon asserts that "some are very respectable and decent in their manner . . . some very steady" (104). Glennon confirms that resurrection men inform on each other but denies that they inform on surgeons (104), whom Glennon praises as "generally kind enough" (105). Magistrate Thomas Halls asserts that resurrection men might "not be the best characters" but denies any personal knowledge of thieving (93). On being asked whether he had ever adjudicated a case in which a thief pretended to be a resurrection man to cover his crime with respectability, he replies, "Certainly not" and later expands on this point: "I have heard that it has been done but cannot name the instances" (93). At the same time, Halls admits that surgeons are not treated as criminals, because of the legal precedent that there is no property in a body and no accessory in a misdemeanor, leaving the only the principals (resurrection men) liable to arrest (94). This testimony seems to position resurrection men as criminals; however, the resurrection men themselves emerge at times as hard-working tradesmen (despite the tide tending to view them as criminals). While the anatomists blamed resurrection men for crime and thievery, the witnesses repeatedly note that officials often ignored resurrection at surgeons' request, which permitted crimes of all sorts to flourish. The anatomists' very testimony indicates that they knowingly sponsored illegal activities and encouraged, in their own view, terrible gangs of men to further vice.

Throughout the novel, Victor seems plagued by similar guilt.[48] Ellen Moers argues that Shelley's novel is a "birth myth" about a "mad scientist who locks himself in his laboratory and secretly, *guiltily*, works at creating human life."[49] She describes Victor's "feverish and *guilty* activity" as he "collects bones and other human parts from the slaughterhouse and the dissecting room."[50] Of what crime is Victor guilty? Victor is

40   certainly a body snatcher, but his guilt seems greater than this. Anne K. Mellor claims that Victor's experiment is a "rape of nature," and Mellor argues that nature attacks Victor with madness in recompense.[51] Mellor concurs with Shelley that those sensitive to nature are rewarded, in Shelley's words, with "a calm and peaceful mind. . . . If the study to which you apply yourself has a tendency to weaken your affections, and to destroy your taste for those simple pleasures in which no alloy can possibly mix, then that study is certainly unlawful, that is to say, not befitting a human mind."[52] Victor may be viewed as guilty of transgressing nature or of usurping female procreation; however, on a more mundane level his guilt strongly resembles that of the anatomists, who simultaneously were and were not responsible for the criminal acts of resurrection men.[53] Like the anatomists before the Select Committee on Anatomy who distanced themselves from resurrection men, Victor distances himself from his creature's crimes; however, he is inconsistent. Despite his protests that he is not responsible for the creature's crimes (and legally speaking, no father is responsible for his son's crimes), Victor views himself as a criminal once-removed. When he destroys the female creature, Victor confesses, "I felt as if I had committed some great crime, the consciousness of which haunted me. I was guiltless, but I had indeed drawn down a horrible curse upon my head, as mortal as that of crime" (142). Victor "tore to pieces the thing on which I was engaged" (145) and returns to his laboratory saying, "I almost felt as if I had mangled the living flesh of a human being" (148). He says, "I felt as if I was about the commission of a dreadful crime, and avoided with shuddering anxiety any encounter with my fellow creatures" (149). Victor has not murdered anybody, since the female creature was not alive; however, in this instance body snatching, anatomy, and murder seem to blend together, just as Maccartney's mob slid quickly from accusations of body snatching to kidnapping to burking as they attacked his dissecting theater. Victor also views the deaths of his friends and relations as his fault: "Justine also was a girl of merit, and possessed qualities which promised to render her life happy: now all was to be obliterated in an ignominious grave; and I the cause!" (79). He writes of Justine's verdict, "The tortures of the accused did not equal mine; she was sustained by innocence, but the fangs of remorse tore my bosom, and would not forego [sic] their hold" (82). While it is difficult to imagine that his sufferings really exceed Justine's, Shelley clearly represents Victor as a guilty creature, albeit unsure exactly for what crime: "But I, the true murderer, felt the never-dying

worm alive in my bosom, which allowed of no hope or consolation" (85). At the same time, Victor enacts the slide from body snatching to fraud to murder. He certainly body snatches to procure parts for his creature, and then he engages in deception during Justine's trial, during his voyage with Henry, and during his engagement to Elizabeth, allowing his family and friends to attribute his sorrow to grief rather than to guilt. He finally attempts to murder the creature himself, saying, "[S]tay, that I may trample you to dust!" and "[C]ome on, then, that I may extinguish the spark which I so negligently bestowed" (93). The creature rightly identifies Victor's true murderousness when he exclaims, "You purpose to kill me. How dare you thus sport with life?" (93). After Elizabeth's death, Victor actually fires a pistol at the creature (168), and, of course, the quest that brings him to Walton's ship is avowedly to kill the creature (178). In her representation of Victor in these instances, Shelley seems to collapse the distinction between anatomist, body snatcher, and murderer. Like the anatomists, Victor is not technically guilty of his creature's crimes, but Shelley shows anatomy to be complicit in the worst sorts of criminal activity, descending a slippery slope from body snatching to murder.

Although the Select Committee on Anatomy's inquiry occurred prior to the Burke and Hare case, an article in the *Westminster Review* mentions Astley Cooper's remarks (and those of other witnesses) as anticipating Burke and Hare: "Warning was given to the legislature of the deeds that were likely to be done; the discovery of the actual perpetration of such deeds, on a scale of magnitude, and with a cool and even scientific deliberation that are truly appalling, has indeed too soon come to justify the truth of the prediction" (129).[54] In this article, blame lies with the legislature for not acting in time rather than with the anatomists: Parliament "has so well protected the dead, as to have produced a most appalling insecurity to the living" (130). The *Westminster Review* calls those who blame surgeons for Burke and Hare's crimes "too contemptible to deserve notice" and argues that "they can mislead only the most vulgar and ignorant, and that only for a day" (130). Instead, the reviewer reinforces anatomy's scientific nature and social benefit: "[D]issection must be practiced; the wants of the community imperiously demand it, and always will demand it; society can no more go on without the supply of subjects for the anatomist, than it can go on without the supply of corn for food" (135). In this review, anatomy connotes progress, benefit, and even beauty: "[T]here is no such thing as

42   a natural aversion to dissection. . . . There is nothing in the process or in its result calculated to inspire horror. It is an exquisitely delicate operation, and its effect is to display a mechanism so complicated and so beautiful, that there is no study at all comparable to it" (141). While the *Westminster Review* uses the Burke and Hare case to reinforce anatomy's positive connotations and to separate resurrection and anatomy further, its attempts to vindicate anatomy imply that many blamed anatomists for burking and that burking undermined anatomy's claims to prestige. It is to burking that I now turn.

In 1828, William Burke and William Hare murdered sixteen people in Edinburgh and sold their bodies to anatomist Robert Knox. Friends of the last victim reported Burke and Hare to the police; Hare turned informer and implicated Burke, who was hanged and anatomized. There is no evidence that Burke and Hare were resurrection men prior to these incidents. Knox and his anatomy students claimed that they did not know that the bodies were murdered, and they were not charged. The case generated the verb *to burke,* which the *Oxford English Dictionary* defines as "To murder, in the same manner or for the same purpose as Burke did; to kill secretly by suffocation or strangulation, or for the purpose of selling the victim's body for dissection."[55] Ruth Richardson argues that the Burke and Hare case is "critically significant" because it contrasts the "clinical 'scientific' view" of the body and the "importance of the corpse and its integrity in popular culture."[56] Richardson mentions the opinion of a committee of inquiry charged with investigating Knox, which rested "in the belief that neither Knox nor his staff entertained any suspicion of the murders."[57] This section explores the implications of such conclusions on anatomy. The issue is not whether Knox knew or did not know about burking but what his denials signified. If aware of burking, Knox was guilty of collusion with Burke and Hare. In this case, burking, especially the Burke and Hare case, undermines the rhetoric of separation that attaches immorality and crime to resurrection men alone. Anatomy itself becomes attached to criminality and thus to quackery (the configuration of quackery outlined by Ludmilla Jordanova earlier as associated with immorality and greed). If he was unaware, Knox's ignorance draws into doubt the very utility of anatomy as a science. In this case, burking leads to serious questions about anatomy's very status because its supposed knowledge and discovery are revealed as exaggerations, blinds used to inflate surgeons' status and power rather than a legitimate study.

Such deception is the hallmark of quackery, where quackery is lack of knowledge or exaggeration of knowledge for gain.

Several contemporary commentators used burking to undermine anatomy's claim of beneficence, although these accounts maintain or even reinforce anatomy's association with science. For example, Knox's porter, Paterson, claims that the doctor knew, or should have known, about the murders: "[I]f the Doctor saw these bodies, he is either horribly ignorant of his profession, or he willfully withheld that information he ought to have given. I will ask any other professors of anatomy, candidly and honestly, that if two men, of the appearance of Burke and Hare, had brought them ten or a dozen bodies, with the same appearance as those brought by B. and H. [sic] must have had, what would be their opinion? I am certain of one thing, that it would, at least, have a great tendency to rouse their suspicions."[58] Critic Suzanne Shultz calls Knox "unfortunate" for his involvement with Burke and Hare;[59] however, Paterson argues that Knox was complicit. Paterson contends that any competent anatomist would have known about the murders and that only an anatomist "horribly ignorant of his profession" could have failed to recognize the signs. Later in this pamphlet, Paterson claims that Knox knew of the murders because Knox immediately ordered the dissection of the body of a well-known victim, Daft Jamie, as soon as word of his disappearance became public.[60] A contemporary ballad describes Knox's conduct succinctly; "Nor did he question when or how / The persons brought had died!" and then advises Knox, "Nor ever more in word or deed / Wink at such tricks again."[61] The word *wink* implies that Knox knew of the murders and deliberately refrained from questioning the situation to avoid losing his specimen. The exclamation point implies skepticism and outrage at Knox's failure to ask questions. The *History of the London Burkers* (1832) also connects anatomy and immorality through Knox: "What opinion, then, can we form of the surgical professor, who can have a human corpse offered to him before it is scarcely cold, destitute of all the distinctive marks of exhumation, and without any of the concomitant signs of corruption, coolly and deliberately purchasing the same, without instituting the slightest inquiry . . . whether he was not himself actually abetting and encouraging a human wretch in the crime of murder. . . . [W]e cannot designate this conduct by any other term than a bonus held out for the crime of murder."[62] In this passage, Knox "coolly and deliberately" purchased the bodies, knowing that they were evidence of murder, because of his expertise in anatomy. Knox

44   was thereby "abetting and encouraging" murder by offering money, "a bonus," to the murderers. In these documents, Knox appears particularly immoral because anatomy reveals the signs of murder to him yet he fails to act appropriately. To these commentators, Knox's conduct seems particularly galling because of an unspoken assumption of anatomy's beneficence: where his skill in anatomy should have led Knox to spot the murderers and to have prevented more murders by informing police, his rapacity for anatomical specimens led to his complicity. From this point of view, the evident bitterness toward Knox derives from the thwarted assumption that anatomy was beneficent. At the same time, Knox reinforced anatomy's scientific value: because of anatomy, they argue, Knox knew the truth, hence the outrage at his lack of questions.

What of Knox's claims of ignorance? The *History of the London Burkers* questions the relationship between burking and anatomy in general: "We know of the existence of human shambles, where the leg, or the arm, or the head of a human being, can be purchased with the same facility as a leg of mutton or a sirloin of beef, we may then with shame ask ourselves the question—Can this be England—the most enlightened, the most civilized country of the globe?"[63] In this passage, anatomy degrades humans to animals, an enlightened nation to shameful barbarism. The language of degradation contrasts sharply with anatomists' claims that anatomy represents knowledge and progress. Here, the term connotes the very opposite. But the text goes on to question whether anatomy is a science at all: "The whole business, however, resolves itself into this simple question: is it, or is it not in the power of a professed surgeon, to whom a body may be offered for sale, to determine, on the very first view of it, whether the subject died a natural death, or whether force or violence has been used to effect the destruction of life? If the question be answered in the negative, that the surgeon has no means of arriving at a just conclusion, what then becomes of the boasted superiority of medical science over that which was possessed by our forefathers?"[64] In this passage, anatomy is a pseudoscience because anatomists cannot tell whether a body died recently or several days before or whether a body was murdered violently or buried and exhumed. The passage compares surgeons trained in anatomy with those who were not and finds little difference between them. This implies that anatomy's scientific value is exaggerated or even false, its scientific reputation a mere strategy for gain. This single text does not prove that there was a widespread belief in anatomy as quackery; however, it does suggest that anatomy might

have connoted in some circles exaggeration or overreaching on the part   45
of surgeons. This passage questions the value of anatomy and concludes
that the "boasted superiority of medical science" may have indeed been
a *boast*, that is, attention-getting, exaggerated, and vainglorious.

Other texts hint that anatomy's status as a science may have been
exaggerated, akin to the embellishments of the medicine show. An 1839
text about quackery lists dissection as a quack practice, since "the inutil-
ity of dissection is well known to every well informed man . . . though
it would be fruitless to attempt to expose this popular folly of the day,
(which like all other follies or fashions will 'have its rage' until its own
enormity cures itself)."[65] George MacGregor's well-known *The History of
Burke and Hare and of the Resurrectionist Times* reproduces ephemera from the
period, including several ballads that question the nature of anatomy.[66]
In one lyric, anatomy seems barely scientific:

> Or should'st have known, if true thy Science says,
> That marks of death by Murder any ways
> May well be seen, when the dissecting knife
> Opens all the sure and secret seats of life.[67]

In this verse, the value of anatomy ("thy Science") to the "secret seats of
life" is questioned, since, if truly a science, anatomy would have revealed
the murders to the anatomists. Another ballad also questions the value
of learning anatomy:

> Ye great men of learning, ye friends of dissection,
> Who travell'd through blood to the temple of gain,
> And bright human life for your hateful inspection,
> O give to the poor friends the white bones of the slain.

> But woe to the riches and skill thus obtained,
> Woe to the wretch that would injure the dead,
> And woe to his portion whose fingers are stained
> With red drops of life that he cruelly shed.[68]

In these verses, anatomy is not completely ineffective as a science, but
it is cruel (to the "poor friends" and to the injured dead) and bloody
("blood," "hateful inspection," "red drops of life," and "cruelly shed").
The fingers in the latter verse may be Knox's or Burke's, since "injure

46   the dead" implies anatomy but "drops of life" implies murder. There is a question about whether Burke or Knox is the murderous tiger: "Some may survive him whose hearts are as callous / O, who will be safe if the tigers are free."[69]

The 1832 *Westminster Review* article that eagerly defends anatomy also raises questions about anatomy's effectiveness as a science. The article blames burking on the resurrection trade: "Their most unnatural calling prepares them for most unnatural crime" and "all the guilt, and ignominy, and ruin, which these desperate men have incurred, should rest upon the shoulders of the law," which is here called the "birth and parentage" of both Burke and the London Burkers, Bishop and Williams (491).[70] The article defends anatomy as the "scape-goat of a nation's folly"; however, the article contends that in the Burke and Hare case, "no medical witness of sufficient information could extract the least tittle of criminating evidence" and "the method of extinguishing vitality, to which Burke and Hare had recourse, sets equally at defiance chemistry, physiology, and anatomy" (492). The article explains in detail the anatomical differences between the Burke and Hare murders and the Bishop and Williams murders, in which anatomists testified to their suspicions: "[I]t is probable that some of the medical evidence given upon these murderers [*sic*] trial has betrayed the public into the belief that Burking cannot be performed without exposing the Burker to detection by the knife of the anatomist. But they may rest assured that there never was a more mistaken notion" (493). This "mistaken notion" becomes the basis for pleading for more anatomical specimens: "[S]eal up the sepulchre which contains your dead children, and he [the burker] will steal into the apartment that contains your living ones" (496). This peculiar line of reasoning implies that scientists in anatomy, chemistry, and physiology are not as knowledgeable as popularly believed and might encourage kidnapping and murder, if not adequately supplied. In pleading for anatomy, this writer ironically undermines claims of knowledge, progress, and beneficence made on behalf of anatomy, making even a skilled and renowned practitioner such as Knox appear bumbling, inept, and inhumane.

In the style of Swift's "A Modest Proposal," "The Philosophy of Burking" (1832) laments Hare's fate. It claims that Socrates, Galileo, and Hare "may be considered victims to their ardent love of science" (52).[71] Like Columbus and de Gama, Hare in this essay finds "the particular department of science best suited for his display of his talents" and must rescue anatomy from "the preposterous and bigoted aversion which the people had to the art of dissection" (53). Unless anatomy is defended, "the sciences dependent upon it . . . would immediately sink into a state of barbarism . . . and there would be vast loss of life, and a great and unnecessary degree of human suffering" (53). As Hare weighs methods of killing, he apparently thinks, "I must shelter myself for the chance of falling a prey to ignorance and bigotry. If I do not, what avail my efforts in the cause of anatomy?" (54). The narrator assures readers that Hare acts not "from any selfish motive, but purely from an unbounded devotion to science and the true interests of his country" (55). The praise is clearly ironic, but the victim of the irony may be either Hare or anatomists themselves, whose familiar claims of beneficence and scientific progress are here repeated to great effect. Although Hare is the obvious target, the complaints of public prejudice, of anatomy's misunderstood nature, and of the anatomist as the unsung benefactor of society are familiar from anatomists' own testimony before the Select Committee on Anatomy. The warnings of terrible consequences should the public interfere with anatomy are also familiar, although here they point to the terrible events that have already occurred. The article brilliantly shows the two-edged nature of such language, which may praise anatomy as the queen of the medical sciences or condemn it as a blind for exploitation, greed, self-interest, and even murder.

This chapter does not argue that anatomy was considered quackery by most commentators during the heyday of burking or afterward; however, these documents suggest through rich description that anatomy's connotations were not under control of official discourse but displayed contradictory tendencies. The latter section displays the ways in which burking in general, and the Burke and Hare case in particular, questioned anatomy's association with beneficence and science. Approached through the discourse of burking, anatomy appears to have been a vainglorious practice, more bent on aggrandizing its practitioners than on discovery and beneficence. Whether criminal or merely ignorant, anatomists in this discourse appear to have been engaged in gross quackery. The former section displays the connection between anatomy, scientific discovery, and public beneficence. Most practitioners concurred in anatomy's usefulness to surgery and medicine; however, testimony before the Select Committee on Anatomy displays a range of positions on issues such as the body, burial, the Murder Act, the Anatomy Bill, resurrection, and others. Both strands resonate strongly with Mary Shelley's *Frankenstein*. On the one hand, Shelley values anatomy and imagines a

48   more empathetic way of conducting it so as to maximize its great potential for human knowledge, but, on the other hand, Shelley questions the very status of anatomy as science. Victor Frankenstein is an anatomist and a remarkably successful experimenter but also a body snatcher, a liar, a potential murderer, and a remarkably ineffective medical practitioner. In this sense, the novel exemplifies the very complex constellations of signification surrounding anatomy during the early nineteenth century. Exploring anatomy in *Frankenstein* reveals not only anatomy's multiplicity of meaning but also the instability of orthodoxy and quackery. In the novel, as in early nineteenth-century culture, quackery may signify ignorance, partial knowledge, and lack of skill. Quackery may also signify immorality or criminality on the part of practitioners, even those quite competent in their profession. Quackery seems highly dependent on circumstances, because the nature of morality is subject to cultural standards and because quackery may indicate wrongdoing or incompetence. Finally, quackery and orthodoxy are difficult to extricate from each other, because the same term may generate connotations of orthodoxy and quackery simultaneously. This chapter asserts that terms such as *anatomy* are not stable concepts dictated by the medico-legal establishment but carry layers of meaning that are dynamic and unruly. In this model, neither public nor scientific sources offer the "right" meaning. As such, anatomy is not a contested field between science and society but an example of the nuances of language that make issues of orthodoxy and quackery thorny and complex.

Chapter Two

Doctoring in *Little Dorrit* and *Bleak House*

> The quacks are on their last legs. . . . The clean will now
> be separated from the unclean, and they fear to be cast
> out into a wilderness of scorn and impecuniosity.
> —From "Quackery on Its Death-Bed," *Lancet,* 1858

> Medicine, as we all know, is one of the saddest of trades
> and the most noble of professions.
> —From "Important Educational Changes," *Lancet,* 1858

This chapter examines the complexities of doctoring in two novels by Charles Dickens, *Bleak House* (1853) and *Little Dorrit* (1857). According to the *Oxford English Dictionary,* the verb "to doctor" may denote "to treat, as a doctor or physician; to administer medicine or medical treatment to" and also "to repair, patch up, set to rights."[1] Thus, "to doctor" may suggest either the administration of medicines, procedures, and interventions (whether successful or unsuccessful) or the concept of amelioration (which is always beneficial). Alternatively, the verb may denote doubtful enterprise or even harm: "To treat so as to alter the appearance, flavour, or character of; to disguise, falsify, tamper with, adulterate, sophisticate, 'cook.'"[2] Written shortly before the Medical Act of 1858, which created the first register of orthodox practitioners in Britain, *Little Dorrit* and *Bleak House* employ language that conflates medical treatment and the ability to "set to rights" by representing medicine as healing. This language emphasizes amelioration over technical intervention, the outcome of which is doubtful. In uniting medical

50 treatment and amelioration, these novels displace doubt onto nonmedical professions, and both novels are saturated with the fraudulent "doctoring" of financial, governmental, and legal systems.[3] In his readings of finance in George Eliot's novels, Richard D. Mallen describes a "necessary symbiosis" between trust and its opposite, suspicion.[4] In displacing fraud onto other professions, Dickens creates in Little Dorrit's Physician and in Bleak House's Dr. Woodcourt a version of the medical professional capable of healing the diseased systems of modern life. Dickens's physicians are less professional doctors than professional healers, a term that implies both the artificial (professionalized, systemized, marketed, and potentially fraudulent) and the organic (natural, personal, authentic).[5] The professional doctor may stitch (using proper technique and for a fee), but time, nature, and Dickens's physicians heal.[6] The ways in which these novels represent physicians raises questions about professional medicine at a significant moment in its development. How did medicine redeploy the language of healing to craft a trustworthy professional ethos? What were the implications of such language for professional medicine's negotiation of financial, scientific, and social interests? How was professional trust developed, and how could the requisite trust be maintained alongside a healthy skepticism?

As a professional author, Dickens was keenly sensitive to issues of authenticity.[7] In his preface to Bleak House, Dickens defends his use of spontaneous combustion, which had been criticized by G. H. Lewes as impossible, saying, "I have no need to observe that I do not willfully or negligently mislead my readers, and that before I wrote that description I took pains to investigate the subject."[8] Dickens lists several noted instances of spontaneous combustion and then alludes to several "distinguished medical professors" who supported the idea.[9] Fiction implies both deliberate lying and imaginative storytelling, but Dickens emphatically rejects the former implication.[10] His response implies that while some authors may mislead readers, he stakes his personal reputation on truthfulness ("I have . . . ," "I do not . . . ," "I wrote," "I took pains" [emphasis added]). At the same time, Dickens claims that he has "no need" to assert his truthfulness, because professionalism assumes good faith, and he is a professional. Dickens's defense of spontaneous combustion appeals to professionalism in medicine as well as in writing when he refers to medical professors who support his view. Was medicine so trustworthy? Richard Quain's Harveian Oration used recent scientific breakthroughs to vindicate medicine's checkered reputation, which implies a more complex relationship between professionalism, medicine, and science.[11] Other critics also identify a complex relationship between scientific advances and medicine's increasing social power during this period.[12] According to W. F. Bynum, English science maintained a vexed relationship with professionalism because science was "pursued on a part-time basis" in the "creative amateur tradition."[13] Thus, Dickens's appeal to medico-scientific testimony may not only generate truth-claims about spontaneous combustion but also invest medical practitioners with disinterestedness, devotion, and integrity, the sense of higher purpose often associated with religious calling. Janis McLarren Caldwell notes the overlap in natural theology between pre-Darwinian science and other ways of knowing, including Christianity.[14] Association with science buoys medicine's claims of trustworthiness not only by discovering new treatments but also by elevating practitioners above mere marketplace concerns. In another way, the Medical Act of 1858 also addresses this issue. Roy Porter claims that the 1858 Medical Act "symbolically at least, united the much-divided medical profession, by defining them over and against a common Other."[15] According to Porter, the act changed the terms of medical orthodoxy by dividing a previously tripartite profession (apothecaries, surgeons, physicians) along new lines, the orthodox and the unorthodox, by placing the former in and excluding the latter from the medical register. Porter describes a change from the terms of marketplace politics to the terms of authenticity. Science was a dominant epistemology during this period in its power to support truth-claims, but it also appealed to other epistemologies. Nineteenth-century science drew upon Christian notions of a calling rather than merely paid work. Thus, medical professionalism encompassed scientific truth-claims and good-faith values, marketplace interests and vocation.

Were such attitudes common in mid-nineteenth-century medical culture? There are provocative suggestions that the language of Christian vocation was deployed by those eager to craft a sense of medical professionalism. For example, a doctor identifying himself as "A Surgeon" complains to the *Times* about pressure from the police in a case in which a woman in labor was wanted for burglary. He asserts that he "is the healer and the comforter, not the spy and thief-taker—the minister of hope and mercy, not of vengeance."[16] The words *healer, comforter, mercy, hope,* and *minister* describe not scientific or technical skill but a "higher calling," elevating him above the demands of even the state. A doctor

52   in the 1858 *Lancet* bluntly outlines the social disadvantages of medicine: "Medical men, as a body, are not regarded as gentlemen; they are not visited as such; they are not treated as such . . . but the great body of the profession is looked down upon by the upper classes as about a shade better than respectable tradespeople."[17] This doctor's complaint views the equating of medicine and trade as social and moral degradation. Another doctor complains that his Poor Law board voted to pay him only 3£ for his services in stemming a cholera epidemic instead of the 25£ he had been promised.[18] While this complaint is explicitly financial, it emphasizes the doctor's trust in the Poor Law board's honor and his victimization by sharp tradesmen whose hard bargains value a few pounds above fair play. An article from the popular-press *Fortnightly Review* similarly contrasts the "guardians, who are small tradesmen, chiefly anxious to save the rates" and the doctors; "We desire to speak with all respect of the medical officers. Assuredly, no more hard-working and ill-paid officials exist in this country."[19] An article in the *Cornhill* magazine describes physicians working in state-run hospitals: "All these gentlemen are men of great eminence, holding the first rank in the profession, so that the poorest man, woman, or child that seeks help is given the benefit of the best advice in the kingdom, and the sick costermonger or ailing chimney-sweeper is enabled gratuitously to command services which many a wealthy man cannot purchase."[20] The physicians here are men of *eminence*, a term also used to describe church officials, and they offer philanthropic equality of treatment, above financial or social considerations. Always an advocate for professionalization, the *Lancet* describes the Medical Act of 1858 in biblical terms as able to separate the "clean" (licensed) from the "unclean" (unlicensed).[21] As an epigraph to this chapter states, medicine is the "most noble of professions," and the *Lancet* continues on to warn its readers; "let us beware, then, how we degrade it to the level of a trade, and let us be strenuous in laboring to elevate it as a liberal profession."[22] While these few examples do not prove that there was a concerted campaign to define medical orthodoxy using terms appropriated from Christianity, they indicate that writers within and outside of the profession both explicitly and implicitly contrast medical practitioners with Poor Law boards, police, and tradesmen in order to distance medicine from the marketplace and conflate Christian virtue and professional duty in medicine.

Although this chapter examines medical orthodoxy in two Dickens novels, Charles Dickens's most famous medical character is (arguably)

Martin Chuzzlewit's (1844) frowzy midwife and nurse, Sairy Gamp. In that   53
novel, medicine is strongly associated with charlatanism, a representation similar to those that Richard Quain considers responsible for the
degradation of medicine in the public mind, "so often regarded with
skepticism and want of confidence, and so often treated with satire and
even with contempt."[23] This chapter does not seek to minimize or to
disregard medical quackery, fraud, and adulteration during this period,
nor to ignore Dickens's critique of medical quackery in other novels and
essays. However, as Miriam Bailin shows, Dickens's representation of
medicine is not always invested in verisimilitude. Bailin reads Dickens's
sickroom as a "kind of provisional or preliminary heaven" that allows the
recovery of a personal and community wholeness, "the hallowed ground
of matrimonial, filial and self-unification."[24] Bailin contrasts the feverish
and confused wanderings of sickness, or "dissolving boundaries," with
the sickroom's restoration of "order and distinction."[25] This chapter examines the ways in which Dickens asserts professional boundaries using
the terms of vocation, recognizing that during this period science and
Christianity were not viewed as adversarial. Rather, medical orthodoxy
was constructed in important ways by the language of Christian vocation as well as from rhetoric associated with progressive science, using
Christianity and amateurism to craft a configuration of medical professionalism that contrasted with other trades and emerging professions.

Fraud at Home in *Little Dorrit*

In *Little Dorrit*, the financial wizard Mr. Merdle commits suicide
rather than face exposure as a forger and fraud. His body is identified
by a minor character called Physician, a wealthy society doctor who at-
tends the best dinners with the best (corrupt) statesmen and financiers:

> Few ways of life were hidden from Physician, and he was oftener
> in its darkest places than even Bishop. There were brilliant ladies
> about London who perfectly doted on him, my dear, as the most
> charming creature and the most delightful person, who would have
> been shocked to find themselves so close to him if they could have
> known on what sights those thoughtful eyes of his had rested within
> an hour or two, and near to whose beds, and under what roofs, his
> composed figure had stood. But, Physician was a composed man,
> who performed neither on his own trumpet, nor on the trumpets of

other people. Many wonderful things did he see and hear, and much irreconcileable [sic] moral contradiction did he pass his life among; yet his equality of compassion was no more disturbed than the Divine Master's of all healing was. He went, like the rain, among the just and unjust, doing all the good he could, and neither proclaiming it in the synagogues nor at the corners of streets.[26]

In his readings of finance in George Eliot's novels, Richard D. Mallen discriminates between "tacit trust," based in personal experience, and "express trust," based in professional systems, both of which are required for the middle class to "enjoy a stable ethos of trust."[27] Physician is a fantasy of personal and professional virtue sorely lacking in the superficial world of Society. Physician enters more dark corners than Bishop, displacing moral guardianship onto medicine because of its long-standing association with healing (the "Divine Master . . . of all healing"). He stands beside beds and under roofs, and he rests his eyes on patients, as if his mere presence benefits sufferers. This appeal to healing (rather than to active medical treatment) downplays the role of modern institutions (education, science, registration) and grounds his professionalism in Christian virtue, not technical skill or scientific knowledge. Physician is absolutely just ("like the rain") and without self-interest (neither expressing nor trumpeting nor proclaiming his accomplishments to his hostesses or to the public). Yet Physician is a professional, because his name implies a profession, not an individual, just as the other dinner guests are identified by their professions (such as Bishop), although Physician does not appear here as a professional man with scientific training and financial concerns.[28] Despite this world's "irreconcilable moral contradiction," Physician appears to reconcile professional and personal interests happily, glossing over the conflicts between and within each.

Physician is a minor but significant figure because he is implicated in two prominent tropes in the novel: disease and finance. Critics have addressed finance to a greater extent than disease; for example, Amanda Anderson claims that Little Dorrit illustrates the dangers of cosmopolitanism, which severs "ties of love, community and nation."[29] In the novel, Merdle himself claims that there must be the "purest faith between man and man; there must be unimpeached and unimpeachable confidence; or business could not be carried on" (590). However, as Anderson notes, Merdle has few personal ties. Despite his devotion to "Society," Mrs. Merdle reprimands him for his social awkwardness, and his butler

recognizes something amiss in his air: "Sir, Mr Merdle never was the   55
gentleman, and no ungentlemanly act on Mr Merdle's part would sur-
prise me" (678). Merdle's stepson, Edmund Sparkler, claims that Merdle "carries the Shop about . . . like a Jew clothesman" (386). Merdle's
business, or shop, interferes with his social life, and the reference to
Jewishness seems to reinforce Anderson's view of Merdle as a symbol
of cosmopolitanism.[30] However, Merdle is associated not only with finance but also with disease in a chapter entitled "Merdle's Complaint."
Merdle's ongoing "complaint" is both physical illness and financial fraud,
as Dickens's notes reflect (803). Merdle is unable to eat or drink: he eats
only "eighteenpence" worth of dinner (246) and drinks only "twopen-
nyworth of tea" (249). The monetary value of his food highlights his
physical disorder. He also habitually performs nervous gestures, such as
putting spoons up his sleeves and convulsively grasping his own wrists
(541). In the chapter entitled "The Progress of an Epidemic," Merdle's
investment scheme is called a disease, and it infects Arthur Clennam and
other hardworking tenants of Bleeding Heart Yard: "That it is at least as
difficult to stay a moral infection as a physical one; that such a disease
will spread with the malignity and rapidity of the Plague; . . . is a fact as
firmly established by experience as that we human creatures breathe an
atmosphere. A blessing beyond appreciation would be conferred upon
mankind, if the tainted . . . could be immediately seized and placed in
close confinement . . . before the poison is communicable" (547). Where
Physician is compared to "the Divine Master . . . of all healing," Merdle
is variously called a "graven image" (465), a "Deity" (533), and the rich
man "already entered into the kingdom of Heaven" (587). To worship
Merdle is to worship the "Devil" (680). In his examination of property
in *Little Dorrit*, Jeff Nunokawa concludes that "grave losses result less from
accident or avarice than from laws of the marketplace situated beyond
the province of human error."[31] Christopher Herbert, however, notices
a paradox in which money appears simultaneously both filthy and divine, an ideal to grasp and a symbol of moral degradation indicative of
two incompatible cultural systems: bourgeois capitalism and evangelical
Christianity.[32] Nunokawa and Herbert capture the financial aspect of *Little Dorrit* but not its connection to disease. In this novel, financial losses
are not merely a function of exchange but of fraud, a result of deliberate
subversion; thus, Physician is an important character, because he com-
bats Merdle's physical disease and also offers readers an ideal in Merdle's
world of fraud. In this representation of Physician as a physical and

56   spiritual healer, Dickens asserts medicine as an authentic and trustworthy profession, a cure for the sick systems embodied both in Merdle's
diseased body and in his fraudulent business.

Monica F. Cohen reads business in this novel as a rather sinister
occupation. For it to produce any good, according to Cohen, business
must develop personal relationships; however, the relationship between
personal and business in this novel is vexed.[33] At the Marshalsea debtor's
prison, to offer a "testimonial" is to give money (91) and to "pay a compliment" is to pay money (230). Terms of respect signify cash. When
an honest prison guard's son, John Chivory, falls in love with mild Amy
Dorrit, the Dorrits "turned it to account" by accepting favors from his
father and cigars from John himself (212). The word *account* implies an
exchange of love for goods. Mr. Dorrit expresses affection for pauper
Mr. Nandy by calling him his "pensioner," suggesting the exchange of
both affection and money (356). Pancks plays "fortune-teller" to Amy
because he reads her palm and later brings an inheritance to her family, a play on the meaning of *fortune* as both destiny and wealth (283).
Professional companion Mrs. General offers the Dorrits "the tribute of
my thanks," recalling the wealth extorted by ruling empires rather than
simple gratitude (577). Fanny Dorrit asserts her "spirit" by accepting
bracelets from her high-born lover's mother to break off the relationship; she explains to Amy, "Make her pay for it, you stupid child; and do
your family some credit with the money!" (241). To Fanny, *spirit* means
goods, and *family credit* means money, not merely a good name. Similarly,
Miss Rugg receives twenty guineas in a breach of promise suit after her
lover breaks off their engagement (290). Well-born but penniless Henry
Gowan evaluates acquaintances according to his "book-keeping . . . a
careful little account of Good and Evil" (205). Henry Gowan catches
wealthy but middle-class Pet Meagles in "Society's matrimonial market";
"what scheming and counter-scheming took place for the high buyers,
and what bargaining and huckstering went on" (381). This "bargaining" and "huckstering" degrades marriage to buying and selling, with the
implication that the buyer should beware. Similarly, Merdle's marriage
is a matter of marketing; Mrs. Merdle's bejeweled bosom, often called
simply "the bosom," is "not a bosom to repose upon, but it was a capital
bosom to hang jewels upon. . . . [Merdle] bought it for the purpose"
(244). The word *capital* implies both praise and money. This novel sen-
sitizes readers to words customarily used in both personal relationships
and finance. Words such as *credit, testimonial, account, tribute, market, fortune,*

capital, and *compliment* are revealed to be more than mere descriptions of   57
harmless social tit for tat; instead, they come to symbolize the degradation of human relationships to the level of transactions, and transactions
in this world are fraudulent. Mrs. Merdle's bosom may carry capital (expensive jewels) upon it, but it is not a "capital bosom" in any affective
sense. Fanny's notion of family credit is little short of extortion. John
Chivory's respect is squandered on the Dorrits, whose pretenses mask
their selfishness and vulgarity. In these relationships between personal
and business, Dickens questions the social and affective consequences
of modernity.

Just as this world is saturated by finance, so too is it saturated by
disease. The novel opens with Arthur Clennam and the Meagles family
in quarantine in Marseilles (28). Clennam's return to his mother's house
of business in London is greeted with Sunday bells tolling "as if the
Plague were in the city and the dead-carts were going round" (41). He
wonders "how many sick people" die listening to the bells (41). Clennam's mother, Mrs. Clennam, suffers from a mysterious complaint that
confines her to her room. During his first visit to the Marshalsea prison,
Clennam imagines prisoners sickening and dying (96). Although slow-
witted Maggy admires the hospital because of its "chicking" and broth,
she is mentally a ten-year-old due to a childhood fever (109).[34] After he
has been ruined by Merdle, Clennam literally becomes sick, and Dickens compares his sickroom to the "fevered world" outside (766). Disease
appears to manifest the corruption at the heart of the financial system;
however, Dickens complicates this paradigm in landlord Mr. Casby, "a
crafty impostor" who owns Bleeding-Heart Yard but is far from a bleeding heart (151). Pondering Casby's benign forehead, "a mere Inn sign-
post without any Inn" (151), Clennam thinks, "[I]n the Royal Academy
some evil old ruffian of a Dogstealer will annually be found embodying
all the cardinal virtues, on account of his eyelashes, or his chin, or his
legs, . . . so in the great social Exhibition, accessories are often accepted
in lieu of the internal character" (151). As in the portraits at the Royal
Academy, the world of this novel is inauthentic, its "cardinal virtues"
mere painted surfaces without depth, complicating a reading of disease
as simply a marker of corruption or fraud.

Two examples display the synergy of fraud, finance, and disease in
this novel: the Dorrits and the Clennams. Mr. Dorrit spends over twenty
years in the Marshalsea because of a business partner's fraud (70), and he
eventually loses his great inheritance to Merdle. Although Dorrit is the

58   victim of fraud in these cases, his life so saturated by impersonation and pretense that he cannot recognize or appreciate authenticity. Jennifer Ruth examines the "double discourse of value" in which finance offers one sort of value and culture another.[35] Constant fraud blinds Dorrit to the values outside of finance, although he is alive to the value of impersonating culture. When he unexpectedly inherits his great fortune, Dorrit scrupulously pays his literal debts: "I will not go away from here in anybody's debt. All the people who have been—ha—well behaved towards myself and my family, shall be rewarded" (404). Dorrit cannot comprehend an affective economy. In prison, Dorrit survives on Amy's salary, literally taking food from her plate (89), and on Clennam's charity, but he never thanks either, so that he may uphold the pretense that he is a gentleman (105).[36] In contrast, Arthur Clennam lauds Amy more than the great inheritance as he tells Dorrit the good news; "I congratulate you with all my soul on this change of fortune, and on the happy future into which you are soon to carry the treasure you have been blest with here—the best of all the riches you can have elsewhere—the treasure at your side" (403). To Arthur Clennam, Dorrit's "fortune" is luck and newfound wealth, but Amy's affection is also "treasure" and "riches." The now-wealthy Dorrit, in contrast, concurs with superficial Mrs. General's opinion that Amy lacks "force of character" and "self-reliance" (456). The narrator imagines a more appropriate reply: "[A]sk me, her father, what I owe to her; and hear my testimony touching the life of this slighted little creature" (456). The word *testimony* recalls Dorrit's financial testimonials at the Marshalsea. Having reduced testimonials to cash value, Dorrit cannot now comprehend the value of testimony as truth-telling. Amy describes the melancholia and mental suffering created by her inauthentic life as a wealthy girl: she describes tears and regret at being estranged from her old friends, particularly Maggy (452). She suffers a "wandering" feeling of disorientation and severe loneliness in her new life that leaves her unable to feel "pleasure" in any of her relationships or occupations (453). Her uncle, Frederick Dorrit, recognizes her quiet suffering and criticizes Dorrit; "I protest against ingratitude. I protest against any one of us here . . . setting up any pretension that puts Amy at a moment's disadvantage, or to the cost of a moment's pain. We may know that it's a base pretension by its having that effect. It ought to bring a judgment on us. Brother, I protest against it, in the sight of God!" (467). Frederick Dorrit sees the cost of the family's pretenses in terms of Amy's mental health, but Dorrit cannot participate in this economy. Ironically, Dorrit

himself suffers a strokelike incident at a grand dinner party. Unable to remember his real wealth, he begs the dinner guests for financial testimonials, as he had in the Marshalsea (621). In the end, his damaged mind becomes estranged from reality and trapped in the Marshalsea prison.

Similarly, Mrs. Clennam becomes literally and figuratively trapped by fraud. Arthur claims, "I am the only child of parents who weighted, measured, and priced everything: for whom what could not be weighed, measured and priced, had no existence" (33). Mrs. Clennam's spirituality is transactional; "Forgive us our debts as we forgive our debtors, was a prayer too poor in spirit for her. Smite thou my debtors, Lord, wither them, crush them; do Thou as I would do, and Thou shalt have my worship" (57). In Mrs. Clennam's provocative application of the Lord's Prayer, debt must be repaid, without forgiveness or grace: "[L]et him [Arthur] look at me, in prison, and in bonds here. I endure without murmuring, because it is appointed that I shall so make reparation for my sins" (60). Word such as *prison, bonds,* and *reparation* imply that her disease is divine punishment, that God imprisons her just as financial debtors are imprisoned in the Marshalsea. Arthur views her illness as self-inflicted punishment for defrauding another, possibly Dorrit. He imagines his mother's thoughts: "He [Dorrit] withers away in his prison; I wither away in mine; inexorable justice is done" (96).[37] Arthur worries about how to pay his mother's figurative debts:

> [L]et us examine sacredly whether there is any wrong entrusted to us to set right. . . . In grasping at money and in driving hard bargains—I have begun, and I must speak of such things now, mother—some one may have been grievously deceived, injured, ruined. . . . If reparation can be made to anyone, if restitution can be made to any one, let us know it and make it. . . . I have seen so little happiness come of money; it has brought within my knowledge so little peace to this house, or to any one belonging to it; that it is worth less to me than to another. It can buy me nothing that will not be a reproach and misery to me, if I am haunted by a suspicion that it darkened my father's last hours with remorse. (59)

Words such as *buy, worth, ruined,* and *reparation* recall the dual meaning of financial terms in the novel. Arthur weighs remorse, peace, and happiness against wealth and recognizes that wealth is not unrelated to these concepts but not equivalent to them either.

60   For all her moral accounting, Mrs. Clennam is a fraud: because of her malice toward Arthur's real mother, whom she has impersonated since his birth, she has hidden the codicil to a will that would enrich Amy Dorrit. Like Merdle, she unites disease, fraud, and finance, and, again like Merdle, Mrs. Clennam's fraud destroys her health, her relationships, and her house of business (it literally collapses in a heap). However, Mrs. Clennam is also a victim: she is blackmailed by Blandois, an assassin from Marseilles, and by her own business partner, Flintwick, who has stolen papers that prove her misconduct. Amy learns the truth, but she does not reveal his mother's impersonation to Arthur. Monica F. Cohen reads Amy's suppression of Mrs. Clennam's secret as the tragic stifling of Arthur's personal growth.[38] Alternatively, perhaps Dickens positions Amy's refusal of Mrs. Clennam's debt as the culmination of the novel's pattern of transactional relationships; Amy says to Mrs. Clennam, "I forgive you freely," and the word *forgive* applies both to finance (Amy will not collect her legacy) and to Christianity (753). She begs Mrs. Clennam, "Be guided only by the healer of the sick, the raiser of the dead, the friend of all who were afflicted and forlorn, the patient Master who shed tears of compassion for our infirmities" (756). The word *healer* appears here, as in the description of Physician. In recognizing Christ as a compassionate healer of physical and spiritual infirmity, Amy corrects Mrs. Clennam's misapplication of the Lord's Prayer. Amy does not refuse to tell Arthur the truth about his mother; she merely refuses to tell her own "business," resolving that Arthur "should come to know all that was of import to himself; but, he should never know what concerned her, only" (773). Amy's remonstrance complicates the relationship between finance and disease in the novel: whereas Mrs. Clennam, and perhaps readers, see disease as a literal punishment for fraud, Dickens here rejects such heavy-handed application by dwelling on healing and compassion as well as affliction and infirmity. Dickens links fraud and disease in this way not to endorse punishment and misery but to advocate the healing of people and society.

          Amy and Physician defy marketplace values through healing. Amy's nursing is described as "inspired" to "be something which was not what the rest were . . . for the sake of the rest" (80). Akin to the "poet" and "priest," inspiration originates in a place elsewhere, a place apparently "lowliest" but drawing upon Christian language of elevation, devotion, and sacrifice (80). Monica F. Cohen recognizes Amy's homemaking in the prison as "vocational domesticity" and critiques Dickens's mystification of women's work.[39] But, Amy's nursing is explicitly not her profession, unlike the drunken, violent Mrs. Bangham, who is explicitly a nurse and midwife. Amy is a seamstress by trade, and her healing activities occur outside of the financial economy (if not outside a moral or affective economy). Amy nurses her father, Maggy, Pet, and, we are told, her brother, who later dies in the Marshalsea. She also nurses Arthur in the Marshalsea during his sickness, both having lost their fortunes to Merdle's fraud.[40] Amy tells Arthur, "[T]he greatest joy I can experience on earth, [is] the joy of knowing that I have been serviceable to you, and that I have paid some little of the great debt of my affection and gratitude" (726). Arthur replies that "liberty and hope would be so dear, bought at such a price" (726). Here again the language of finance dominates the text, but the debt that is paid is not money but gratitude, which is too "dear" to be "bought." The scene recalls Amy and Arthur Clennam's previous conversation in his rooms when she secretly visits him to offer thanks for paying her brother's debts. At that time, Amy says that she does not know, cannot thank, and cannot kiss her brother's benefactor. But in saying this, she kisses the hand of Arthur, who, of course, is the mysterious benefactor, as both well know. Arthur in turn claims that the unknown man is grateful to *her* for the opportunity to be of service. This curious conversation does not offer thanks while offering thanks and does not accept thanks while accepting it. In doing so, it, like the final proposal scene, resists the logic of exchange and subverts the financial language that dominates relationships in this novel: here, no thanks are thanks and to do service is to become indebted. In both cases, the constellation of service, debt, and indebtedness gestures toward an excess of meaning that cannot be contained by financial metaphor. In positioning Amy Dorrit in this manner, Dickens celebrates affect over finance, amateurism over professionalism, and vocation over job. If Amy is his ideal, can Dickens craft medical professionalism out of the same language that celebrates amateurism, radical self-denial, vocation, and femininity?

Jennifer Ruth identifies a paradox in which professionals disown the marketplace yet create a marketplace, "chicken-and-egg fashion."[41] Using the language of vocation, Dickens distances Physician from the financial marketplace, with its fraudulent relationships and immorality; however, Physician fails both as a physician and as a moral force in society. For example, he visits Merdle but cannot diagnose him, supposing him "unwell without reason" (250). He handles Merdle's suicide with grace, but he does not prevent it. When asked by Bishop about preventing throat pain in new clergymen, Physician answers, "[T]he best way to

62   avoid it is to know how to read, before you make a profession of reading"
(546). Physician here advocates professional authenticity, because to be
personally what one is professionally is to retain one's physical health
and one's moral authority. Just as in Physician's own case, the personal
and professional, the physical and moral, must be in harmony. Even as
he advocates authenticity to Bishop, he hobnobs with the Barnacles, a
political family whose Circumlocution Office is a model of corruption.
Society figure Ferdinand Barnacle even praises fraud, saying, "[A] little
humbug, and a groove, and everything goes on admirably" (706). Physician's passivity is sharply contrasted with Blandois's activity in bringing
Mrs. Clennam's fraud to light. Blandois calls himself her "doctor" and
reads in the pounding of Mrs. Clennam's pulse the truth of her fraud
and of her malicious nature (736). When Mrs. Clennam learns that Blandois has left copies of her papers for Arthur and Amy, she literally runs
from her sickbed to prevent the discovery. In this incident, Blandois's
blackmail actually achieves more than any of Physician's ministrations,
yet Dickens is hardly advocating a model of medicine based on fraud
and cruelty. Even Amy's activities are rarely successful: she cannot cure
Maggy, help Pet, inspire Tip, guide her father, or advise Fanny. If healing is the hope of modernity, why is it so ineffective?

In *Little Dorrit*, Dickens finds little to admire in the professional systems of modernity, such as finance, which spread a miasma of fraud over
human relationships at every level of society.[42] In many ways, medicine is the beneficiary of this critique of professional finance, because
its connection with healing allows Dickens to imagine it a trustworthy
profession, both inside and outside of modernity. Medicine becomes
an exemplary profession not because of its modernity but because of
its ancient associations with Christian healing. This configuration of
medicine recalls the language from the *Lancet* and other publications
that advocates for increased social power and prestige for medical practitioners based on selflessness and virtue. However, this novel reveals
the limitations of delineating medical orthodoxy using the language of
vocation, because it offers little help in articulating the conflicts of professional medicine. How does Physician pay for the grand dinners he
gives for the Barnacles? How does he maintain his philanthropy despite
the physical and financial pressures of maintaining a practice? Many of
the letters in the *Times* and *Lancet* refer to such dilemmas, but Physician
offers no model for solving such problems. Even Amy's vocation results
in little change, although it temporarily softens misery. In configuring

medicine as the opposite of other modern professions, Dickens crafts an utterly trustworthy profession, but it is only nominally professional. If medicine benefits from exaggerated vocational language, it also is limited by it to passivity and inaction, a kind of professional amateurism. Can Dickens imagine a more effective medical professionalism using the terms of vocation?

Physician Abroad in *Bleak House*

As in *Little Dorrit*, modern systems in *Bleak House* are rife with fraud and disease. In this novel, a case before the Chancery court investigates (rather than remedying) fraud, impersonation, blackmail, and murder, while the slum Tom All-Alone's, a Chancery property, becomes a source of smallpox infection. Fraud and disease are combated both by Esther Summerson, whose nursing recalls Amy Dorrit, and by Dr. Woodcourt, whose virtues recall Physician.[43] Like *Little Dorrit's* Physician, Dr. Woodcourt is a fantasy of authenticity in a fraudulent world; however, there are significant differences between *Little Dorrit* and *Bleak House*. For example, Woodcourt has urban and imperial practices, and this allows Dickens to craft a more active, masculine medical profession out of the language of vocation, which is associated in *Little Dorrit* with Amy.[44] Bruce Robbins's perceptive essay "Telescopic Philanthropy: Professionalism and Responsibility in *Bleak House*" argues that the impersonal Chancery system is the villain of this novel, which features "a substantial case against the professions, and especially against the legal profession."[45] Although the medical profession seems "an unqualified ideal," Robbins argues that medicine betrays "a certain inhumanity," akin to that of Chancery at times.[46] Robbins's persuasive argument contrasts medicine and law, although in the end both share in Dickens's critique of professionalism. This section examines the deployment of vocational professionalism in *Bleak House*. Unlike *Little Dorrit*, this novel presents the financial and social complexities of medical practice while maintaining the link between Christianity and medicine. How does joining Christianity and imperialism allow Dickens to craft medical orthodoxy in more powerful terms? How does Dickens complicate the vocational paradigm? What are the implications of this rhetoric on the emerging concept of professional medicine?

Dr. Woodcourt first appears alongside a crusty, Scottish medical man who has been summoned to the deathbed of the mysterious clerk, Nemo.

64   Woodcourt lingers at Nemo's bedside to deplore the man's poverty and suffering in Standard English, and the Scottish doctor announces, in "broad Scotch tongue," "I'm nae gude here" and walks away to finish his dinner.[47] Because Edinburgh was a center of medical education, the reader might assume that the Scottish doctor is well trained; however, Woodcourt's sympathy and Englishness imply that he is a more desirable doctor. This Englishness is emphasized in his personal life by his mother, who is comically preoccupied with her aristocratic Welsh ancestry, to Woodcourt's embarrassment (222). At the deathbed, Woodcourt also shines in comparison to the aptly named landlord, Krook. Woodcourt tactfully labels Nemo's opium overdose an "accident" while Krook literally smacks his lips at the excitement of a suicide (130). The last man present is a lawyer, Tulkinghorn, whose remorseless hounding of Lady Dedlock led to the discovery of the body. Like Tulkinghorn, Woodcourt displays a keen sense of observation, and, like the lawyer, Woodcourt's expertise allows him to uncover his patients' hidden secrets. Later, he, too, joins in the search for Lady Dedlock. Yet Dickens differentiates medicine from trade, law, and the police by emphasizing Woodcourt's compassion. The unflattering portraits of tradesmen and lawyers in this scene reinforce the doctor's union of Christian compassion and professional knowledge. The Scottish doctor complicates the boundaries of medicine by asserting the importance of Englishness in defining medical orthodoxy: while many doctors might be well-trained, only those who, like Woodcourt, perform Christianity and Englishness are ideal practitioners of medicine.

Dickens's critique of the Chancery system benefits medicine by displacing doubt and potential fraud onto law. If the law is estranged, impersonal, and often fraudulent, medicine emerges as Christian, personal, and authentic. Symbolized by the convoluted lawsuit Jarndyce and Jarndyce, the legal profession is "trickery, evasion, procrastination, spoliation, botheration, under false pretenses of all sorts, there are influences that can never come to good" (5). Indeed, the Chancery characters seem bereft of personality entirely: the names Chizzle, Mizzle, and Drizzle and Boodle, Coodle, and Doodle seem eminently interchangeable. Lady Dedlock says that Tulkinghorn is "mechanically faithful without attachment" (475). Humanitarian Mr. Jarndyce (who adopts the orphan wards of the suit, supports illegitimately born Esther Summerson, and patronizes freeloading Harold Skimpole) describes the lawsuit's effect on one of the wards of Jarndyce and Jarndyce, Richard Carstone: "[I]t is in the subtle poison of such abuses to breed such diseases. His blood is infected" (457).

When Mr. Jarndyce criticizes the Chancery system, Kenge, his lawyer, argues that "this is a very great country, a very great country. Its system of equity is a very great system, a very great system" (785). In explicitly nationalist terms, Kenge defends the inefficient court system as "great" because it is orderly, systematized, and complex—in short, accessible only to professionals. Clearly, Dickens does not endorse such professionalism as an English virtue. Vholes, the unfortunate Richard's lawyer, perhaps most clearly embodies the critique of the legal professional. To Vholes, the Chancery court exists "to make business for itself," without personal, emotional, national, or humanitarian aims (509). Vholes's claim to professional respectability rests on the fact that he "never misses a chance in his practice . . . never takes any pleasure . . . [and] is reserved and serious" (509). Although Voles mentions his daughters and family, he allows no intermixing between his professional life and his personal feelings.[48] As Esther says, Vholes (and by extension, Chancery) is a "Vampire" (763), one who drains blood from the healthy body of the individual and the state.

The irony of Chancery is that its main concern is authenticity, yet it seems to spawn fraud and crime. In the same way as Jo bites Lady Dedlock's guinea to see if it is real (210), one of the reasons for Jarndyce and Jarndyce's longevity is the need to validate every document, and there are "great heaps, and piles and bags and bags-full of papers" (321).[49] Chancery tests every document for authenticity but produces only more suspicion, to the point of breaking down human relationships. When Gridley's long-standing Chancery case flounders over questions of authenticity, Gridley tries and fails to employ personal appeals to "My Lord" or to Tulkinghorn, only to be told, "*He* is not responsible. It's the system" (200 [original italics]). The rag-and-bottle shop run by Krook is full of questionable papers, but Krook himself is so suspicious that he will not hire a teacher to teach him to read, because he fears he may be defrauded. Krook's skepticism proves no more effective than Gridley's personal trust, because Krook has Lady Dedlock's incriminating letters and Jarndyce's latest will, two authentic pieces of textual evidence that he cannot read. A document for the Jarndyce and Jarndyce case copied by a poor law writer, Nemo, instigates imposture, fraud, blackmail, murder, and misery. Nemo is really Captain Hawdon, Lady Dedlock's former lover and the father of her illegitimate daughter, Esther, whom Lady Dedlock's sister, Mrs. Chadband, claims died at birth. Pursuing the truth about this document uncovers the truth about Esther but also leads Lady Dedlock to impersonation, disgrace, and death. Similarly, Tulkinghorn's quest to uncover Lady Dedlock's secret ends with his death. At one point, Tulkinghorn encourages Lady Dedlock's maid, Hortense, to impersonate Lady Dedlock, and this reveals the truth to Hortense, who blackmails and later murders Tulkinghorn. Mr. Smallwood, who inherits Krook's shop after his death, uses Lady Dedlock's letters and Mrs. Chadband's testimony to blackmail Sir Dedlock. Establishing the authenticity of Nemo's document generates a chain of suspicion, blackmail, imposture, and murder that links Nemo's and Lady Dedlock's deaths, the two events that bookend the narrative.

If Chancery is associated with fraud and imposture, medicine is associated with authentic relationships based in Christian virtue.[50] Whereas Vholes refuses to become emotionally involved with Richard, Woodcourt visits Richard as a "sacred trust" that he performs at Esther's request and without pay (641). Vholes asks Esther if Woodcourt's visits to Richard are "professional attendance, medical attendance," and she states that Woodcourt's visits are those of a "disinterested friend" (763). To Esther, and perhaps to Dickens, professional, medical, and friendly visits are the same. After Esther is disfigured by smallpox, Mr. Guppy, a law clerk, asks Esther formally and publicly to refuse his earlier offer of marriage by reciting her name, her place of abode, and a statement of renunciation before a witness. Woodcourt's reaction to her disfigurement is quite different; she observes that he "had greater commiseration for me than I had ever had for myself. It inspired me with new fortitude and new calmness" (580). Woodcourt does not treat Esther medically, but he helps to heal her by inspiration, the method of the faith healer.[51] When he meets a bricklayer's beaten wife, Jenny, in the slum Tom All-Alone's, Woodcourt speaks to her in a manner that restores her confidence, "avoiding patronage or condescension or childishness" (584). His hands intermingle medical skill and the touch of the miracle healer; Woodcourt "laid his fingers on the wounded place," as he cleans, dries, and dresses her cut face, "touching her with his skillful and accustomed hand" (584). Not only does he refuse payment, Woodcourt concludes by offering her money (585). Woodcourt provides medical care for the anonymous Nemo, the deranged Miss Flite, the suffering Jenny, the crazed Richard, and the homeless Jo free of charge, uniting medical skill and Christian charity.

Similarly, Woodcourt mingles medicine and the Lord's Prayer at the deathbed of the orphaned street-sweeper, Jo (603). Woodcourt's behavior at Jo's deathbed contrasts with Skimpole's. A former doctor turned social parasite, Skimpole suggests throwing the boy out when he arrives, sick, at Jarndyce's house. Later, Skimpole informs Detective Bucket of Jo's whereabouts in exchange for money. In contrast, Jo describes Woodcourt's visits in his poor English: "[H]e come fur to giv me something fur to ease me, wot he's allus a-doin on day and night, and wen he come a-bendin over me and a-speakin up so bold, I see his tears a-fallen" (601). The "ease" Woodcourt offers is both physical and spiritual, and it is offered regardless of rank, wealth, or literacy. Woodcourt is not alone in caring for Jo: Snagsby, George, and Esther also display considerable charity toward the boy, but only Woodcourt performs charity as part of his profession. Dickens implies that impersonal, modern systems are responsible for the boy's death in his satirical announcement of Jo's death: "Dead, your Majesty. Dead, my lords and gentlemen. Dead, Right Reverends and Wrong Reverends. . . . Dead, men and women" (604). In this announcement, Dickens blames the crown, the government, the church, and society for Jo's suffering, but medicine is significantly absent from the rogues' gallery. While Woodcourt's personal charity seems to be his motive for helping Jo, Dickens specifies that Woodcourt personally shrinks from the boy because Jo infected his sweetheart, Esther, with smallpox. Woodcourt's attendance is due not to personal feeling but to his professional obligation as a physician to aid the sick. In Jo's sickness and death, Dickens displays the worst consequences of modern systems, but this critique benefits medicine, because medical professionalism, as embodied by Woodcourt, heals and comforts individuals that other systems dehumanize and cast away.

Woodcourt's personal virtues and professional duties appear to blend seamlessly into a fantasy of professionalism; however, Woodcourt also suffers from problems that were very common in Victorian medicine, such as low pay and severe competition. Woodcourt undertakes a voyage to China as a ship's surgeon because he has no practice of his own and is thus too poor to propose marriage to Esther. At first, Woodcourt's voyage seems to offer Dickens another opportunity to emphasize medicine's Christian virtue by allowing Woodcourt more activity than *Little Dorrit's* Physician.[52] Woodcourt's ship is wrecked, and he "saved many lives, never complained in hunger and thirst, wrapped naked people in his spare clothes, took the lead, showed them what to do, governed them, tended the sick, buried the dead, and brought the poor survivors safely off at last!" (465). Miss Flite praises Woodcourt by saying, "[M]y dear physician was a hero" (465), and Esther says to him, "You have been in shipwreck and peril since you left us. . . . [B]ut we can hardly call that a misfortune which

68   enabled you to be so useful and so brave" (580). Prior to his voyage, Esther enthused, "I am sure he will take the best wishes of all our hearts with him wherever he goes. . . . [A]nd though they are not riches, he will never be the poorer for them" (639). Dickens seems to introduce Woodcourt's professional difficulties and foreign voyage only to create an opportunity for the physician to heal the sick and clothe the naked, drawing a parallel between the urban slums and foreign countries as objects for Woodcourt's charity.[53] When Esther meets Woodcourt in the slums as she searches for Lady Dedlock, she says, "It was like hearing his voice in a strange country" (747). Tom All-Alone's is a strange country of disease and misery, unfavorably compared with the "coral reef in the Pacific" (206) and the "British dominions" (583), because of its "infection," "contagion," "pestilential gas," "obscenity," and "degradation" (583). In treating patients abroad and in the slums, Woodcourt becomes a Christian hero, although Woodcourt rejects such language. He describes the result of his voyage as having "gone out a poor ship's surgeon, and come home nothing better" (580). Yet Woodcourt does enjoy material gain from his adventures abroad. Grateful shipwreck survivors offer Woodcourt a practice in Yorkshire, "a very very commonplace affair, my dear, an appointment to a great amount of work and a small amount of pay" (760). Is the Yorkshire practice an improvement over Woodcourt's urban and imperial practices?[54] The practice pays little and demands much, implying that medicine demands vocation, regardless of location. Woodcourt's rejection of praise may also serve to highlight the view that medicine is the "saddest of trades" and "most noble of professions."[55]

 This novel appeared during the same decade as urban cholera outbreaks, the Crimean War, the so-called Indian or Sepoy Mutiny, and the Medical Act of 1858, all of which drew attention to the emergence of professional medicine. The language of imperial medicine and heroic sacrifice resonates with Dickens's representation of Woodcourt's experience, and authors in both mainstream and medical literature link imperial war zones and domestic poor zones as twin beneficiaries of professional medicine's sacrifices. An article from the *Times* describes medicine thus: "[T]here is no class of the community generally so free from mercenary motives as the members of the medical and surgical professions."[56] The article complains of lawyers and clergymen but claims that "the medical has attained the highest character for disinterestedness."[57] Similarly, a doctor describes his struggles during a domestic cholera epidemic: "[I] laboured and toiled incessantly; I never went to bed till 3 or 4 in the morning, and frequently had to rise before an hour's sleep had taken possession of me."[58] The Crimean War offered writers a new location for this otherwise domestic service. An officer in the Crimea describes a doctor working in a hospital ship: "Will it be believed that these 250 men had only one surgeon (Dr. Furlong) and a young assistant to attend them? They were sent on board without an orderly to help them, and with 100 bandages to dress their wounds. Dr. Furlong naturally went on shore to remonstrate, and when he said he had cut-off the bandages with which the wounds had first been dressed, he was accused of wasting public property; . . . Dr. Furlong works from morning till night, and from night till morning; still it has been found impossible for him to do justice."[59] Always a supporter of professionalized medicine, the *Lancet* deploys hyperbolic language to describe the difficulties of surgical practice in war zones and in poor zones:

> British surgeons are scattered over the whole earth, from the Arctic Pole to the continent of Victoria, as well as in each dependent colony of the Crown. In all scientific expeditions, whether it be proposed to search amid the snows of Lapland or in the wilds of Arabia, surgeons are always found cheerful and ready to take their part in the danger; and though the medical faculty has shown again and again its zeal and willingness to advance science and do good to our kind, yet our most useful and indispensable profession, appears still to be reserved for the contumely, the ignorance, and the sneers of society. . . . Obstacles on all sides to reasonable emolument and just ambition: gratis advice—gratis medicine—gratis operations; bickerings in villages, jealousies and rivalry in towns. Wearisome attendance upon persons who will not, or do not, pay; and the incessant and depressing drudgery of an Union."[60]

These references suggest that Dickens drew upon a wider cultural current in his representation of Woodcourt's urban and foreign practices and of his Christian charity and self-sacrifice. In addition, several articles above employ a rhetorical technique similar to that of *Bleak House*: just as physicians and surgeons benefit from comparison with inept army officers and greedy ratepayers, so too does Woodcourt benefit from Dickens's critique of Chancery and of its lawyers and clerks.

Is Dickens simply endorsing vocation over profession in this novel, as in *Little Dorrit*? Dickens complicates vocation through Mr. and Mrs.

70 Chadband, Mrs. Pardiggle, and Mrs. Jellyby.[61] These men and women are not professionals in the same manner as the men of Chancery; however, their systematized vocations are, perhaps, worse than Chancery, because they are masks for selfishness and cruelty. Mrs. Jellyby is so focused on African charity that she ignores her daughter's wedding, her husband's bankruptcy, and the many accidents that befall her son, Peepy. Mr. Jellyby advises his neglected daughter, Caddy, on her wedding day, "Never have a Mission, my dear child" (392). Mrs. Pardiggle forces her children to give their allowance to charity, ignoring their misery and hostility, and she insults poor Jenny. Esther attributes Mrs. Pardiggle's offensiveness to her "mechanical way of taking possession of people" like an "inexorable moral Policeman" (100–101). Mrs. Chadband abuses Esther because of her illegitimacy, heedless of Esther's personal virtue and generous nature, and later she uses her knowledge of Esther to blackmail Sir Dedlock (684). Mr. Chadband calls Jo "a brother and a boy" in a parody of the abolitionist slogan, but Chadband only uses the boy as an example for his sermons and ignores Jo's ragged and starving state. In contrast, Snagsby, a law stationer, privately offers Jo half-crowns and food (251, 333). The ridiculousness of pursuing vocation in this manner recalls Mr. Turveydrop, who religiously practices deportment without practicing the genuine consideration for others of which deportment is supposedly only the outward sign. Unlike Esther, Snagsby, and Jarndyce, who offer charity privately, the Pardiggles, Chadbands, and Jellybys claim charity as a vocation in a quasi-professional manner, and vocation in this sense is a mere excuse for selfishness and fraud. In fact, Eric G. Lorentzen calls Jarndyce the "ideal domestic reformer" and views Woodcourt's connection with Jarndyce as significant.[62] In these characters, Dickens warns of the dangers of vocation as self-involvement and self-righteousness, more akin to the impersonal systems of Chancery than to Woodcourt's medical profession.

If Dickens complicates vocation in the Pardiggles, Chadbands, and Jellybys, does he also complicate professionalism? In Inspector Bucket, Dickens seems to mingle professional duties with genial conduct, but, unlike Woodcourt, Bucket's friendship is untrustworthy.[63] Bucket routinely masquerades as other people to extract information, pretending to be the son of a servant to induce Lady Dedlock's footman to reveal her whereabouts (671), to be a cellist to arrest George (630), and to be a doctor to arrest Gridley (328). As he arrests George, Bucket "seems to be really fond of him" because of his "friendly hold" (630), but this friendliness masks a restraining grip. Bucket warns George that "duty . . . 71 is one thing, and conversation is another. It's my duty to inform you that any observations you may make will be liable to be used against you. Therefore, George, be careful what you say" (630). Bucket explicitly warns George that duty compels him to use George's comments against him, but Bucket's use of George's name and his advice to "be careful" generate a tone of personal concern for George's situation. In George's arrest, Dickens reveals the potentially deceptive nature of displays of personal affection in a professional context. Dickens describes "an element of forefinger" beneath Bucket's geniality, indicating that despite his good nature Bucket points the finger of blame (662). Woodcourt enfolds the personal into his professional attendance on patients, such as Richard and Jo; however, Bucket reveals that the personal may signal untrustworthiness, not authenticity. Bucket says to Hortense at her arrest, "I'm surprised at the indiscreetness you commit, you'll say something that will be used against you, you know. You're sure to come to it. Never you mind what I say till it's given in evidence" (686). Is Bucket's advice to Hortense merely a repetition of his advice to George, a rote recitation given to all suspects? Is it a ruse to elicit a confession? Or is it a genuine aside, an intrusion of Bucket's personal opinion? Bucket's personal feelings seem to intrude when Bucket encounters Mrs. Rouncewell. Dickens calls Bucket's remarks an "aside," in which Bucket reassures her that George will be released and that George was "game" at his arrest (710). Why does Bucket reveal personal feelings for George or relieve George's mother's anxiety? Similarly, in his description of Hortense's activities, Bucket offers details about his wife that do not bear on the case but express his personal admiration for her (689). Alexander Welsh notes that the detective and the blackmailer are opposites in that both seek secret information but one retains power through secrecy and the other through revelation.[64] Bucket seems to be an agent of revelation, and perhaps this accounts for his tendency toward personal revelation, as well. For example, Bucket and Tulkinghorn both come to occupy positions of trust in the Dedlock house, and both pursue Lady Dedlock; however, Tulkinghorn is a kind of blackmailer who uses secrets to force Lady Dedlock to stay in her marriage. Conversely, Bucket reveals Lady Dedlock's secret to Sir Leicester (684), yet he advises paying blackmail money to Smallweed and Chadband rather than pursuing legal action (684). Should Bucket advocate legal action instead? Is this advice pity rather than professional thinking? In Bucket's case, revelation may be as

72   dangerous as secrecy. Bucket's friendliness is more deceptive than the obvious impersonality of Chancery, and his explicit claims of professional duty are often counteracted by suggestions of personal feelings, which may or may not be genuine. Bucket complicates Dickens's view of professionalism, as symbolized by Chancery, because Bucket reveals the dangers of the personal in the professional sphere.

In this novel, vocation may be as systematized and as fraudulent as professionalism, and personal relationships in the professional sphere may signify emotional manipulation, not Christian virtue. This view complicates medical orthodoxy, by displaying the pitfalls of vocation as well as the dangers of systematized professionalism. Lauren M. E. Goodlad argues that *Bleak House* displays "the diminished power of modern individuals," and, although Dickens advocates social pastorship, he is unable to imagine a governmental body or organized charity capable of such responsibility (*Victorian Literature*, 87). Goodlad argues that this novel lacks "the charismatic, semi-entrepreneurial/ semi-professional heroic expert . . . determined to push through deadlock in order to provide much-needed pastoral care" (103). This reading dismisses Woodcourt's "private paternalism" as "conservative" rather than innovative (104). Dickens's deployment of Christian vocation may draw upon even more conservative epistemologies than Goodlad's reading of sanitary health imagines. In Woodcourt, Dickens imagines the physician as a Christian hero, capable of ameliorating (if not curing) the systemic ills of modernity in urban and imperial settings. Goodlad recognizes an overlap between feminine domesticity and medicine; however, Woodcourt's imperial and slum adventures, as well as his relationship with Esther, resist the passive virtue that is so prominent in *Little Dorrit*'s Physician (109).[65] As in *Little Dorrit*, Dickens praises vocational nursing by women; however, Esther is also a victim of disease herself, and she requires Woodcourt to heal her visible scars. Dianne F. Sadoff notes that Esther falls ill twice in the novel, emerging without identity and face after her smallpox until her marriage with Woodcourt restores her beauty in the "mirror of her husband's love" (59).[66] In contrast, Michael S. Gurney notes that Dickens's representation of Esther's recovery of her good looks is not inaccurate, due to the fading over time of the hyperpigmentation associated with smallpox scarring.[67] Like Amy Dorrit, Esther inspires others with her personal charity, often symbolized by her amateur nursing. Esther nurses Richard, Caddy, Caddy's baby (also called Esther), Jo, and her own maid, Charley. Unlike Amy Dorrit, Esther contracts disease herself, catching Jo's smallpox after nursing Charley through it. Jenny describes Esther's "angel temper" and blames Jo for infecting her (587). Esther does not nurse Woodcourt, but her virtue inspires him, also. When he proposes to Esther after her illness, Woodcourt recalls the moment "when I came back [from China], no richer than when I went away, and found you newly risen from a sick bed, yet so inspired by sweet consideration for others, and so free from a selfish thought" (775). Esther's "sweet consideration" is described (as Amy Dorrit's nursing is also) by the word *inspired*, which carries religious connotations. Woodcourt's unfinished sentence implies that he is inspired by her example. Whether or not her scars actually fade, Esther needs Woodcourt to heal her after her illness and to direct her future charity. Although Esther at first rejects Woodcourt's offer of marriage, she says, "I aspired to be more worthy of it" (775). Upon hearing of his shipwreck, Esther enthuses, "I felt so triumphant ever to have known the man who had done such generous and gallant deeds; I felt such a glowing exultation in his renown; I so admired and loved what he had done; that I envied the storm-worn people who had fallen at his feet and blessed him as their preserver" (465). In this description, Esther desires to worship Woodcourt with "glowing exultation" as a "preserver," language that imagines Woodcourt more as a saint than a skilled professional. She cherishes Woodcourt's flowers secretly, because she believes her scarring renders her unmarriageable, drawing from them hope despite her condition (468). After her marriage, Mrs. Woodcourt's new station as "doctor's wife" provides her with the personal support she requires and enables her to perform vocational nursing to the Yorkshire poor. In Esther and Woodcourt's union, and their occupation of the Bleak House given to them by the humanitarian Jarndyce, Dickens imagines medicine as masculine, active, and professional, yet personal, vocational, and Christian (818). In Woodcourt and Physician, Dickens points to the differences between professions, observing that critique of one profession, or even of professionalization itself, benefits medicine, because of its conservative, Christian connotations. These representations highlight the power of Christian language during this period, despite the oft-repeated claim that medical orthodoxy gained power through association with science. On the contrary, medicine in these novels gains not from its progressive aspect but from its conservative resonances, displacing doubt and fraud onto other modern professions, such as the police, law, and business.

Chapter Three

Legerdemain and the Physician in
Charlotte Brontë's *Villette*

> A physician should "know no legerdemain, do no conjuring tricks."
>
> —Robert M. Glover, *Lancet*, 1851

*A*s the sickly, secretive, first-person narrator of Charlotte Brontë's *Villette* (1853), Lucy Snowe is often connected both to medicine and to narrative unreliability but only rarely to fraud.[1] Athena Vrettos examines Lucy in the context of nineteenth-century nervous disease, arguing that Lucy's narrative concretizes the vague symptoms of hysteria, a disease particularly associated with intellectual women such as writers. Acknowledging that nervous diseases were controversial, Vrettos mentions only briefly the contemporary connection between nervous disease and charlatanism.[2] Instead, Vrettos finds in Lucy's narrative symptoms that express a "dis-order of the self," resulting in a narrative that is both "a truth and a lie."[3] Similarly, Sally Shuttleworth examines *Villette* in the context of "acute public concern" about insanity and nervous disease.[4] Despite the contemporary controversy about phrenology, Shuttleworth equates John's "medical authority, calmly confident of his ability to define inner experience from outer signs," and Paul's phrenological reading of Lucy as twin male sciences interpreting female nature (314). In Shuttleworth's reading, Lucy's refusal to accept John's diagnosis of her nervous disorder symbolizes Lucy's resistance to medical power, although John's view echoes the language Lucy uses in her own narrative to describe her experience (327). Thus, John asserts the "pre-defined categories of suitable female behavior" through his professional power, and Lucy's narrative rejects the "traditional division between external social process and inner mental life, revealing their fictional status" (328, 331). Alternatively, Nicholas Dames reads *Villette* in the context of nineteenth-century phrenology; in this reading, the word *quackery* crops up several times, most notably in a footnote describing the "stain of quackery" on Brontë's own phrenological report.[5] Despite phrenology's questionable status, Dames recognizes in phrenology "one of the nineteenth-century's visual theories" and an "ideal starting point" for his study of nineteenth-century hermeneutics (368). Calling phrenology a "pseudoscience," Dames nevertheless finds in it a "clinical epistemology" for reading a novel about the very nature of seeing and reading (369). In acknowledging then dismissing quackery, these readings reproduce one of *Villette*'s narrative strategies. Like her critics, Lucy recognizes quackery only to disregard or to minimize it, most notably in her physician and kinsman, John Graham Bretton. Because of modern medicine's epistemological power, critics tend to read John as a marker of the stable boundaries of masculinity, Englishness, propriety, and normality.[6] In identifying medical quackery as a context for this novel, this chapter suggests that John actually represents the instability of these boundaries. Mid-Victorian culture worried about quackery's ability to confound the division between orthodoxy and quackery, not simply reversing the territories of orthodoxy and quackery but revealing the fluid nature of supposedly stable cultural formations. In failing to discriminate between medical orthodoxy and quackery, John signals the instability of other cultural formations that Lucy associates with him. Far from occupying a stabilizing role, John symbolizes the slippery nature of boundaries that Lucy's narrative attempts to reinforce but ultimately cannot maintain.

To some, the 1850s was a period of medical professionalization; for example, the *Lancet* triumphantly announces, "Quackery on Its Death-Bed" because of the new Medical Act, which created a register of orthodox practitioners.[7] Similarly, the *British Medical Journal* celebrated October 1, 1858, as the date on which the Medical Act would "collect the scattered sheep of the profession into one fold, and put on them—as far as the law can do so—a mark by which they may be known from pretenders."[8] In contrast, others view the mid-nineteenth century as the heyday of quackery. For example, physician Robert M. Glover describes several flourishing quack systems, including homeopathy, hydropathy, phrenology, mesmerism, teetotalism, and vegetarianism.[9] Glover encourages orthodox physicians to regulate their own language and conduct,

76   because any trickery on the part of physicians, even in the patient's best interest, promotes quackery. He quotes the *Lancet* when he asserts, "A Physician should 'know no legerdemain, do no conjuring tricks.'"[10] The *Oxford English Dictionary* defines *legerdemain* as "sleight of hand; the performance of tricks which by nimble action deceive the eye; jugglery; conjuring tricks" and "trickery, deception, hocus-pocus."[11] *Hocus-pocus* and *sleight of hand* may connote entertainment, the pleasure of witnessing nimble juggling or skillful magic, for example. However, the words *trickery* and *deception* carry connotations that are more sinister. Dwelling on the latter, Glover warns orthodox practitioners against employing even rhetorical *legerdemain*, since quacks "take note of all positive facts and . . . disregard negative ones, to avail themselves of whatever favoured their doctrines."[12] Like Brontë, Glover is concerned with drawing and maintaining the boundaries between harmless and harmful, authentic and inauthentic. In this context, John Graham Bretton may not offer a stable point in Lucy's narrative but represent Brontë's engagement with the slippery nature of medical boundary making.

Why might Glover employ a foreign-sounding word, *legerdemain*, instead of one of the many English terms available, such as *quackery, fraud, charlatanism, cheat, trickery, deception,* or *sleight of hand?* Victorian commentators sometimes appeal to other (supposedly) stable, self-evident categories, such as foreignness, in their struggle to define quackery. In his examination of the conflict between phrenologist George Combe and philosopher William Hamilton for the chair of metaphysics at Edinburgh University in 1836, Thomas Gieryn attributes Combe's defeat to his disrespect for rhetorical boundaries.[13] Gieryn argues that while Hamilton's rhetoric maintained the cultural boundaries between professor and layperson and between politics and religion, Combe's campaign attacked these customary and socially accepted divisions. To Gieryn, Combe's stinging defeat was not due to the realization that phrenology was unscientific so much as to fear of social disorder.[14] In Dr. John Graham Bretton, Lucy creates a guardian of medical orthodoxy, Englishness, and Protestantism in the French-speaking, Catholic city of Villette; however, John's frequent lapses indicate that he might not be as reliable as Lucy claims. After all, Lucy's narrative employs considerable rhetorical *legerdemain* to maintain John as a touchstone of authenticity, which encompasses both medical orthodoxy and English propriety. However, Brontë's narrative questions the ways in which such authenticity is constructed by undermining first John's medical orthodoxy and then, implicitly, the other boundaries he supposedly defends. Thus, *Villette* offers an important addition to midcentury medical discourse because of its examination of the ways in which orthodoxy and quackery informed each other, because of its depiction of medicine's interaction with wider cultural discourses (notably, foreignness), and because of its exploration of language's ability to create and to destabilize supposedly self-evident truths.

Legerdemain, Orthodoxy, and Quackery

Published in 1853, *Villette* emerged from a culture struggling to articulate quackery's scope and nature. On one hand, repeated calls for reform suggest widespread faith in stable, fixed boundaries between orthodoxy and quackery; on the other hand, commentators bewail quackery's pernicious resistance to categorization.[15] Roy Porter identifies two simultaneous shifts in the discourse of mid-Victorian quackery: first, the culmination of a campaign for legislation to define orthodoxy, which had begun in the 1820s and resulted in the passage of the 1858 Medical Act; and second, a new proliferation of elaborate systems of quackery in which "ideology, philosophy, and morality moved centre stage."[16] For example, the notorious James Morison, creator of Morison's Vegetable Pills, developed a complex system based on the relatively simple notion of corrupt blood and deliberately confounded divisions between quack and orthodox: his British College of Health recalled the Royal College of Physicians; his Hygeian system borrowed its name from Greek mythology just as orthodox medicine employed the staff of Asclepius; his medical manuals and monthly magazine rivaled the *Lancet* and *British Medical Journal*.[17] Helfand calls Morison one of the "most important innovators" in quackery, and Porter calls Morison "the first quack to exploit the nineteenth-century passion for organizations and institutions."[18] During the 1850s (after Morison's death), Morison's followers called for a public monument to him, just as orthodox physicians and scientists received posthumous public recognition. At the same time, Morison's so-called articles appeared in the advertisement section of the *Times*, alongside traditional quack advertisements for nostrums and devices, rather than in the print columns.[19] The *Lancet* laments that Morison is treated "precisely as though MORISON's pills had been a discovery such has [sic] the steam-engine or spinning jenny, . . . instead of a nostrum which may have sent thousands to premature graves."[20] Medical concern about the public's confusion between quack and orthodox practitioners was more

78 widespread than just the case of Morison's Pills, however. Physician Robert M. Glover opines to the *Lancet's* readers that "if 'Professor' Holloway [another notorious quack] became only rich enough, he might be made a baronet as easily as Dr. Bright or Dr. Chambers."[21] Another article in the *Lancet* laments "shameful impostures" by quacks; "He [the quack] may have been a felon, or a thief, or a cobbler; but of what consequence is that, so long as he dresses as a staid and respectable person, utters lies with sufficient assurance, and advertises his cures with sufficient audacity?"[22] This article characterizes quackery as a recalcitrant disease, stating that "the most potent agents of cure . . . are totally powerless against such diseases" (605). Although these articles unhesitatingly use the term *quack*, they reveal frustration at quackery's apparent ability to defy easy recognition and concern at apparently widespread inability to discriminate between quackery and orthodoxy using markers such as dress, conduct, wealth, and prestige. The articles nevertheless seem to hold out confidence that such categorization might successfully combat quackery if only pursued with vigilance and enthusiasm.

If quackery was difficult to identify, orthodoxy was hardly simpler. The apparently lamentable situation regarding quackery was compounded by the lack of unity on the part of orthodox practitioners themselves. Christopher Lawrence divides medical orthodoxy into elites and rank-and-file, two groups with divergent interests and modes of conduct: "All sides claimed to be custodians of the authentic knowledge and methods . . . even though such authentic knowledge and methods might look quite different according to who was claiming to possess them."[23] An article in the *Lancet* laments "professional quackery," in which college members participated in advertising for patent medicines, a practice strongly associated with quackery such as Morison's Pills.[24] The article describes one such advertisement as having "three names adorn[ing] it: the owner's, a Frenchman's, and last, though not least, that of a F.R.S. and physician to a London hospital!" (319). Faced with such conduct on the part of Fellows of the Royal Society and elite London practitioners, the writer questions, "How can we expect the public to recognise the profession, by right, as a body of educated gentlemen, if we reduce ourselves to nothing better than a set of touting tradesmen?" (319). According to this writer, "*testimonializing*" and "huckstering, bartering, trade-driving projects" are widespread, with advertisements posted alike "in provincial towns" and in "the West end" (319). William H. Helfand identifies a tradition in which orthodox practitioners including Hans

Sloane (founder of the Royal Society) and the developers of Dr. James's Fever Powders, Dr. Radcliffe's Royal Tincture, and Dr. Hooper's Female Pills engaged in the marketing of patent medicines.[25] To the *Lancet*, testimonials and advertising are markers of quackery, even when authored by college members. Were these collegians quacks? To what extent was publishing quackery? If these quacks refrained from publishing, would they become orthodox? Roy Porter notes similar issues in Wakley's own campaign for antiquackery legislation in the *Lancet*.[26] Porter calls Wakley's writing "messianic" in tone and argues that Wakley both spurred medical professionalization and "helped to sell his journal."[27] Thus, Wakley simultaneously advocated professionalism and emulated quackery in his exploitation of heated rhetoric for greater sales, an ironic situation that reveals the slippery nature of writing in marking the boundaries of medical orthodoxy. The specter of professional quackery draws other behaviors associated with quackery into doubt, even when undertaken by supposedly qualified and regular practitioners.

Two articles published several years earlier in *Fraser's Magazine* reveal the long-standing nature of the debate over writing, particularly testimonials, and quackery in both lay and professional circles. William H. Helfand defines testimonials as "words of praise from contented users" and contends that they were a long-standing form of quackery.[28] Helfand claims that testimonials by physicians were preferred, followed by endorsements by well-known and respectable people, whether "real or imaginary."[29] The first article from *Fraser's Magazine* describes notorious quack John St. John Long's career but explicitly excludes reprinting testimonials about his (in)famous anti-consumption ointment because "no person of sense could endure to read them, and none of the dupes of quackery would derive any benefit from them."[30] The article claims that although quackery cannot "be rooted out by any exposure, we yet hoped that something might be done to prevent their [the victims'] infatuation from spreading so contagiously."[31] Like the *Lancet*, the article metaphorically connects quackery and infection (both spread "contagiously") and also acknowledges its own powerlessness (to convince "dupes" and to "root out" quackery). The second article from *Fraser's Magazine* likewise links testimonials and quackery, stating that "the followers of quacks are the cause of quackery. . . . One simpleton bears testimony to Mr. Quackall's virtues; another of his manners; a third attests his wonderful cures."[32] If, as Helfand asserts, testimonials had long-standing association with quackery, why did writers assert and reassert their unreliability? Were

80   these repeated attacks merely a rhetorical device that established the author's own orthodoxy? These articles display the public, as well as medical, concern over the nature of writing as a marker of quackery, more so since it was used by credentialed as well as by avowedly unorthodox practitioners.

Writing in 1862, G. H. Lewes blames quackery's persistence on the language not of quacks but of orthodox physicians who are "glib about 'vital forces,' 'tone,' 'electricity' and many other words which veil ignorance."[33] Publicity, testimonials, and unscientific methods here indicate quackery: "He [the quack] proclaims with emphasis some absurd proposition, some theory, which is meant to justify his practice. Thus, for example, he affirms that 'all diseases are owing to impurity of the blood,' and his panacea purifies the blood. . . . These bold theoretic assertions are supported by an ostentatious list of cures. Jones was suffering from lumbago, he took the pills, and is now in health. . . . Such cases are multiplied and paraded."[34] Here, Lewes alludes to Morison's Pills, which supposedly purified corrupt blood. Morison can be identified as a quack, according to Lewes, by his tendency to "proclaim" and to publish, as well as by his absurd medical theory. Similarly, well-known surgeon Benjamin Brodie, writing in 1861, asserts that quackery should be fought by avoiding "errors of diagnosis" on the part of orthodox practitioners.[35] Brodie contends that the orthodox can diminish quackery if they "act honourably" and are never "induced, either by good nature or by any motives to self interest, to appear to give their sanction to a system which they know to have no foundation in reality" (340). Like Glover, Brodie associates trickery with dishonor and thus with quackery; for example, Brodie attacks homeopathy for taking credit for healing hypochondria, which resolves "under no treatment at all" (338). Unlike earlier articles, Brodie's relies almost solely on the regulation of orthodox conduct to quash quackery: "There was a time when many of the medical profession held the opinion that not only Homoeopathy, but all other kinds of quackery, ought to be put down by the strong hand of the law. I imagine that there are very few who hold that opinion now. The fact is, that the thing is impossible" (340). Brodie and Lewes offer lay and medical opinions about how to differentiate between orthodoxy and quackery that draw heavily upon familiar markers of quackery, notably, language and conduct. Written after the Medical Act of 1858, neither calls for legislation to solve the problem; indeed, Brodie explicitly speaks out against such an approach. On the contrary, both abandon legal devices aimed at quashing quacks and advocate even stricter regulation of orthodoxy's conduct and language than before, since earlier articles also warned about testimonials and advertisements while these regulate even private communication between doctors and patients. At the same time, Lewes's reference to Morison's Pills reveals the persistence of a familiar paradox in this discourse; to Lewes and Brodie, quackery (such as Morison's Pills and homeopathy) is self-evident, yet its boundaries cannot be easily identified for those not already in the know (as the persistence of Morison's Pills illustrates).

Several articles resort to ad hominem attacks as a way to identify and to combat quackery. According to Helfand, itinerancy was a common feature of patent-medicine quackery, and foreignness is one of many epithets traditionally aimed by orthodox practitioners at quacks, who are described as "empirics, illiterate, ignorant, often foreign."[36] An 1848 article in *Fraser's Magazine* entitled "Quackery and the Quacked," for example, singles out first-person testimonials, advertising, and foreignness as signs of quackery. Here, testimonials are unreliable because of their narrators, "a class of people sanguine, credulous, and enthusiastic."[37] This article refrains from reprinting testimonials, because "to refute such nonsense as this would be an insult to the understanding of our readers."[38] Instead, the article offers brief biographies of Hahnemann (from Saxony), who developed homeopathy; Priestnitz (from Germany), who championed hydropathy; and Perkins (from the United States), who introduced tractors, which are metal devices placed on the skin. The article undermines these quack systems through biography, revealing that the quacks were foreigners and thus unreliable. Nevertheless, Helfand notes that quacks often exploited the "appeal of the exotic" to market their nostrums.[39] For example, one advertisement for Morison's Pills turns foreignness into an advantage. Although it appears in the *Times*, it is entirely in French and addresses citizens of Russia, Austria, and Prussia.[40] Another includes testimonials from Moldavian, French, and German aristocrats: Prince Johanniza Sturza, Princesse Kalou de Cantacuzene, and Conseiller Honoraire de Zielinski.[41] Are these names intended to imply glamour and prestige? Did these names exploit the attraction of aristocracy while also nodding to the reader's skepticism about testimonials? As with other markers, foreignness failed to establish a stable boundary between orthodoxy and quackery. Despite its traditional association with quackery, foreignness also displayed quackery's resilience and innovation.

82   This chapter does not attempt to offer an exhaustive survey of attitudes toward quackery during this period, only to suggest contexts that may inform Lucy Snowe's narrative. As K. Codell Carter asserts, quackery in early nineteenth-century medical periodicals is associated with certain behaviors, notably, secrecy and advertising. Yet Carter describes the social pressures that drove licensed physicians to give testimonials in favor of nostrums, to use secret medicines, and to advertise.[42] Carter calls such practices "regular" and "irregular" quackery, in which delineation regular quacks are trained physicians and irregular quacks arc a "quasimedical fringe," and Carter asserts that during this period the regular quacks were perceived as more worrisome than the irregular; indeed, Carter notes that institutional medicine seemed to demand quackery since it relied on Latin terminology and its accompanying secrecy.[43] Although medicine enjoyed increasing power and prestige in the nineteenth century, it also had strong associations with charlatanism and trickery. Aside from the slippery nature of notorious quacks, such as Morison, even qualified and registered college members faced scrutiny from both the public and their colleagues for perceived quackish conduct, because of the specter of professional quackery. If John is Lucy's marker of orthodoxy, as critics assert, then his status in this discourse deserves close attention, especially because both Lucy's narrative and quackery emphasize questions of textual reliability, and Lucy's first-person narrative is a sort of testimonial. John's activities as a physician draw upon associations that foreground the difficulty in drawing boundaries between orthodoxy and quackery, English and foreign, proper and improper, sincere and deceptive. In this context, John allows Brontë to examine the ways in which language constructs categories such as quack and orthodox and the difficulties of maintaining such distinctions.

Dr. John and Mrs. Sweeny's Indian Shawl

At first glance, John Graham Bretton seems to stand for both medical orthodoxy and English values, both of which appear natural, self-evident, and unchanging. John is a "Bretton of Bretton," his name conflating his English village, his family name, and his personal identity, since he is the only surviving male Bretton.[44] Lucy claims that he has a "Celtic (not Saxon) character" (13). His name, Bretton, announces him to be a true Briton, and his Celtic origins recall the natives of the British Isles rather than the continental conquerors, the Saxons. Like Rupert

Brooke's soldier, whose body makes the foreign soil England, John's body exhibits authentic Englishness even abroad. When she unknowingly encounters him on the continent, Lucy does not merely see him as an "English gentleman" but hears in his voice "Fatherland accents" (56) and finds "goodness in his countenance," "honour in his bright eyes," a "frank tread," and a "nature chivalric" that together act as "a cordial" (57). John's very body speaks through what Lucy later calls his "English complexion, eyes, and form" (88). Lucy's use of the word *cordial* to describe John reveals the overlap in this novel between Englishness and medicine. Medicine as well as Englishness is part of John's inheritance, since Lucy tells us that he is the son of an English physician (3). This "true young English gentleman" is able to ameliorate Lucy's situation at the dockside, where she is seasick, lonely, unemployed, and ignorant of the local language and customs (57). In describing John, Lucy claims, "I should almost as soon have thought of distrusting the Bible" (57). Through John, Lucy connects medicine, nation, family, and personal identity in a unified and stable whole.

Because of his profession, John acts as Lucy's bulwark in the strange, French-speaking, Catholic city of Villette. Monica F. Cohen notes that John is accorded special privilege at Mme. Beck's school because he is a physician.[45] John successfully treats Fifine's broken arm, Georgette's fever, and Blanche's and Angélique's migraines, despite Lucy's assumption that Mme. Beck would not allow a handsome young man to visit her pupils (92). When Lucy becomes ill, John takes her into his home, merely because she is an English teacher whom he recognizes as an acquaintance (173). Lucy describes John as a "philanthropist" who accomplishes a "world of active good" in his visits to the charity hospital (186). John's description of Père Silas, a Catholic priest, sheds light on his own conduct: "[Silas] was a man I have often met by the sickbeds of both rich and poor: and, chiefly, the latter. He is, I think, a good old man, far better than most of his class" (173). John's statement about Silas's attention to the poor reveals his own; in addition, his interjection "I think" legitimizes Lucy's view of Silas as an exceptionally kind Catholic. John also aids Polly Home when she is crushed by a panicked crowd at a theater. The terms upon which John treats the then-unknown Polly are revealing: John states that Mr. Home should "trust her with me; I am a medical man" (246). Like the girls at the school, Polly is implicitly safe from impropriety with John, because he is a physician. This trustworthiness is reinforced by Mr. Home's enquiry, "You are an Englishman?"

84   (246). To Mr. Home, a physician is trustworthy, and an English physician apparently even more so. In these instances, John appears to affirm the boundaries between orthodoxy and quackery, English and foreign, Protestant and Catholic, proper and improper. By representing John as the embodiment of these categories, Lucy naturalizes them, rendering them stable, inevitable, and tangible.

Critics note that John is sometimes inconsistent in his conduct, but these lapses are often interpreted as slight or accidental. Amanda Anderson calls John's insensitivity "myopia."[46] Rogers and Dames accept Lucy's view that John is blind to her feelings.[47] The metaphor of blindness exculpates John from wrongdoing; his insensitivity becomes a blind spot he cannot help rather than deliberate or culpable action. John's lapses deserve serious attention because in the context of Victorian medicine, misconduct by orthodox practitioners is a form of quackery. Physician Robert M. Glover contends that even trickery in the patient's best interest is quackery. For example, Glover criticizes a well-known physician who tricked a lady into needed exercise by leaving her stranded on an outing; "It would astonish the popular admirers of this man, were they to read the expressions of disgust which the orthodox LANCET once thought right to utter, in reference to this transaction."[48] Similarly, the *British Medical Journal* prints a letter from F. J. Brown warning about the use of the "bread pill" and the "sugar globule" to trick patients.[49] Brown argues that "it was immoral to act deceitfully to sick men, as much so as to deceive men in good health. I fully believe that it is immoral to deceive children and lunatics."[50] John displays just such trickery in his treatment of Mme. Beck's mischievous daughter, Désirée, who is perfectly healthy but amuses herself by feigning sickness. John repeatedly visits her and writes what Lucy calls "harmless prescriptions" for the child (89). This might seem to be the mere flattering of a childish whim, but Lucy's language, like Robert Glover's indictment of the fashionable doctor, condemns the charade. In her sickbed, Désirée "lounged like a Turk, . . . throwing her shoes at her bonne and grimacing at her sisters—overflowed, in short, with unmerited health and evil spirits—" (89). In using terms such as *unmerited* and *evil*, Lucy implies that this pretense is not a childish whim but a facet of Désirée's violent and dishonest nature, which also manifests in lying, theft, and vandalism (85). In comparing the child to a Turk, a non-Christian, Lucy implies that unrestrained desire, a word apparent in the child's name, transgresses Christian morality. When Mme. Beck, who prefers surveillance to remonstrance, fails to explain to the child what Lucy calls "the evil of such habits" (86), Lucy condemns her, saying that "she had not rectitude of soul to confront the child with her vices" (86). Lucy repeatedly uses words such as *soul*, *vice*, and *evil*, and, in doing so, Lucy implies that there are serious consequences to trickery, both for Mme. Beck and for her daughter.

What then of John's harmless prescriptions? Readers may dismiss John's conduct as a minor matter; however, given the odium attached to misconduct on the part of orthodox practitioners, John's prescriptions deserve reflection. When he agrees to participate in this scheme, John consents "tacitly to adopt Madame's tactics and to fall in with her maneuvers" (89). These tactics and maneuvers have been suspect since Lucy first arrived at the school. On her very first night, Lucy is hired to replace Mrs. Sweeny, an Irish teacher of English impersonating a native Englishwoman. Mme. Beck hired Mrs. Sweeny because of her "*real Indian shawl*" (64 [original italics]). For Mme. Beck, the shawl's authenticity acts as a guarantee of Mrs. Sweeny's authenticity until secret surveillance can ferret out the truth. Contemplating Mme. Beck's methods, Lucy states, "All this was very un-English: truly I was in a foreign land" (64).[51] What does John's participation in Mme. Beck's trickery reveal? Lucy sees John's "comic doubt" and "an interval of self-consultation" before he consents "with a good grace to play his part in the farce" (89). According to Lucy, Mme. Beck is willing to keep her daughter out of trouble "at any price," but Lucy wonders "that Dr. John did not tire of the business" (89). Lucy recognizes John's unease with his situation but softens John's ethical struggle by using terms such as "farce" and "comic doubt" of which he may "tire," implying that the charade is lighthearted albeit tedious. Lucy also glosses over the pecuniary benefit implied in the phrase "at any price," in terms of both John's fee for his daily visits to Désirée and his future fees if he is retained as the school's physician. Like Mrs. Sweeny's Indian shawl, John becomes an authentic object in a fraudulent scheme, Mme. Beck's passion for "*Angleterre*" substituting for her appreciation of textiles (66). Benjamin Brodie warns that physicians should never even appear to sanction false conduct, so John's actions should raise questions about his professionalism. These questions are furthered by his affiliation with foreign methods, because foreignness is an epithet associated with quackery. In this context, John's prescriptions do not seem quite harmless, because they contribute to Désirée's corruption and because they destabilize his own status as an orthodox physician and an English gentleman.

Another of John's lapses involves his liaison with a student at Mme. Beck's school, Ginevra Fanshawe. A physician's seduction of members of a patient's household has long-standing associations with misconduct because, aside from the strict rules of Victorian propriety, medicine has its own standards regarding sexual relations. For example, the Oath of Hippocrates forbids intermingling of professional and personal: "Into whatever homes I go, I will enter them for the benefit of the sick, avoiding any voluntary act of impropriety and corruption, including the seduction of women or men, whether they be free men or slaves."[52] Monica F. Cohen differentiates between John's roles as lover and physician, but his use of professional visits for romantic encounters indicates an uneasy overlap between these two roles. In this case, as in the case of Désirée Beck, Lucy minimizes John's misconduct, but Brontë provides hints that John's conduct is inappropriate.[53] For example, Lucy describes little Georgette's suffering as Georgette waits, feverish and crying, for John's visit (94). Upon hearing John at the main door below, Lucy waits to question him before giving Georgette a draught of medicine, and she says that her "heart ached" to see the child's suffering (94). When John does not immediately appear in the sickroom, Lucy goes in search of him, hears him pleading with his lover in English, and sees him emerging from a room, "his fair English cheek high-colored" (95). Whether blushing from excitement or frustration, John conducts himself in a way that is doubly improper: it is a betrayal of Mme. Beck's trust and of his duty to Georgette. He should not prolong a child's suffering, even briefly, to pursue his own affairs, and perhaps his blushing English cheek betrays knowledge of wrongdoing as well as sexual frustration. Lucy minimizes John's lapse by imagining that Mme. Beck is John's lover, although Lucy does not recognize John's lover as Mme. Beck and Mme. Beck does not speak English. But imagining Mme. Beck as John's mysterious lover excuses only his breach of trust toward her as mistress of the school: it does not excuse John's delay in attending to Georgette, whose suffering reveals the impropriety of his conduct.

But John is guilty of a breach of trust toward Mme. Beck, and he compounds his lapse by flirting with her. Lucy reassures readers that John does not "curry favour" (89). Yet Lucy sees his "mischievous half-smile" and his "masculine vanity" (94) and asserts, "With all his good looks and good nature, he was not perfect; he must have been very imperfect if he roguishly encouraged aims he never intended to be successful. But, did he not intend them to be successful?" (94).[54] Of course,

John has no intentions of marrying Mme. Beck, as she eventually realizes with some mortification (96). In the midst of Lucy's excuse, Brontë employs the word *roguishly*. The *Oxford English Dictionary* defines *rogue* as an "idle vagrant or vagabond," "a dishonest, unprincipled person," but also as a "mischievous person."[55] While the former two definitions connote socially and morally unacceptable conduct, the latter definition may apply either to genuinely undesirable conduct or to charming misconduct, for example, to a child who is beloved as well as censured. For physicians, vagrancy, dishonesty, and mischief may be markers of quackery, whether professional quackery or outright rejection of orthodox practice. The word *roguery* even appears in the *Lancet* as a synonym for quackery.[56] The *British Medical Journal* warns the reader that any failure to "love his neighbour" and "to do to all men as he would that they should do to him" will "increase the obscurity of the cloud which we have described as overshadowing medicine."[57] According to the *British Medical Journal*, ethical lapses, even those not explicitly medical, bring medicine as a whole under the cloud of quackery. Lucy uses the term *roguishly* to connote John's high spirits (96); however, John's flirtation transgresses the norms of orthodox medical conduct, and readers might question Lucy's easy dismissal of John's conduct as charming rather than morally and professionally suspect.

Brontë repeatedly uses language that implies untrustworthiness in describing John's conduct at the school. When John follows a billet-doux dropped into the school's garden, Lucy calls his presence there "sacrilege" and "intrusion" (104), but she concludes, "No matter whether he was to blame or not; somebody, it seemed to me, must be more to blame" (105). To Lucy, John's culpability is of "no matter," a claim undermined by words such as *sacrilege* and *intrusion*. Similarly, when Rosine, the porteress, questions John about the billet-doux, he bribes her, yet Lucy blames Rosine for "chattering like a pie to the best gentleman in Christendom" (113).[58] At Mme. Beck's ball, John asks to dance with a student, but Mme. Beck forbids it; "'Come, Wolf; come' said she, laughing: 'You wear sheep's clothing, but you must quit the fold, notwithstanding'" (133). Mme. Beck's view of John as a wolf in sheep's clothing contrasts with Lucy's view of him as he wanders among the young girls: "[T]here was about him a manly, responsible look, that redeemed his youth, and half expiated his beauty" (133). Where Lucy minimizes John's sexuality, Mme. Beck sees him as both sexually aggressive and duplicitous. At the dance, Mme. Beck places John among the other young, single men

88   behind a cordon, but John escapes, the only man to cross the boundary. He finds Ginevra and offers a shawl in what Lucy describes as his "English voice" (137). John's use of the shawl as a pretext for his transgression of Mme. Beck's cordon recalls Mrs. Sweeny's use of her shawl as a mask for fraud. Yet Lucy scolds Ginevra; "Is it possible that fine generous gentleman—handsome as a vision—offers you his honorable hand and gallant heart . . . and you hang back—you scorn, you sting, you torture him!" (137). In Lucy's view, Ginevra is duplicitous: "You are only dissembling: you are not in earnest; you love him; you long for him; but you trifle with his heart to make him more surely yours?" (138). In these incidents, Brontë hints that Lucy's view of John as an ideal physician and gentleman is not the only view, nor, possibly, the correct one. John's exploitation of medical authority for personal interest undermines his status as an orthodox physician and an ideal English gentleman and troubles Lucy's status as a reliable narrator.

John Kucich notes the untrustworthy nature of passion in Brontë's work and contends that expression and repression of passion in this novel are "identically opposed to direct self-revelation."[59] Lucy chastises Ginevra for playacting passion, but John's passion is also partly deceitful. From the beginning, Ginevra admits to Lucy that she feigns passion for John, whom she calls Isidore, to extract presents of bouquets, gloves, and jewelry (83). Ginevra claims that she is too "coquettish, and ignorant, and flirting" to marry John; "je ne serai jamais femme de bourgeois, moi!" (84).[60] Lucy calls this conduct "very wrong—seriously wrong" (83), and she chides Ginevra. At the time, John tells Lucy that he believes Ginevra too "disinterested" and too "simpleminded" to know the value of his gifts (182), although Lucy sees "a blue subtle ray" from his eye that "half led me to think that part, at least, of his professed persuasion of Miss Fanshawe's naïveté was assumed" (183). John later confirms that his passion was at least partly assumed: "Do you remember our conversation about the presents? I was not quite open with you in discussing that subject: the warmth with which you took it up amused me. By way of having the full benefit of your lights, I allowed you to think me more in the dark than I really was. It was that test of the presents which first proved Ginevra mortal. Still, her beauty retained its fascination: three days—three hours ago, I was very much her slave" (205). Only in retrospect is John's duplicity clear.[61] Far from a brief lapse in conduct, John engages in an ongoing charade designed to manipulate both Lucy and Ginevra. His confession prompts a reappraisal of his entire conduct. For example, at the school play, Ginevra and Lucy perform the part of lovers onstage while John watches from the audience.[62] At the time, John appears sincere, but in retrospect, John is performing as much as either Lucy or Ginevra, because both women are responding to his cues as the "sincere lover" (130). Lucy hints that this role may not encapsulate him entirely: "There was language in Dr. John's look, though I cannot tell what he said" (130). Although John's deception in this instance is not medical in nature, his conduct magnifies the tendency toward deceit and manipulation that is also evident in his professional life. What began with a harmless prescription for a child snowballs into all-encompassing duplicity.

John is not a quack in the sense of one who peddles nostrums or adheres to discredited systems of health.[63] However, John's association with trickery and deception complicates his status as an orthodox physician. Perhaps the novel's most potent symbol of trickery is the nun, which John diagnoses as a figment of Lucy's diseased mind.[64] Sally Shuttleworth argues that John embodies the "gaze of medical authority" and that despite his diagnostic error the "authority of science is not . . . thereby erased from the text."[65] If the authority of science is unchallenged by the nun, however, John's place (and medicine's place) in relation to that authority is challenged. John's error foreshadows Benjamin Brodie's warning about the damage caused by misdiagnosis and G. H. Lewes's concern about glibness and quackery. The nun is perhaps less a sign of medicine's power than a symbol of its limitations. Near the novel's conclusion, the nun is revealed to be Ginevra's lover, Colonel de Hamal. Ironically, Lucy initially censures de Hamal as "the doll—the puppet—the manikin—" (137), and in the same way that a doll can be dressed in multiple ways for make-believe, he dresses up as a nun to visit Ginevra, an enterprise that echoes John's own duplicitous entries onto school grounds. Ginevra and de Hamal's deception is also foreshadowed at the opera, when John classifies Ginevra's glance at de Hamal as "not flirtation: it was a look marking mutual and secret understanding—it was neither girlish nor innocent" (211). Viewed as trickery rather than symptom, the nun reproduces orthodoxy's ongoing difficulty in coping with quackery. Just as medicine cannot cope with impersonations such as Morison's system of health, John cannot penetrate his rival's masquerade. What the *Lancet* says about quackery may be applied to the nun: "Humbug in its every shape has always been petted, applauded, and patronized by all classes of society; and so long as it is harmless, it merely excites our smile or arouses our derision; but this system of imposture is by no means harmless, and

90   inflicts great and irreparable injury upon all who become its victims and dupes."[66] Part amusement and part cruelty, the nun exposes the harm in the apparently harmless love of trickery, medicine's limitations as a way of knowing, and the pernicious nature of quackery.

This is not to say that Lucy is wholly well throughout the narrative, only that John's diagnosis of the nun is inadequate. Lucy seems genuinely ill when she collapses in the street and is brought to John's house, where he diagnoses her with "[h]ypochondria" and prescribes "cheerful society" and "plenty of exercise" (172). Lucy thinks that his opinion bears the "well-worn stamp of use" (172). Lucy's unspoken thought anticipates Benjamin Brodie's warning about imaginary or self-limiting disease as a boon to quackery (338). It also recalls earlier warnings about quackery's exploitative curing of disease that is not disease but boredom or overwork, "the two great evils of our social system."[67] Lucy's comment about John's well-worn diagnosis and prescription suggests skepticism about his actual insight, despite his confident manner. Lucy's doubts are magnified when the nun appears. John dismisses "material terrors" such as "fears of robbers" out of hand and diagnoses the nun as a symptom of "nerves" (234), a "spectral illusion" brought about through "mental conflict" (235). John orders Lucy to "cultivate happiness" (235). However, Lucy thinks to herself, "What does such advice mean? Happiness is not a potato" (235). Lucy's unspoken play on the word *cultivate* suggests that Lucy is skeptical of John's diagnosis.[68] Although she does not verbally challenge John, Lucy's subsequent thoughts reflect the resistance of the Victorian patient. Christopher Lawrence notes that financial concerns, overcrowding, and a "flourishing army of unqualified healers" gave patients considerable power during this period.[69] Lucy is far from a passive patient: although she is disturbed by John's diagnosis, she does not accept it uncritically. Instead, she continues to ponder whether the nun is a person, a ghost, or a symptom (237). Lucy's unspoken critique, John's trickery, and his diagnostic patter together unsettle the line between quackery and orthodoxy.

Brontë signals John's misdiagnosis to readers by highlighting John's trickery during his consultation with Lucy. When the nun appears, Lucy drops the letter she was reading, a letter from John himself. John secretly picks up and conceals the letter, then watches Lucy become increasingly distressed over its loss. When he finally restores it to her, Lucy sees "a new sort of smile playing about his lips—very sweet, but it grieved me somehow—a new sort of light sparkling in his eyes: not hostile, but not reassuring" (234). John claims, "You don't know my skill in sleight of hand: I might practice as a conjuror if I liked. Mama says sometimes, too, that I have a harmonizing property of tongue and eye; but you never saw that in me—did you Lucy?" (234). By representing John as a conjuror just at this moment, Brontë points to the falsity of his confident dismissal of material terrors such as burglars. Lucy's agitation over the nun is pronounced, yet John upsets her further by this trick, and with evident enjoyment.[70] This recalls his earlier deception over Ginevra when Lucy was recuperating at his home. John taxes Lucy's patience with false praise of Ginevra at a time when Lucy says that "illness and weakness had worn it and made it brittle" (178). Finally, Lucy snaps, "[Y]ou merit no respect; nor have you mine" (178). John then allows Lucy to apologize; "He showed the fineness of his nature by being kinder to me after that misunderstanding than before" (180). John's verbal manipulation and actual sleight of hand with the letter undermine his reliability as a physician by recalling the association between trickery and quackery. In the case of Désirée Beck, John's trickery compounds the child's naughty tendencies; in Lucy's case, it contradicts his own prescription for cheer and happiness. In both, John's trickery transgresses medical norms for orthodox practitioners.

The nun displays John's trickery as well as de Hamal's: she appears as Lucy reads John's letter, before Lucy goes to the theater with John, when she buries John's letter, and as she lingers over the burial spot pondering her relationship with John. Each appearance marks Lucy's growing dissatisfaction with John's diagnosis. When the nun appears before the theater, Lucy thinks, "[I]t was all optical illusion—nervous malady, and so on. No one bit did I believe him, but I dared not contradict: doctors are so self-opinionated, so immovable in their dry, materialist views" (241). When she buries John's letters, Lucy acts on her own belief that the nun is not a figment: "I advanced one step. I stretched out my hand, for I meant to touch her" (279). Later at the same spot, Lucy ponders her relationship with John, thinking it a "curious one-sided friendship . . . only on one hand truth, and on the other perhaps a jest?" (341). Although Lucy mentally questions John's diagnosis, she repeats it to M. Paul, saying that she is "constitutionally nervous" (345).[71] However, Paul acknowledges the supernatural quality of the nun while maintaining the logical proposition that she may be merely a person: "Whether this nun be flesh and blood, or something that remains when blood is dried and flesh wasted, . . . I mean to make it out" (346). When Paul questions his

92 "morbid fancies" about the nun, Lucy finally speaks her own view, which contradicts John's: "I believe a perfectly natural solution of this seeming mystery will one day be arrived at" (383). If readers believe John, the nun is an expression of morbidity, either Lucy's or Paul's or both. Yet de Hamal's nun perhaps better acts as a symbol of trickery, both de Hamal's and John's. Like de Hamal, John employs trickery to pursue Ginevra, transgresses the boundaries of the school grounds, and causes Lucy distress. Just as de Hamal and John are rivals for Ginevra, so too does John call the nun his rival for Lucy and states that "he was determined to dispute with her her prey. . . . [H]e was determined to try whether he or she was the cleverest" (239). According to Lucy, the nun affords John opportunity to treat Lucy "scientifically in the light of a patient" and to use his "professional skill" and "natural benevolence" (239). Yet the nun equally exposes John's lack of knowledge, skill, or benevolence as she symbolizes the cruelty of *legerdemain*, which, like John's sleight of hand with the letter, may provide amusement but also cause genuine distress.

John's courtship of Polly further exposes his unreliability.[72] In the guise of both a physician and a childhood friend, John enters a secret relationship with Polly, betraying Mr. Home's trust just as he had Mme. Beck's. Polly confesses to Lucy that John has written to her, and she describes his letter as a "ewe lamb" (351). Her metaphor recalls King David's sexual aggression and betrayal and also Mme. Beck characterization of John as a wolf in sheep's clothing.[73] Polly forbids his letters, but he continues to write and she to respond (399). When Mr. Home discovers their clandestine correspondence, he characterizes John as a "Highlander and a chief, and there is a trace of the Celt in all you look, speak, and think. You have his cunning and his charm. The red—(well, then, Polly, the *fair*) hair, the tongue of guile, and brain of wile, are all come down by inheritance" (407). Like Mme. Beck, Mr. Home sees in John a wolf in sheep's clothing, possessing "cunning," "guile," and "wile"; however, Mr. Home sees duplicity as a Celtic trait. John asserts, "I *feel* honest enough" (407 [original italics]), and Lucy says that "a genuine English blush covered his face with its warm witness of sincerity" (407). Is John blushing for sincerity? Or is he blushing because he was caught in duplicity? Is redness (of cheek and hair) a sign of Englishness or of foreignness, honesty or deceit? Is John the embodiment of English virtue or of Celtic wile? Home's characterization of the Celts contrasts with Lucy's view of John as Celtic and therefore trustworthy. Home's estimation of John, like Mme. Beck's earlier, thus undermines

Lucy's too-favorable interpretation. For Lucy, John is an ideal, and his status as a physician importantly grounds her estimation of his personal and moral qualities. However, there is ample evidence that John is not an ideal physician; in fact, he signally transgresses medical norms when he becomes involved with his patient, Polly, and deceives her father. In this instance, as in previous ones, John muddies the very boundaries that Lucy claims he embodies, an embodiment also undermined by Mr. Home's view. Through trickery and deceit, John draws into doubt the very boundaries that Lucy says he defends.

Lucy's Narrative as Testimonial

In John, Brontë troubles the boundary between orthodoxy and quackery. In Lucy, Brontë reveals the considerable *legerdemain* required to establish and maintain such boundaries. If John's *legerdemain* muddies orthodoxy and quackery, Lucy's narrative *legerdemain* in covering for John questions the very nature of boundary making itself.[74] Critics such as Sally Shuttleworth contend that John asserts predefined cultural boundaries, but in the context of quackery, John allows Brontë to foreground the difficulties of boundary making in medicine and in culture. Just as she cannot sustain John within the boundaries of orthodoxy without considerable effort, Lucy admits that she cannot draw a clear boundary between acting as John's "faithful narrator" and acting as his "partial eulogist" (186).[75] Lucy's conundrum recalls the medical testimonial, a suspect genre that explicitly claims authenticity despite its long-standing association with falsehood. Although Lucy privileges "faithful narrator" over "partial eulogist," Lucy, like John, admits the pleasures of trickery. John Kucich argues that Lucy's apparent relinquishment of acting is belied by her "repressions that become invested with this relish for self-negating dramatic performance."[76] Lucy openly relishes misleading Ginevra about John's affection: "There was pleasure in thinking of the contrast between the reality and my description" (224). She offers false praise of de Hamal to goad John (140) and expresses false interest in the portrait of Cleopatra to goad Paul; "I had a certain leisure in keeping cool, and working him up" (190). When Paul asks Lucy whether she is upset, she denies it with a "neat, frosty falsehood" (300). When she recognizes John as the Graham of her youth, she confides, "To *say* anything on the subject, to *hint* at my discovery, had not suited my habits of thought, or assimilated with my system of feeling. . . . I liked entering his presence covered with

94   a cloud he had not seen through, while he stood before me under a ray of special illumination" (164 [original italics]). Lucy's confession of her own trickery paradoxically parades honesty but reveals the tempting power of falsehood. In confessing to these false narratives, Lucy leaves the reader unsure about how to read her apparent frankness.

Nevertheless, Lucy's narrative features ambiguous confessions that may not be trickery so much as lack of insight. For example, when Lucy goes to the theater with John, she both confesses and denies doubts about the propriety of their outing: "And away I flew, never once checked, reader, by the thought which perhaps at this moment checks you: namely that to go anywhere with Graham and without Mrs. Bretton could be objectionable. I could not have conceived, much less have expressed, to Graham such thought—such scruple—without risk of exciting a tyrannous self-contempt; of kindling an inward fire of shame so quenchless, and so devouring, that I think it would soon have licked up the very life in my veins" (240). Is the possibility of a sexual relationship with John really so inconceivable to Lucy? Or is this a confession of thoughts Lucy is ashamed to acknowledge? When Lucy later buries John's letters, she symbolically relinquishes a desire she denied ever harboring. Regarding John's insensitivity toward her, Lucy confides, "[I]n quarters where we can never be rightly known, we take pleasure, I think, in being consummately ignored. What honest man on being casually taken for a housebreaker, does not feel rather tickled than vexed at the mistake?" (91). Is Lucy confessing secret delight at John's callousness or confessing her hidden vexation? The latter seems to dominate her later, vehement refusal to act as John's "officious soubrette," saying in powerful block capitals and italics, "NO. I could not" (298 [original italics]). When asked her opinion of John, Lucy again replies in italics, "I never see him" (398), an admission contradicted by her detailed narrative itself. Her most questionable confidence is her union with Paul at the end of the novel, an ending Philip Rogers reads as a hoax on readers. However, Lucy's omission of Paul's fate is only the most obvious of her many incomplete confessions. While Lucy openly confesses to tricking Ginevra, John, and Paul, her deceptive confidences lead readers to question whether she is deliberately deceptive or genuinely unaware of the truth of her own experience. Lucy's confessions privilege revelation over concealment, but they complicate the nature of revelation, since they exhibit incomplete knowledge which may or may not be deliberate.

Defenders of medical orthodoxy, such as the *Lancet*, Glover, Brodie, and Lewes, call for linguistic reform to discriminate between orthodoxy and quackery. They assert that deliberate trickery, such as the placebos John offers Désirée Beck, should be avoided, and they censure those who write false testimonials for money. However, Brontë complicates the nature of this type of reform by suggesting that matters of narrative trickery are not simple matters of outright lying so much as a no-man's-land between Lucy's categories of faithful narrator and partial eulogist. Medical commentators chastise writers of testimonials as liars or as "dupes," "simpleton[s]," or "sanguine, credulous, enthusiastic" persons.[77] Far from being a dupe, a simpleton, or a sanguine, credulous enthusiast, Lucy is deeply concerned with narrative truth and falsehood. For example, Lucy asserts strict boundaries between English and foreigners, Protestants and Catholics, reliable and deceitful.[78] The French practice "insolence and deceit," an "oilier glibness with which flattery and fiction ran from the tongue" (75). Lucy describes their confessions in this way: "J'ai menti plusieurs fois" (75).[79] Lucy attempts to teach her students that "falsehood" is worse than missing church, but the Catholics reject her apparently English, Protestant value for truth (77). Similarly, Lucy scolds the students and teachers in Mme. Beck's school: "Vive l'Angleterre, l'Histoire et les Héros! A bas la France, la Fiction et les Faquins!" (322). For England, Lucy claims history and heroes, but for France she sees only fiction and fops. To Lucy, the English are factual as history and the French are deceitful as fiction.

Despite her best efforts, Lucy's narrative cannot maintain these boundaries. For example, Lucy disapproves of foreigners but approves of the "cosmopolitan" nature of Villette and of Mme. Beck's school, in which "the young countess and the young bourgeoise sat side by side" (75). Although she censures Ginevra's deceptiveness, Lucy praises Ginevra's frankness (135). Most significantly, Lucy cannot easily categorize M. Paul. He says of Lucy, "[W]e are alike—there is affinity" (345). Paul praises Lucy's frankness, just as Lucy praises Ginevra's: "It is well— you do right to be honest. I should almost have hated you, if you flattered and lied" (325). Although Lucy claims honesty as English, she deceives readers about Paul's many gifts to her of flowers, books, and chocolates (326). Conversely, Paul scorns deception: "Now I knew, and had long known, that the hand of M. Emmanuel's was on intimate terms with my desk. . . . The fact was not dubious, nor did he wish it to be so; he left signs of each visit palpable and unmistakable" (323). Lucy admits

96 Paul's resistance to her categories; "I thought Romanism wrong, . . . but it seemed to me that *this* Romanist held the purer elements of his creed with an innocency of heart which God must love" (393). Considering Paul's conduct, Lucy ponders the slippery nature of perception: "If he *really* wished for my confidence and regard, and *really* would give me his—why, it seemed to me that life could offer nothing more or better" (382 [original italics]). She continues, "When he spoke, the tone of his voice, the light of his now affectionate eye, gave me such a pleasure as, certainly, I had never felt. I envied no girl her lover, no bride her bridegroom, no wife her husband; I was content with this my voluntary self-offering friend. If he would but prove reliable, and he *looked* reliable, what, beyond his friendship could I ever covet? But, if all melted like a dream, as once before had happened—?" (382). The italicized terms *really* and *looked* indicate considerable anxiety about the nature of truth and falsehood, despite Lucy's rigid categories.

Lucy's own conduct cannot maintain her supposedly inviolable categories of truth and deception. For example, when asked to hold Fifine's broken limb, Lucy describes her courage as "feigned" (87). She watches Mme. Beck rifling through her possessions as she "feigned" sleep, thus appropriating Mme. Beck's foreign methods of deception just as John adopts them in the matter of Désirée (63). Lucy's first English lesson exemplifies her situation. Lucy asserts that in her "own tongue" her voice "could make itself heard, if lifted in excitement or deepened by emotion" (73). However, Lucy cannot teach English using straightforward English methods. Instead, Lucy resorts to trickery, melodramatically ripping up a student's essay and pushing a particularly rowdy student into a book closet (73). Dolores, the student Lucy locks up, is doubly a foreigner to Lucy, since she is not from Villette but from Catalonia (74). Is Lucy containing foreign influence when she locks up Dolores, or is she participating in it by appropriating its methods? Is she teaching English to these students or being schooled in Villette's duplicity? In medicine, Brontë finds a discourse deeply invested in questions of authenticity and language. As a physician, John apparently embodies Lucy's ideals; however, John's *legerdemain* draws his status as an orthodox physician into question and thus undermines the values he ostensibly symbolizes. More important is that John signals to readers a way of approaching the novel that, far from reinforcing Victorian norms, uncovers the instability of these categories. Whereas medical commentators suggest that quackery deals in lies or stupidity, Brontë explores the slippery nature of language itself.

What Lucy's narrative makes clear is that reform of orthodox language is   97
unlikely to quash quackery, because the hallmarks of quackery may easily apply to orthodoxy itself. In Lucy's narrative, Brontë acknowledges
the considerable *legerdemain* involved in constructing and maintaining
categories such as orthodox and quack, and Brontë's achievement in this
novel lies in this realization about the potentially uncontrollable nature
of communication, even as medical commentators call for ever-more-
stringent regulation of language and conduct.

Chapter Four

Poisons and the Poisonous in
Wilkie Collins's *Armadale*

I cannot draw the distinction between a poison and a
medicine, but I can point out, from my experience, what
has caused death during the last 30 years.

—Alfred Swaine Taylor before the Select Committee
of the Chemists and Druggists Bill, 1865

It is said it must be some kind of poison; but what is
a poison? It is something which, as administered, is
destructive or injurious to human life. There is hardly
any active medicine which may not be so; and on the
other hand, there is hardly any poison which may not, in
certain quantities, and in given circumstances, be salutary.

—"What Is a Noxious Thing?" *British Medical Journal*, 1880

oison is a tricky entity. *Dorland's Medical Dictionary* defines *poison* as "a substance which, on ingestion, inhalation, absorption, application, injection, or development within the body,
in relatively small amounts, may cause structural damage or functional
disturbance."[1] Thus, a poison is a chemical either foreign or native to
the body distinguished by quantity (small amount) and by capacity for
physical disturbance (symptomatic or not). The *Oxford English Dictionary*
offers other perspectives: "Material that causes illness or death when
introduced into or absorbed by a living organism, esp. when able to kill
by rapid action and when taken in small quantity."[2] *Dorland's* mentions

only small amounts and physiological disturbance (with or without symptoms); however, the *OED* specifies "illness or death" following exposure to a specifically foreign substance. This more sinister configuration of poison continues: "To hate intensely, detest"; "A drink prepared for a special purpose; a medicinal draught; a potion"; and "A principle, doctrine, influence, etc., which is harmful to character, morality, or the well-being of society; something which causes harm; something which is detested."[3] Here, *poison* signifies not only physical disturbance to an individual but also moral or social harm to the social body, perpetrated by the hated or the ostracized. Nevertheless, *poison* is also defined as a "medicinal draught" and a "potion," one connoting medical care and the other magic. From intrinsic and asymptomatic to extrinsic and harmful to immoral and antisocial, *poison* is a multivalent entity.

In poison, Victorian culture confronts what Mary E. Fissell calls the shifting meanings of medical goods.[4] Victorian Britain recognized a relationship between poison and medicine, and in the Arsenic Act of 1851, the Poisons Act of 1857, the Pharmacy Act of 1868, and various similar but unsuccessful bills, Victorians struggled to define and to regulate poison. In his essay "Plato's Pharmacy," Jacques Derrida deconstructs the meaning of *pharmakon*, showing it to signify both medicine and poison.[5] But the word *poison* in medical practice carries important ramifications for people and groups in culture. Calling a substance a poison alters its commercial potential, its accessibility, and its status by attaching negative connotations to it. At the same time, the developing pharmaceutical profession demanded that poisons be dispensed by licensed druggists alongside medicines, a connection that seems to complicate *poison* as a pejorative, since both substances may apparently be handled safely by experts. As legislators endorse or restrict given uses for a particular chemical, they also profoundly affect individuals and groups, professionalizing some and criminalizing others. Judith Knelman connects the genesis of the Arsenic Act of 1851 with anxiety about domestic poisoning because "poisoning was a time-honoured way for women, who were in charge of a family's food, to do away with people."[6] According to Knelman, women charged with poisoning were labeled "monsters" because of their transgression of the supposedly natural role of women.[7] Peter Bartrip suggests that poison legislation is connected to the Pharmaceutical Society's attempt to monopolize dispensing.[8] In this way, Bartrip accounts for Victorian legislation restricting pharmaceutical poisons but not industrial poisons. In her reading of Christina

100   Rossetti's "Goblin Market," Rebecca Stern views the goblins' tainted fruit
not simply as a metaphor for sin but as a social issue that "emphasizes
the proximity of economic and domestic concerns."[9] In Stern's reading,
poisoned fruit becomes a "signifier that *all* commodities and people that
vended them were potentially poisonous."[10] Stern rightly emphasizes
two aspects of poisoning: the ways in which poisoned food collapses
boundaries between public and private and the connections between
the identity of goods and persons. However, Stern's excellent reading
takes for granted the nature of poison itself, which emerges as always
already harmful and dangerous.[11] Is a poison always a poison? Why do
some substances, such as arsenic, come to be widely accepted as poison
when other potentially dangerous substances, such as opium, do not?
This chapter examines the ways in which poison is created, not as a
self-evident entity defined by scientists, but through cultural processes
in the public sphere.

Wilkie Collins's *Armadale* (1866) reflects poison's resistance to categorization.[12] The novel focuses on a murderess, Lydia Gwilt, and a quack,
Mrs. Oldershaw, who together plot to steal a naïve aristocrat's fortune
using elaborate ruses, marriage, and murder. This is a novel about slippery identities and about the difficulty of discriminating between friends
and foes. The novel begins with two cousins, both named Allan Armadale, who are rivals for the inheritance of an estate and for the hand of a
woman. One Allan wins the estate, and the other Allan wins the woman
with the help of a deceptive young maid, Lydia Gwilt. Bitter at the loss
of his sweetheart, the now-wealthy Allan Armadale murders the successful lover Allan Armadale before dying prematurely at a mountain spa.
Prior to his death, murderer Allan Armadale dictates a letter confessing
his crime and warning his young son to avoid at all costs the son of
his victim, for both men have sons named Allan Armadale. The second
generation of Allan Armadales grow to maturity, become friends in unlikely circumstances, and, like their fathers, become rivals for the hand
of a woman, who turns out to be Lydia Gwilt in disguise. After a life of
crime, Lydia Gwilt reemerges with a scheme to become a rich widow by
marrying and then poisoning wealthy Allan Armadale with the help of
her accomplice, Mrs. Oldershaw. But Lydia and Mrs. Oldershaw do not
realize that wealthy Allan Armadale is protected by a mysterious friend,
Ozias Midwinter, who is really the second Allan Armadale and who has
his father's letter describing the events of twenty years earlier and is
determined to prevent a second tragedy. Piya Pal-Lapinski argues that

Armadale takes full advantage of poison's ubiquity in Victorian culture and of its slippery nature.[13] Pal-Lapinski argues that prosecuting Victorian poisoners was difficult because of the inaccuracy of toxicology tests, and she argues that substances such as opium may be "masquerading as medicine and recreation."[14] This approach acknowledges the limitations of Victorian medicine; however, it fails to address pharmacy. Poison's difficulty is not merely that it is hard to identify or available in multiple forms but that it is not reliably poisonous. This chapter argues that it is not poison that creates the poisoner, but the poisoner who, by employing a given chemical in murder, creates the poison. In this configuration, poison emerges as a culturally determined artifact, not a stable, chemical entity. This reading challenges the idea that medicines are cut-and-dried facts; instead, it argues that *Armadale* displays the fallacy of such conventional wisdom, and it pursues the implications of this fallacy for those whose identities are linked to pharmaceuticals.

Poison as Medicine: Medicine as Poison

Near the climax of *Armadale*, adventuress and poisoner Lydia Gwilt tours sinister Dr. Downward's asylum, just prior to the arrival of her prospective victim, wealthy Allan Armadale, ostensibly to visit his sweetheart, whom he believes is a patient. Downward shows Lydia and other visitors his dispensary: "'There is nothing to interest you inside,'" he said. 'Nothing but rows of little shabby bottles containing the poisons used in medicine which I keep under lock and key. Come to the kitchen, ladies, and honour me with your advice on domestic matters below stairs'" (641). Downward's motive is to provide Lydia with information about how to poison Armadale while maintaining deniability for himself, since the information is innocently given during a tour. His diversion of the tour from the dispensary to the kitchen is telling. Downward attempts to distinguish the male preserve of medicine, and its poisons (which he alone controls), from the site of female activity, the kitchen, where chemistry of a different sort occurs. At the same time, readers are fully aware of the fictitious nature of this division. The medicines *are* interesting to Lydia and probably to the other women on the tour. Despite Downward's conventional separation of pharmacy and cooking, the idea of a woman poisoning via food was a well-known concept of the day. Downward protests too much when he asks, "My dear lady, what interest can you possibly have in looking at a medical bottle, simply because it happens to be a bottle of poison?" (641). When he returns to Lydia in the dispensary, Downward instructs her in that which he previously stated was of no interest to women; "There are all sorts of medical liquids and substances in those bottles—most innocent, most useful in themselves—which, in combination with other substances and other liquids become poison as terrible and as deadly as any that I have in my cabinet under lock and key" (641). Downward points Lydia not to the locked cabinet of poisons but to an unsecured bottle he calls his "Stout Friend":

> He is freely dispensed every day to tens of thousands of patients all over the civilized world. He has made no romantic appearances in courts of law; he has excited no breathless interest in novels; he has played no terrifying part on the stage. There he is, an innocent, inoffensive creature, who troubles nobody with the responsibility of locking him up! But, bring him into contact with something else—introduce him to the acquaintance of a certain common mineral Substance, of a universally accessible kind, broken into fragments; provide yourself with (say) six doses of our Stout Friend, and pour those doses consecutively on the fragments I have mentioned, at intervals of not less than five minutes. . . . [O]ur Stout Friend will kill him in half-an-hour! Will kill him slowly, without his seeing anything, without his smelling anything, without his feeling anything but sleepiness. Will kill him, and tell the whole College of Surgeons nothing, if they examine him after death, but that he died of apoplexy or congestion of the lungs! What do you think of *that*, my dear lady, in the way of mystery and romance? Is our harmless Stout Friend as interesting *now* as if he rejoiced in the terrible popular fame of the Arsenic and the Strychnine which I keep locked up there? (642)

Downward's statements are seconded by his Resident Dispenser, who innocently bustles to procure the necessary mineral in hopes of performing an experiment for the attractive Lydia (643). Under the guise of educational information, Downward is instructing Lydia about how to poison Armadale, but Downward's lecture reveals a more worrisome fact about pharmaceutical chemistry. As Downward shows, the word *poison* is not particularly meaningful in chemistry, despite its romantic and legal potency. The locked poisons are medicines and the unlocked medicines are potential poisons, if compounded correctly. Pharmaceutical chemistry is about malleability. Even Downward's language is unstable: the pronoun *he* that at first describes the chemical ("he is freely dispensed") slides into the identity of the murder victim, Allen ("will kill him"). In the pharmacopoeia, no entity is reliably an "innocent, inoffensive creature."

This ambiguity is evident later when Lydia investigates the bottles of chemicals Downward has left for her: "She drew out the wand, and cautiously touched the wet left on it with the tip of her tongue. Caution was quite needless in this case. The liquid was—water" (644). Lydia's caution displays both awareness about the difficulties of identifying poisons and naïve trust in taste as an identifier. But is water harmless? Collins shows that even water has a role to play in poisoning. Water is being used here to preserve the mineral and to keep it away from the solvent until the correct time. While water is not a poison in itself, it is a participant in the chemical reaction that Lydia will use to kill Armadale. Bottles are substitute markers of identity for chemicals that may lack intrinsic markers such as taste, color, or smell, but, as Downward shows, bottles are unreliable.[15] Tanya Pollard points to the power of bottles in the staged poisonings of the early modern revenge drama, where the bottle symbolizes both the poison it carries within and the moral poison of the woman poisoner, who is a contaminated and contaminating vessel.[16] But here, even the Stout Friend is deceptive: Downward "had privately removed the yellow liquid on the previous day, and . . . had filled up again with a carefully-coloured imitation, in the shape of a mixture of his own" (642). The water bottle, Stout Friend, and Purple Flask exemplify both the need for and the difficulties of reliable identification. In his testimony before the Select Committee on the Sale of Poisons Bill in 1857, pharmaceutical chemist John Abraham describes the dangers of using bottles to identify poisons. Abraham describes a bottle of Burnett's cleaning solution "standing upon a lady's dressing-table, and she took it up instead of a bottle of Dinneford's solution of magnesia, and she died from the effects of it."[17] Unlike Lydia sharply observing the Stout Friend, this lady failed to note the details of the Dinneford's bottle. Both this lady and Lydia fail to realize that taste is unrelated to danger. Alfred Swaine Taylor asks the Lords to mandate use of glass that is colored and of a particular shape for poison bottles: "It is just a balance of whether we can possibly save life at the expense of a little trouble and cost."[18] Irish physician J. M. Neligan suggests mandating the use of angular bottles for poisons and of round ones for other medications, but William Herapath recognizes that patients may prefer to use their own bottles or to subdivide liquids at home.[19] Similarly, Jacob Bell concludes that "it would be very hard upon a patient to deprive him of his liniment because his bottle happened not to be a square one."[20] The question of bottling seems a trivial matter of pharmacy procedure; however, it addresses the question of identity. Bottles add a layer of ambiguity to poisons by bestowing on chemicals a definitive and easily observed identity but also by destabilizing this identity, because there is no guarantee that the bottles will be used as expected. Downward's game with the bottles displays the potential for misuse in even routine pharmacy procedures and undermines the often naïve trust placed in markers of identity, such as bottles, taste, and appearance.

In his introduction to *Armadale*, John Sutherland calls Lydia's use of poison gas produced by carbonic acid and limestone a "modish murder to crown her career—poisoning with style."[21] However, Collins's use of compounding rather than a simple poison such as arsenic exploits a countercurrent to the prevailing push to segregate, label, and regulate poisons. In his testimony before the Select Committee on the Sale of Poisons Bill in 1857, Neligan argues, "Poison is not like medicine: medicine may be required in a hurry, but for poison a person can afford to wait."[22] Conversely, a representative of the Pharmaceutical Society, Jacob Bell, claims that poisons are very much like medicines and that "nine out of ten of the substances which we sell are poisons, if taken in too large a dose" (5). Bell later asserts, "It seems to be impossible to include the whole list of poisons, and all the precaution that can be taken must only be an approximation to safety, and selecting such poisons as are most capable of being used, or likely to be used, for criminal purposes" (22). Similarly, professor of chemistry William Thomas Brande testifies, "Your Lordships are well aware of the extreme difficulty of defining a poison" (82). Because of the many substances that may harm an individual if ingested, F. Crace Calvert claims, "you cannot prevent poisoning; you can only restrict the facility of poisoning" (67). William Herapath contends that "the vast number of things introduced into this schedule would embrace half, or at least a very large proportion, of the articles to be sold in a druggist's shop" (44). Although the purpose of this report was to create a list of drugs to be labeled poisons and then to develop regulations for these substances, witnesses acknowledged the difficulty of defining poisons amid the variety of chemicals available in the marketplace with the potential for harm.

In an 1865 report by the Select Committee of the Chemists and Druggists Bill, the line between medicine and poison is similarly unclear. Toxicology expert Alfred Swaine Taylor claims, "I cannot draw the distinction between a poison and a medicine, but I can point out, from my experience, what has caused death during the last 30 years."[23] When asked to define *drug*, Taylor responds, "[I]t includes all things, animal, vegetable, and mineral" (15). In this broad definition, poison is merely a type of drug with social cachet, as Herapath, Calvert, and Brande implied earlier. Asked whether the law can prevent "murder by chemicals," Taylor asserts, "No, I do not believe it could; I do not suppose you could suppress poisoning by legislation. But, I believe, you would reduce the number of cases, and render detection more easy" (14). Taylor further advocated dividing chemicals into the categories "poisonous" and "non-poisonous" and restricting the former to sale by chemists and druggists only. By also forbidding compounding of the latter by unlicensed persons, Taylor would attempt to forestall the Downwards and Gwilts of the world from creating poisons out of nonpoisonous chemicals. Member of the Medical Council Richard Quain similarly supported restriction of compounding to chemists and druggists, because "[s]imples, by being compounded, may become dangerous" (35). After describing the results of a dispensing error, Quain was asked whether the substance involved was "poisonous," and his answer reinforces the limitations of such a question by affirming the malleable nature of pharmaceuticals: "Not a poison, but a large dose, and in this instance injurious" (33). Both Taylor and Quain concurred with earlier witnesses about the ambiguous nature of pharmaceutical preparations, which are changeable due to dose and to compounding. In a sense, the Chemists and Druggists Bill reveals the weakness of the earlier Arsenic and Poisons Acts by realizing that merely restricting the sale of a short list of so-called poisons is ineffective if compounding is unregulated, since compounding creates dangerous substances out of innocuous ones. Both Taylor and Quain advocated for the restriction of compounding and dispensing to trained men because of the danger represented even by supposedly safe drugs.

In his "Address in Therapeutics" at the 1858 meeting of the British Medical Association, Robert Christison describes the unstable nature of materia medica. Christison complains about the lack of pharmacological knowledge about popular drugs, including digitalis, colchicum, sarsaparilla, and opium, and he argues for the importance of pharmacy in ascertaining the nature of such substances. For example, Christison points out the importance of compounding in the case of colchicum preparations: "We do not positively know which part of the plant, the seed, or the bulb, is the more powerful, and which the more uniform. . . . Some prefer a tincture of the seeds; and this preparation is probably both most energetic and most easily made uniform in energy: others prefer a vinous solution of the bulb: others an acetic solution of the bulb; others of the seed: and we do not yet positively know who is right."[24] The variation in potency that in colchicum is related to plant structure and process used in preparation exists in other plants for several different reasons. Some, such as the cherry laurel, for example, are more pharmaceutically active during specific seasons. Christison observes, "I found that when the flowering is past, the young, imperfectly-developed leaves contain the largest quantity of hydrocyanated volatile oil, and that they yield weight for weight by distillation ten times as much oil as the full grown old leaves from the very same plants."[25] Thus, the same cherry laurel plant may be more poisonous in the spring than in the summer. Christison also experimented on the *Oenanthe crocata* plant, because he wished "to trace the influence of season, or rather the progressive changes in vegetation during the succession of the seasons, on some organs of plants."[26] He was astonished to discover that "[t]he plant throughout every organ, and in every season, appeared to be not poisonous at all. The root, the leaves, and the seeds had no effect on animals, when administered largely."[27] Christison concludes that this variety of hemlock plant might lose some or all of its pharmacological activity in the northern climate (Scotland), although he still does not recommend it as a "culinary vegetable."[28] Christison's address questions the taken-for-granted nature of materia medica and illuminates the artificial nature of all drugs, even those derived from plants. Far from merely natural, self-evident, and stable, these substances are highly variable and dependent on the processes by which they are gathered and prepared. This underscores the unstable nature of even the most widely known poisons and medicines, which, in fact, vary in pharmacological activity.

Synonymous with Poison

Before Lydia attempts to poison Armadale at Dr. Downward's, she attempts to poison him with arsenic. While visiting Lydia and Ozias's home in Italy, Allan asks for wine, and Lydia offers to make him lemonade. He raises the cup to his lips, drops the glass, and collapses into

Ozias's arms (562). Ozias later discusses the incident with Lydia, and she questions him in an agitated manner, "*Do you think I tried to poison him?*" (562 [original italics]). In fact, Lydia put arsenic and brandy into Allan's lemonade because she did not know that Allan has a "nervous horror of the smell and taste of brandy" (562). Confronted with the brandy, he fainted. Lydia reflects on her failure: "I *was* innocent—so far as the brandy was concerned. I had put it into the lemonade, in pure ignorance of Armadale's nervous peculiarity, to disguise the taste of— never mind what" (563 [original italics]). She confesses to her journal, "[T]here will be no brandy in Armadale's lemonade if I mix it for him a second time" (565). In recording this threat, Lydia has apparently re- solved to try again. Collins's representation of attempted murder by ar- senic draws heavily on arsenic's reputation as the quintessential poison; however, the double poisoning (arsenic and brandy) undermines this conventional view.

John Sutherland argues that Collins's depiction of Lydia exploits sev- eral notorious poisoning cases, including those of Madeleine Smith and Sarah Chesham.[29] Judith Knelman describes a spate of well-publicized arsenic poisonings between 1843 and 1851, ending with Sarah Chesh- am's.[30] Chesham, whose hanging attracted ten thousand spectators, was a serial poisoner who helped a father get rid of an illegitimate child, got rid of her own children, killed her husband, and offered to bake "poi- soned pies" for any woman in need of one.[31] Mary S. Hartman links Vic- torian interest in murderesses with fears about "modern women," who poisoned family members, especially children, to gain so-called selfish freedom.[32] Hartman examines the stereotypes surrounding a notorious case from 1857, the year of the Poisons Act, involving Madeleine Smith, a young woman from a prominent Scottish family who was romanti- cally linked to a Frenchman, Emile D'Angelier. Upon her engagement to a wealthy Scottish businessman, Smith asked D'Angelier to return her explicit letters. After he threatened to publicize them instead, Smith was seen buying arsenic. When he fell ill and died, Smith claimed that she had purchased the arsenic as a cosmetic and went free on the Scot- tish verdict of "not proven." Hartman argues that in this case romantic stereotypes worked in favor of the accused woman.[33] In contrast, Karin Jacobson argues that the "not proven" verdict "introduces an element of 'queerness' into the supposedly unambiguous realm of the law, a 'queer- ness' associated with women. Justice does not prevail, as the defendant is left in a morally ambiguous position—neither hanged nor vindicated."[34]

108   Such ambiguity attaches to Lydia Gwilt as well. Having poisoned her previous husband with arsenic and received clemency, Lydia is described by amateur detective Bashwood as "free to do any mischief she pleases, and to poison at her own entire convenience any man, woman, or child that happens to stand in her way" (530). Bashwood questions his infatuated father's desire to marry Lydia: "With the chance of being poisoned, the first time you happened to offend her?" (533). As Bashwood surmises, Lydia is a serial poisoner, like Sarah Chesham, but he is incorrect in that she plans to poison not her husband, sincere Ozias Midwinter, but his friend, wealthy Allan Armadale. Like Madeleine Smith, Lydia is involved with two men. Lydia married Ozias under his real name, Allan Armadale, and she plans to use her marriage certificate to impersonate the wealthy Allan's widow and collect the Armadale fortune, since her marriage to Ozias, Ozias's real name, and the details of Allan's death will be conveniently unknown in England. In Lydia, Collins seems to draw upon the notorious image of arsenic as the definitive poison, an evil entity used by evil women to evil purpose.[35] However, Lydia fails to poison Allan, and this queers, to use Jacobson's term, the supposedly unambiguous nature of arsenic.

During the second reading of the Sale of Arsenic Regulation Bill, the Earl of Carlyle states that "among those classes where the crime was rife, 'arsenic' and 'poison' were looked on as synonymous."[36] A white, tasteless powder, arsenic is similar to domestic staples, such as flour and soda, and the Earl of Carlyle argues at the bill's third reading that "several deplorable accidents had occurred from young children and female servants being sent to purchase it."[37] Six years later, before the Select Committee on the Sale of Poisons, Alfred Swaine Taylor similarly recalls domestic accidents such as "white arsenic being put into a teapot or a plum-cake instead of carbonate of soda."[38] Jacob Bell imagines that arsenic could be "sprinkled into tea or gruel," and George Waugh describes arsenic put into puddings.[39] The Arsenic Act of 1851 required shops to keep a register of arsenic sales, to sell to adults only, and to color white arsenic with indigo or soot. Although these measures intended to fix the identity both of the purchaser and of the poison, in 1857, Waugh argued that coloring white arsenic only added to the ease of poisoning by offering false security: "[P]ersons get accustomed to this black arsenic. We know that, with great ease, we can separate the arsenic. If I wished to poison, I should be less likely to be found guilty of criminal poisoning now than I should have been two or three years ago before the Arsenic

Act."[40] Addressing another select committee, the Select Committee of
the Chemists and Druggists Bill, in 1865, Alfred Swaine Taylor asserted
the failure of earlier legislation to stem domestic accidents: "The worst
of arsenic is that it is almost tasteless, and it is white and mixes with anything. Although the Act [Arsenic Act of 1851] says it is to be coloured
blue or black, that Act is avoided to my knowledge."[41] The committee
then asked Taylor whether the earlier Arsenic Act is a "dead letter," to
which he replied, "To a great extent it is; I have had to examine bodies
after death, and I have found white arsenic without colouring matter."[42]
Given arsenic's notoriety, the number of poisonings involving food, and
the ease with which white arsenic could be obtained despite the Arsenic
Act, why should Collins depict an experienced poisoner such as Lydia
masking the taste of arsenic with brandy in Allan's lemonade, when it is
so easily introduced into food and so little likely to be tasted?

In Lydia's failed poisoning attempt, Collins queers the term *poison*,
despite arsenic's reputation as the quintessential poison. Lydia's actions
recall famous female poisoners who used arsenic to kill inconvenient
men, but it is brandy that Allan finds noxious. An 1862 article entitled
"Alcohol a Poison" elucidates the dangerous nature of wine, brandy,
and gin. It describes the stages of inebriety, ending in coma and death,
and recommends stomach pumping, ammonia by inhalation, and coffee
as remedies, "as in case of poisoning by opium."[43] If a poison is a substance that produces illness in relatively small quantity, then brandy is
a poison to Allan. Brandy's noxious nature emerges earlier in the novel,
when Allan is given brandy by a medical practitioner, Mr. Hawbury; "A
marked change in Allan's face, as he suddenly drew back and asked for
whisky instead, caught the doctor's medical eye" (117). Allan is "foolish
enough" to be "a little ashamed" of his symptoms, but Allan turns "sick
and faint" regardless of "[with] what diluting liquid the spirit was mixed"
(117). Words such as *diluting* and *liquid* seem to connote a chemical reaction rather than a mixed drink in the social sense. In Allan's aversion to
brandy, Collins reveals the noxious nature of even common substances.

Collins's depiction of alcohol reveals the multivalent nature of even
supposedly safe substances. For example, wine is a social lubricant for
"common humanity" at Allan's awkward picnic and at his London dinner with lawyer Young Pedgift (250, 336). Yet it is also medicinal; Lydia
takes a "tumbler of claret" to clear her head (166), and Bashwood takes a
"glass of good wine" to steady his nerves (231), flushing red because he
is "not much used to wine" (235). In Bashwood's flush, the telltale flush

of low alcohol tolerance, one surmises that his avoidance of alcohol results from his having been ruined by his wife's alcoholism (234). Alcohol seems to be a noxious substance in Mrs. Bashwood's case, as well as in Allan's. Although avoiding brandy, Allan drinks whiskey to excess, and whiskey is blamed for his impulsive and dangerous decision to take a night cruise. Allan, "on whose harum-scarum high spirits Mr. Hawbury's hospitality had certainly not produced a sedative effect," clarifies the meaning of "hospitality" when he calls out as he and Midwinter sail away, "Your whisky-and-water is delicious" (120). Yet whiskey is also depicted with medicinal qualities. Stranded on the night cruise, Allan uses whiskey from his flask to revive the fainting Midwinter: "The stimulant acted instantly on the sensitive system of the swooning man" (125). Shaking the nearly empty flask later, Midwinter inquires, "[H]ow much of the doctor's medicine did you take while I was up in the mizzen-top?" (132). Later, when Allan is under threat during a mutiny in the Adriatic, he again drinks whiskey as a stimulant to prevent swimmer's cramp (602). Terms such as *medicine, stimulant, sedative,* and *system* connote medicinal activity. Alcohol thus transforms from noxious substance, in the case of Allan's brandy and Mrs. Bashwood's alcoholism, to a social habit, such as at the picnic, to medicine, displaying alcohol's sometimes beneficial and sometimes regrettable influence.

Despite the critical attention paid to arsenic as a secret poisoning agent, it, like whiskey, was considered a medicine as well. Michael Diamond notes that Madeleine Smith's lover, D'Angelier, was known to have used arsenic to prevent cholera, which was widespread at that time, and Peter Bartrip confirms that arsenic was used to treat a variety of ailments including cholera.[44] In his testimony before the Select Committee on the Sale of Poisons, George Waugh complains about the difficulty of simply labeling arsenic a poison because of its popularity as a treatment for ague: "[T]here is Fowler's solution of arsenic, which is, I believe, in frequent use."[45] He complains about the public's inability to understand the overlap between medicine and poison: "A man sees a large label, with the word 'poison' upon it; he will not touch it, and he goes to his doctor, and says, 'You are giving me poison.'"[46] An article in *Chamber's Journal* contrasts the British fear of arsenic, called here "arsenicophobia," with the European habit of arsenic eating, an activity that supposedly bestows "plumpness and good looks."[47] Before the Select Committee of the Chemists and Druggists Bill in 1865, Alfred Swaine Taylor provocatively presented the committee with two packets of arsenic and called

one a "poison" and one a "medicine": "All I can say is, a medicine, in a
large dose, may act as a poison, while a poison, in a small dose, may
act as a medicine."[48] In one sense, arsenic is synonymous with poison,
because of its connection with notorious murders by women; however,
its popularity as a drug and its widespread (virtually unregulated) sales
in defiance of legislation imply that arsenic's identity was not so limited.
If *Armadale* exploits arsenic's notoriety as a poison, it also queers the idea
of poison itself by depicting substances such as alcohol and arsenic as
simultaneously noxious and medicinal.

Opium, Cosmetics, and Women's Pharmacy

Armadale features another substance known for its multivalent nature: laudanum, which is tincture of opium (opium dissolved
in alcohol). In this novel, laudanum is only one potentially noxious
substance associated with the cosmetics vendor Mrs. Oldershaw.[49]
Formerly the wife of a medicine show doctor, Mrs. Oldershaw runs
the Ladies' Toilette Repository, and she offers Lydia laudanum and
"powders and paints and washes," which Lydia rejects as "odious,"
implying that Oldershaw's cosmetics may contain harmful ingredients (162). In addition, Lydia complains to Mrs. Oldershaw, whom
she calls Mother Jezebel, about "*those other men,*" an italicized hint that,
joined to the name Jezebel, connects Mrs. Oldershaw's business with
illicit activity, perhaps prostitution (421).[50] Oldershaw advises Lydia,
"My experience, as confidential adviser of my customers, in various romantic cases of private embarrassment, has shown me that an assumed
name is . . . a very unnecessary and a very dangerous form of deception" (167). Terms such as *romantic, private embarrassment,* and *confidential*
imply sexual impropriety, perhaps unwanted pregnancy or sexually
transmitted disease. Dr. Downward, at this point Mrs. Oldershaw's
next-door neighbor, is described as a "ladies' medical man" (341), and
Lydia claims to know "the risks the doctor runs in his particular form
of practice" (499). Through cosmetics, abortifacients, and opium, Mrs.
Oldershaw raises the specter of poisons in the hands of quacks, particularly female quacks. According to Lilian Furst, women in medicine
have long suffered association with quackery and poison.[51] William H.
Helfand cites examples of female sellers of quack remedies, such as
Oldershaw's cosmetics and medicine show, and of female purchasers
of quack products, such as Lydia. Helfand's collection of ephemera

includes advertisements for "Madam Winneford's Magnetic Maternal Wafer," which promises to restore fertility; "Dr. Wrightsman's Sovereign Balm of Life," which promises easy childbirth; and "Dr. Marchisi's Uterine Catholicon the Female's Friend," which makes no explicit promise but implies general fertility and sexual health.[52] According to Helfand, products aimed at women often promised either abortion or fertility, and women's guilt and shame about such topics made them easy targets for quacks.[53] In Mrs. Oldershaw and Lydia, Collins presents a secretive and rather sinister world of female-centered pharmacy, which both exhibits the power of women as proprietors and as consumers of medicines and indicts women as quacks and murderers.

The 1857 report by the Select Committee on the Sale of Poisons reveals similar concerns about female amateurism, poisons, and the boundary between the domestic and the commercial spheres. This worry was reflected even earlier, during the debate over the 1851 Arsenic Act, when the Earl of Carlyle realized that one of the "deficiencies" of his bill was "that the provisions of the Bill were limited to the sale of arsenic alone, where as it was obvious there were many other kinds of poison which might be used."[54] In 1857, witness William Herapath advocated restricting a group of "secret poisoning" agents, such as arsenic, Fowler's solution of arsenic, prussic acid, strychnia, nux vomica, and also savin and ergot.[55] According to Thomas D. Mitchell's 1857 *Materia Medica and Therapeutics*, concentrated prussic acid kills instantly, but diluted prussic acid is used internally for cough, asthma, and whooping cough and externally for skin disease.[56] Strychnine and nux vomica, which contains strychnine, were used as animal poisons and as treatments for ague, dysentery, palsy, and other conditions.[57] Savin, or savine, induces uterine contractions; Mitchell complained that it was "too frequently employed" for abortion.[58] Similarly, ergot of rye may be used to speed labor or for abortion.[59] In contrast, pharmaceutical chemist John Abraham called nux vomica "one of the safest things that you can give to destroy mice," despite concurring about savin's place on the list of poisons.[60] Abraham's assertion implicitly touches upon the issue of domestic poisoning through food, because he considered bitter strychnine safer than tasteless arsenic despite its considerable toxicity. Police magistrate J. Hammill suggested that the entire project of developing a list of poisons may have been misguided, because of the sheer number of noxious substances available. Hammill mentioned a case in which a husband had procured potash for his wife's abortion and was convicted of murder upon her death.[61] Potash was not considered a poison by any medical or pharmaceutical witness. In the 1865 report of the Select Committee of the Chemists and Druggists Bill, witness Alfred Swaine Taylor mentions several plants familiarly known as "kill-bastard" that induce abortion and, like potash, do not require purchase from a chemist.[62] Fear of criminal poisoning and of accidental poisoning formed the ostensible motives for many of these suggestions, hence the support for restriction of secret poisoning agents and tasteless agents, although, as Mitchell shows, many substances are both poisons and medicines. Yet the unity of opinion on the subject of abortifacients is notable, given that these substances are not implicated in either secret or accidental poisoning. In *Armadale*, Dr. Downward articulates the conventional wisdom that women are inept in pharmacy when he leads his tour from the dispensary to the kitchen; however, the testimony in 1857 and in 1865 before the respective select committees indicates that women were not ignorant of or uninterested in pharmacy but perhaps all too knowledgeable. Witnesses in 1851, 1857, and 1865 seem to confirm Knelman's and Hartman's assertions about widespread fear of secret poisoning by women, but the repeated mention of abortifacients as poisons in need of regulation also indicates concern about women acting as amateur medical practitioners, a concern that similarly finds voice in Collins's depiction of Mrs. Oldershaw's Ladies' Toilette Repository.

Although a murderess, Lydia is also a victim of poisoning, in some sense, because of her own use of laudanum. At first, laudanum appears to be an innocuous substance used for trifling purpose. She complains to Mrs. Oldershaw, "[K]eep your odious powders and paints and washes for the spotted shoulders of your customers; not one of them shall touch my skin, I promise you. If you really want to be useful, try and find out some quieting draught to keep me from grinding my teeth in my sleep. I shall break them one of these nights, and then what will become of my beauty, I wonder?" (162). Laudanum, here called a quieting draught, is more acceptable to Lydia than cosmetics, which may contain harmful chemicals. Lydia later writes, "Send me some more of those sleeping drops, and write me one of your nice, wicked, amusing letters" (289). Like Oldershaw's letters, laudanum seems naughty rather than dangerous. However, matters quickly turn ominous; "My fancy plays me strange tricks sometimes—and there is a little of last night's laudanum, I dare say, in this part of my letter" (417). After a sleepless and despairing night, Lydia writes in her diary,

Who was the man who invented laudanum? I thank him from the bottom of my heart, whoever he was. If all the miserable wretches in pain of body and mind, whose comforter he has been, could meet together to sing his praises, what a chorus it would be! I have had six delicious hours of oblivion; I have woke up with my mind composed; I have written a perfect little letter to Midwinter; I have drunk my nice cup of tea, with a real relish of it; I have dawdled over my morning toilet with an exquisite sense of relief—and all through the modest little bottle of Drops which I see on my bedroom chimney-piece at this moment. "Drops," you are my darling! If I love nothing else, I love *you*. (426 [original italics])

This diary entry represents a shift in tone from trivial to serious issues of pain relief and dependence. Many Victorians indeed owed pain relief to laudanum, but Lydia's excessive attachment seems inappropriate, despite her conventionally feminine activities. Her "modest little bottle of Drops" foreshadows the murderous Stout Friend and Purple Flask at Dr. Downward's asylum, and, like herself, the bottle hides danger beneath a pleasant exterior.

Over time, Lydia becomes moody, melancholy, and unable to sleep, and she asks, "Why don't I take my sleeping drops and go to bed? . . . I don't know—I am tired and miserable; I am looking wretchedly haggard and old" (440). She writes later, "A night's rest, thanks again to my Drops" (442). Feeling "more depressed in spirits than usual," Lydia begins taking laudanum during the day as well as at night; "How am I to get through the weary, weary hours between this and the evening? I think I shall darken my bedroom, and drink the blessing of oblivion from my bottle of Drops" (509). As estrangement grows between Lydia and her new husband, the overworked Ozias, Lydia writes in her diary:

I have shut up my dressing-case again. The first thing I found in it was Armadale's shabby present to me on my marriage—the rubbishing little ruby ring. That irritated me to begin with. The second thing that turned up was my bottle of Drops. I caught myself measuring the doses with my eye, and calculating how many of them would be enough to take a living creature over the border-land between sleep and death. Why I should have locked the dressing-case in a fright, before I had quite completed my calculation, I don't know—but I did lock it. (550)

These passages display a pattern of increasing psychological dependence, physical exhaustion, and mental instability. Lydia first takes the drug by choice, then by necessity. She relies on laudanum to accomplish daily tasks and takes it inappropriately, such as during the day. Finally, laudanum becomes a method of suicide, recalling Lydia's earlier attempt to drown herself and foreshadowing her later suicide by poison gas at Dr. Downward's asylum.

In Lydia's diary, Collins, who habitually used laudanum himself, charts Lydia's downward spiral toward mental breakdown. Michael Diamond speculates that Lydia was "too wicked" for nineteenth-century readers, but her descent into laudanum dependence nevertheless appears marked by loss of control and perhaps pitiable results.[63] Lydia's first request for laudanum is from Mrs. Oldershaw to preserve her beauty, but her last request is to Dr. Downward to preserve her sanity: "Offer me the strongest sleeping-draught you ever made in your life, . . . And leave me alone till the time comes to take it. I shall be your patient in earnest! . . . I shall be the maddest of the mad if you irritate me tonight" (631). Lydia's dissolution is foreshadowed by a very minor character, Ozias's antisocial employer, a bookseller, who is described as a "confirmed opium-eater in secret—a prodigal in laudanum, though a miser in all besides" (96). The man's warped personality and early death are warnings about the danger of opium, which are reinforced by the allusion to the proverbial misfortunes of the prodigal son. Yet despite its negative associations, laudanum is not treated as a poison alongside arsenic or even carbonic acid. Not until the incident with the dressing case does even Lydia view laudanum as a potential poison, and afterward Lydia reverts to treating laudanum as a medicine, demanding sleeping draughts to self-medicate, not to self-destroy. Given its negative representation in this novel, why is laudanum not defined as a poison, too?

Even as arsenic became the focus of an act of Parliament, opium flourished as an agent of secret and accidental poisoning. In his testimony before the Select Committee on the Sale of Poisons in 1857, Alfred Swaine Taylor notes that prior to the Arsenic Act there were more poisonings by opium than by arsenic, the two together forming nearly three-quarters of the total poisonings admitted to Guy's Hospital.[64] Mitchell's 1857 *Material Medica and Therapeutics* warns about using Godfrey's cordial or any other preparation of laudanum for children: "Children without number have had their physical frames ruined by the perpetual exhibition of Godfrey's cordial and the like, to relieve lazy nurses from the task of amusing and quieting the helpless creatures."[65] Witness William Herapath similarly claimed that Godfrey's cordial was used "sometimes to keep them [children] quiet, and sometimes intentionally to destroy them."[66] Sanitary commissioner F. Calvert also mentioned that laudanum was used both to quiet and to kill children.[67] Even nonmedical sources recognize opium's tricky nature, as a contemporary article on Samuel Taylor Coleridge opines: "Opium gives and opium takes away. It defeats the *steady* habit of exertion, but it creates spasms of irregular exertion; it ruins the natural power of life, but it developes [*sic*] preternatural paroxysms of intermitting power."[68] For this writer, opium was responsible for both Coleridge's failures and his successes as a poet, a poisonous influence and an inspiration. Another popular-press article describes the opium trade with China and English intemperance as twin dangers: "We like it the less because it can be likened to English drunkenness—to remind us of our home sins should not make us less lenient to our sins in China."[69] Although habits such as smoking or drinking alcohol might, like the opium trade, have relatively innocent aspects, this author concludes that opium is "a potent poison still."[70] Comparing opium and arsenic reveals the social nature of the word *poison*, since both drugs are defined not by pharmaceutical, medical, or toxicological standards but by practical, financial, and social considerations. In *Armadale*, laudanum, abortifacients, and cosmetics join prostitution and quackery under the aegis of Mrs. Oldershaw's Repository. In the hands of Mrs. Oldershaw and Lydia, laudanum seems poisonous, but the witnesses before the various select committees did not consider opium products on the same footing as arsenic, because if compounded and dispensed by orthodox chemists and druggists, they were already defined as medicines.

Chemists, Druggists, and Quacks

After Lydia's suicide, lawyers Pedgift Junior and Senior correspond about the fate of Dr. Downward and Mrs. Oldershaw. Pedgift Senior discovers Mrs. Oldershaw as a popular, religious-themed public speaker on the subject of "Pomps and Vanities of the World" in a "pious and penitential style" (674–75). Pedgift Senior notes that the audience comprises the "old harridans of the world of fashion, whom Mother Oldershaw had enameled in her time, sitting boldly in the front places, with their cheeks ruddled with paint" (675). In this ironic passage, the religious women are plastered with the very cosmetics that Old-ershaw ostensibly repents selling, although she apparently accepted their money both in the past for the cosmetics and again for the speaking engagement. Pedgift Senior believes Downward "mixed up in the matter" of Lydia's suicide, but he says that Downward "carried things with a high hand, and insisted on taking his own course in his own Sanatorium" (671). Pedgift Senior writes, "I believe the doctor to have been at the bottom of more of this mischief than we shall ever find out; and to have profited by the self-imposed silence of Mr Midwinter and Mr Armadale [*sic*], as rogues perpetually profit by the misfortunes and necessities of honest men" (672). Pedgift Senior ironically addresses his son: "We live, Augustus, in an age eminently favourable to the growth of all roguery which is careful enough to keep up appearances. In this enlightened nineteenth century, I look upon the doctor as one of our rising men" (673). Pedgift's use of the word *rogue* implies quackery behind Downward's medical authority. This description satirizes not only Downward but also the medical field generally, since in Pedgift's estimation, medical authority is "high-handedness" and its respectability mere "appearances."

Amid discussion of famous poisoning cases of the 1850s, including the Madeleine Smith case, Michael Diamond mentions the William Palmer case, calling it "the most famous of all Victorian poisoning cases" and describing public interest so massive that it spurred increases in newspaper circulation and price gouging.[71] A physician, Palmer was convicted of serial poisoning for life insurance money using strychnine, a drug harder to identify than arsenic at the time, and Diamond claims that the "high social standing" of medicine made the case particularly interesting to the public.[72] Just as Downward apparently interferes with the investigation of Lydia's death, so too did Palmer, according to Diamond, use his status as a medical man to interfere with his initial investigation.[73] Diamond's statements about medicine's high standing and about the case's level of fame are perhaps debatable; however, his discussion of Palmer balances the critical tendency to focus on poisoning by women. Palmer's case reminds us that in Downward Collins draws upon the considerable cultural interest in male poisoners, particularly those with a medical background.

Similarly, testimony before the Select Committee on the Sale of Poisons in 1857 paints a troubling picture of commercial and medical poisoning largely by men. Alfred Swaine Taylor claims, "There are people who deal in these drugs in shops who do not know one from the other; they would not know hemlock from parsley."[74] Taylor describes strychnine accidentally given instead of salicine and arsenic given instead of calomel, both with fatal results (139). Irish physician J. M. Neligan describes shops storing white arsenic in open crocks, grinding ginger next to white lead, and selling cream of tartar in place of arsenic (123). Although such accounts of professional misconduct implicate men (because of their dominance in the public sphere), female shopkeepers were sometimes singled out for misconduct, as when Calvert states, "Whenever I have been in the shop, a woman has always served me. . . . I have several times asked her some little questions when I have been in her shop; but she is perfectly unacquainted with the matter" (73). Similarly, Samuel Jessop Burch argues, "In villages in the country, drugs are often sold by females; but they should only be allowed to sell certain things, and to a certain extent" (90). At the same time, magistrate J. Hammill reports failures by druggists themselves, presumably men who are properly trained and vetted: "[P]oison has been most incautiously sold to people whose appearance must, I thought, have denoted to the druggist who sold it that they were in a wretched [suicidal] condition" (59). Calvert implies that even trained persons are unreliable without legal supervision when he states that "the laws are very good, but there is nobody to see that they are carried out" (64). This testimony displays considerable concern with poisoning by male professionals and by male quacks, who pretended to knowledge of dispensing that they did not truly possess, although commercial ventures by women were certainly indicted as well.

In the report of the Select Committee of the Chemists and Druggists Bill in 1865, Alfred Swaine Taylor differentiates between trained and untrained men with regards to poison sales: "The sale of these substances is not so much with the higher class of chemists and druggists as with the lower class, where oxalic acid, and substances of that sort, can be obtained in common shops; grocers, oilmen, and persons of that kind."[75] For example, Taylor points to an error in which an untrained dispenser misunderstood the label "Turc." and gave Turkish opium for Turkish rhubarb, resulting in the death of the patient (2). Similarly, Richard Quain supports restricting poisons to those with proven "competence to deal with drugs and chemicals," especially the "knowledge of the properties of drugs, and the capability of reading ordinary Latin prescriptions" (23). Pharmaceutical chemist John Mackay describes the

Pharmaceutical Society's training in Latin prescriptions, formulations and compounding, chemistry, and materia medica (43). These witnesses avowedly supported the Pharmaceutical Society's claims for the monopoly over dispensing. However, the litany of dispensing errors raised the specter of poisoning even within the ranks of male experts. As testimony in 1857 and in 1865 shows, even trained men sometimes skirted regulations and failed in judgment. In *Armadale*, Downward engages in numerous shenanigans under the guise of professionalism. Lydia commits suicide, but both Oldershaw and Downward thrive; thus, the novel may calm fears of domestic poisoning while stoking those of quackery by men and women in the public sphere.

An 1864 article entitled "Popular Poisons" compares sensation novels to arsenic, laudanum, tobacco, alcohol, and other poisons as a kind of slow poisoning agent.[76] In this article, physical poisons are described as "vulgar" and "harmless" when compared with "indulgences" that are "self-inflicted," and novels are "mental drugs" that corrode morality and "pollute public taste" through "tales of blood, seduction, violence."[77] Thus, "poisoners" are writers who embed their poison in the "honey and syrup" of literature.[78] The vivid language of this article slides between novels as poison and novels as drugs and implies that drugs are poison and vice versa. The pejorative tone applied to novels is shared not only by poisons such as arsenic but also by opium, alcohol, tobacco, and drugs in general, which emerge as quite sinister entities. Critics also connect sensation novels and poison. Lyn Pykett, for example, argues that the "distinctive features" of the sensation novel include "passionate, devious, dangerous and not infrequently deranged heroines, and its complicated, mysterious plots—involving crime, bigamy, adultery, arson, and arsenic."[79] Ann French Dalke argues that the American sensation novel depicts women co-opting male power and creates a role reversal in which the man becomes similar to the heroine of domestic fiction.[80] Like the domestic heroine, this type of man relies on self-control and chastity to avoid the snare of the seductive, mercantile woman; thus, the "psychological pattern so common in temperance literature prevails in city novels as well. The first glass is the fatal one, and ruin is inevitable after it is drunk."[81] In *Armadale*, Collins shows through chemicals such as carbonic acid, arsenic, brandy, wine, and opium that the term *poison* is not a fixed identity but a term of convenience, reflecting not the chemical nature or even the practical uses of a substance so much as its reputation. If the term *poison* also applies to the sensation

120   novel itself, Collins has already robbed it of its sting by showing that *poison* is a mixed, not a wholly negative, entity and one that may be as medicinal as poisonous.

Although *Armadale* draws upon several notorious incidents involving poison, the novel participates in the ongoing cultural conversation about the natures of poison, medicine, pharmacy, and quackery. Collins draws upon the notoriety of arsenic as a weapon of murder, but he also displays many of poison's ambiguities. In this novel, poison is not easily identified, and such substitute markers of identity that are available, such as bottles, are easily manipulated. But poison is more ambiguous than a mere shell game with bottles. Collins's poisons are not reliably poisonous, as Lydia's carbonic acid and laudanum and Allan's brandy show. Notorious poisons such as arsenic appear alongside popular beverages, such as brandy, which emerge as similarly noxious. In displaying poisons in this manner, Collins displays the fallacy of control that underlies both criminal trials and pharmacy regulations, a fallacy of which the witnesses before the various select committees in 1851, 1857, and 1865 were well aware despite their support for increased regulation. Far from being naïve about poisons, many Victorians seem to have been keenly aware of the difficulties of controlling entities that resist social and cultural categorizations such as medicine/poison and domestic/commercial. Indeed, the *British Medical Journal* asked "What Is a 'Noxious Thing'?" in the 1880s, as the epigraph to this chapter exhibits. The implications of this resistance are many. Collins may have drawn upon sensational trials involving female poisoners; however, Lydia's plans are often stymied by laudanum, arsenic, and carbonic acid, all of which escape her control. In Mrs. Oldershaw, Collins emphasizes the medicalization of the private sphere and the power of female amateurs in medicine. Just as the professions of medicine and pharmacy are advocating the removal of poisons from amateur hands, Collins depicts amateurism as quackery. At the same time, Dr. Downward exploits anxiety about the professions themselves. Witnesses before the select committees openly critiqued not only unprofessional vendors but also those whom they deemed inappropriate within their own ranks. There was dissension as well as concordance between pharmacy and medicine and within each. Moreover, repeated testimony by Alfred Swaine Taylor (and a few others) exemplifies the narrow range of practitioners who were able to influence professional and public life in this relatively brief but significant period in pharmaceutical regulation and professionalization, exhibiting the wide gap between the standards

the witnesses advocated and those that were actually practiced. While 121
fears of domestic poisoning are allayed with Lydia's death, quackery
flourishes in the successful careers of Mrs. Oldershaw and Dr. Downward. This novel apparently supports professionalization by demonizing
women in pharmacy and by displaying the dangers of unprofessionalism,
yet it also displays the ongoing power of quackery and the continuing
power of consumers of medicines and poisons.

Chapter Five

The Quackery of Arthur Conan Doyle

The science of medicine and surgery is continually ad-
vancing. The successive learners of one generation become the advanced teachers of the next. . . . The open
book of nature is ever before us, and we gladly welcome
all science, all knowledge, and all truth.

    · —C. S. Hall, "Abstract of an Address," 1885

A distressing feature in the life which you are about to
enter, a feature which will press hardly upon the finer
spirits among you and ruffle their equanimity, is the uncertainty which pertains not alone to our science and
art, but to the very hopes and fears which make us men.
In seeking absolute truth we aim at the unattainable, and
must be content with finding broken portions.

    —William Osler, "Aequanimitas," 1904

Indeed, this state of ignorance and uncertainty, of questions without final answers, remains quite characteristic
of the practice of medicine despite an intensive public-
relations campaign to invest the physician with the
cloak of certitude more correctly worn by the laboratory sciences.

    —Pasquale Accardo, *Diagnosis and Detection*, 1987

*A*t first glance, William Osler's advice to medical students in
"Aequanimitas" seems very practical. Although medicine
lauds truth as an ideal, practitioners make decisions every day based

on incomplete or ambiguous information, and Osler recognized that cultivating equanimity was one way of maintaining stability in emotionally distressing circumstances. At the same time, this advice opens up a vexed question about truth and illusion in medical practice. Pretending certainty in uncertain circumstances seems to bestow upon medicine a scientific certitude and to downplay medicine's day-to-day compromises and guesswork. For example, C. S. Hall powerfully deployed the language of progress and discovery to claim prestige and power by aligning medicine with the laboratory sciences through words such as *science, knowledge, truth,* and *advance,* which connote precision and certitude. Pasquale Accardo identifies the financial and cultural benefits of wearing the "cloak of certitude." For Accardo, the appearance of equanimity in the face of uncertainty gestures toward pretense, a "public relations campaign" that connotes at best salesmanship and at worst deception for personal gain. In this respect, Accardo reverses the connotations of Osler's word, *equanimity,* by transforming it from a mark of professionalism into a mark of quackery, a confidence trick. The dates of the three epigraphs may at first glance imply increasing skepticism toward illusion in medical practice, as if Hall's confidence gave way over time to Accardo's skepticism; however, the question of illusion's scope and nature in medical practice was explored thoroughly by Victorian physician and writer Arthur Conan Doyle.

Critics have long connected Doyle's best-known character, Sherlock Holmes, to Doyle's own medical training and practice during the 1870s and 1880s; for example, Ely Liebow argues that Doyle modeled Holmes on Professor Joseph Bell, a medical doctor, and that this resemblance was obvious to mutual acquaintances.[1] Susan Cannon Harris views Holmes in a medical context and argues that Holmes's medicine allows him to save the day by transforming exotic poisons into beneficial medicines.[2] For example, in "The Devil's Foot," Harris argues, "Holmes is invested with the authority of science, however, he is not a savage 'medicine-man' but a civilized jurist."[3] Harris acknowledges that this may not be the case in "The Blanched Soldier," where Holmes uses medicine as "an illusion," but she suggests that this story is an anomaly in the Holmes canon.[4] Alternately, Paula J. Reiter places the Holmes stories in the context of contemporary physician-poisoner Dr. Thomas Neill Cream and argues that Holmes "encapsulated both a model of expertise and an implicit critique of men *not* fulfilling this model."[5] Reiter contrasts the incompetent, selfish, and irresponsible professionals of the Cream trial with

124 Holmes, saying, "Perhaps most crucially, Doyle characterized Holmes as a man worthy of trust."[6] Reiter concludes that Holmes defends the professional class because he is "above petty profit" and because of his "individual achievement," which combines "expert, specialized knowledge" with "chivalric service and pleasure."[7] In addition, Maria Cairney explores the "slippage" between criminal and patient, doctor and detective in the Holmes stories and finds Doyle "positing medical solutions to moral and social problems."[8] Cairney argues that Holmes allows the healing of society by purging the infected or criminal element. In these readings, medicine strengthens Holmes's power as a symbol of knowledge, service, and professionalism, despite his overlap with evildoers and criminals.

 Whereas Harris, Reiter, and Cairney use Doyle's medical background to bolster Holmes's own claims of rationalism, this chapter finds that Doyle's deployment of medicine in "The Adventure of the Speckled Band" (1892) and in *The Stark Munro Letters* (1895) is more ambiguous. In contrast with Harris's reading of "The Speckled Band," which contends that medicine supports Holmes's rationalism, this chapter concentrates on the overlap between Holmes, Watson, and the evil Dr. Roylott and allows their shared traits to complicate Holmes's well-known statements about reason and truth.[9] In contrast with Reiter's argument that references to medical criminals such as Dr. Cream highlight Holmes's idealized professionalism, this chapter contends that Doyle depicts medicine as a gray area caught between illusion as means of coping with uncertainty (Osler's view) and deception as quackery and crime (anticipating Accardo). As a result, Doyle's medicine does not bolster Holmes's claims of scientific certitude but instead highlights the slippery nature of medical orthodoxy because of the necessity for a little quackery in day-to-day medical practice.

 Like "The Speckled Band," *The Stark Munro Letters* drew heavily on Doyle's early medical training and experience. Set in the early 1880s, when Doyle himself was just starting as a physician, the novel depicts the struggle of medical practitioner Stark Munro to discriminate between the acceptable illusions of professional decorum and the improper illusions of fraud and quackery. In the novel, Munro embarks on a series of failed assistantships before joining the thriving practice of his schoolfellow Cullingworth. Astonished at Cullingworth's quackish methods and confused by Mrs. Cullingworth's hostility, Munro is eventually tricked into quitting. Despite financial hardship, Munro establishes a new practice and succeeds finally in business and in love, until the novel's shocking conclusion. Alvin E. Rodin and Jack D. Key's landmark study of Doyle's medical writing argues that *The Stark Munro Letters* was received from its earliest reviews as autobiographical in nature.[10] Rodin and Key identify the novel's Dr. Cullingworth as a fictionalization of Doyle's own medical partner, George T. Budd, who appears also in Doyle's autobiography and was, Rodin and Key assert, a major influence because of his "eccentricity" and "questionable practices," including seeking publicity, waiving consultation fees, and overcharging for drugs.[11] Similarly, Martin Booth identifies Doyle's "eccentric" medical schoolfellow, Budd, as Dr. Cullingworth and claims that the "ethically dubious" Budd conducted his practice as "a slick operation preying upon the poor" using free examinations, showy premises, advertising, and patent medicines.[12] Booth claims that Doyle was "a welcome foil to Budd's mercurial nature" and was "innocent, naïve, and, consequently gullible," a man "honest and honourable" who "did not consider others capable of willful mendacity."[13] Both Booth and Rodin and Key concur that Budd double-crossed Doyle after reading Doyle's private letters, just as Cullingworth double-crosses and dupes Munro in the novel.[14]

Although valuable, this approach presents several drawbacks for readers of *The Stark Munro Letters*. First, it encourages readers to view Munro as Doyle, and in our desire to vindicate the author of the Sherlock Holmes stories, we may minimize Munro's misconduct. Instead, both "The Speckled Band" and *The Stark Munro Letters* might be approached not as Doyle's celebration of medicine as scientific and rational but as Doyle's exploration of the gap between scientific ideals and daily medical practice, given Doyle's experience with illusion in daily practice both alone and with Budd. Second, contrasts between Budd and Doyle encourage readers to see contrasts between Cullingworth and Munro, although they are not opposites. Cullingworth might be less trustworthy than Munro, but neither man completely eschews illusion or avoids misconduct in his medical practice. Like Holmes, Watson, and Roylott in "The Speckled Band," Cullingworth and Munro share notable qualities, some of which strongly indicate misconduct. Finally, this method downplays Doyle's repeated depiction of illusion as a necessary part of orthodox medical practice, a view perhaps more akin to Osler's philosophy than to Sherlock Holmes's. Rather than aligning medicine with science, both "The Speckled Band" and *The Stark Munro Letters* remind us that medicine is often not the location of scientific precision but a shifty field keenly aware of its own pretenses. Indeed, far from representing Sherlock Holmes, or any medical or quasi-medical figure, as the embodiment of scientific certitude, Doyle may represent medical culture in both "The Speckled Band" and *The Stark Munro Letters* as rife with fraud, illusion, and uncertainty, which medicine ideally opposes but in practice too often exploits.

As a medical practitioner, Doyle was very interested in and far from naïve about illusion in day-to-day medical practice. For example, Rodin and Key note that Doyle "utilized some of the same techniques to attract patients that he ascribed to George Budd."[15] Like Munro in the novel, Doyle drew maps of streets he planned to walk down to become familiar to the populace, drew maps of competing physicians' addresses, placed newspaper ads implying that his brand-new practice was already well established, and sent to the newspapers an account of an accident in which he assisted.[16] Yet Rodin and Key dismiss Doyle's activities as "more likely a recollection of Doctor Budd's behavior than his own."[17] Booth also describes Doyle's public relations campaign to establish his new practice, including the deceptive advertisement and planted newspaper story, and in addition, Booth describes Doyle's memberships in sporting clubs as an attempt to build a public character.[18] Although Booth condemns Budd for publicity seeking, Booth excuses Doyle, arguing that self-promotion was necessary for a new doctor trying to establish a practice.[19] Given Doyle's experience with illusion both as a necessary part of his daily medical life and as a painful personal and professional betrayal by George Budd, his view of medicine in "The Speckled Band" and *The Stark Munro Letters* might offer readers insight into this gray area of medical practice. More than biographical tidbits or simple contrasts between orthodoxy and quackery, *The Stark Munro Letters* and "The Speckled Band" offer an exploration of the overlap between orthodoxy and quackery, given the necessary illusion that was part of day-to-day practice despite medicine's scientific ideals of knowledge and truth.[20]

The Necessity of Quackery in *The Stark Munro Letters*

The Stark Munro Letters opens with American physician Herbert (Bertie) Swanborough's assurance that the letters are faithful transcriptions of those written by his British schoolfellow, Munro. The avowal of truth is a common device of epistolary novels; nevertheless, Bertie's assurance introduces the theme of uncertainty.[21] Whereas Bertie claims absolute trustworthiness, the very first letter highlights Munro's difficulties in establishing absolute truth in a world of uncertainty. Although he admires Cullingworth, Munro reveals that Cullingworth does not obey the rules of rugby but plays a "savage" game that results in censure.[22] Cullingworth is a brawny man with "rough-hewn" features who scorns ties and collars, those marks of civilized society (2): his hair stands "like a fighting terrier's" (6), and he has a "bulldog grip" (7) and runs "fit as a greyhound" (9). Munro writes, "You cannot imagine a more savage-looking creature than Cullingworth is when his temper goes wrong. He gets a perfectly fiendish expression in his light blue eyes, and all his hair bristles up like a striking cobra" (134). In addition to his "fiendish" expression, Cullingworth displays "demoniac cleverness" (5) and an "infernal" temper (6). In the context of eugenics, a major medical and social movement of the period, a man who strongly resembled animals and savages might be connected to degeneration, atavism, or criminality.[23] At the same time, Munro admires Cullingworth's energy and imagination, calling him "the greatest genius I have ever known" (3). Munro mentions Cullingworth's academic achievement despite his "idling ostentatiously" during the day and "reading desperately" at night (3). An amateur naval designer, Cullingworth invents torpedoes that Munro says are technically impossible but "quite plausible and new" (4). Cullingworth raises as many questions for readers as he does for Munro. The bestial and demonic descriptions reinforce readers' sense of Cullingworth as impressive but dangerous, like the snakes and dogs he resembles. Is Cullingworth dangerous? Should Munro's positive assessment be trusted? Is there something in Munro's character that craves Cullingworth's demonic and bestial energy? Although the opening letter seems to offer a contrast between Munro, who is civil, articulate, and confiding, and Cullingworth, who is bestial, violent, and deceptive, Doyle raises questions about both Munro's and his readers' ability to judge in matters of incomplete information. This is magnified by the fact that Bertie does not remember Cullingworth at all. Perhaps Cullingworth's achievements, like his study habits and torpedo designs, may be more illusory than real, since incidents so striking to Munro have been forgotten by Bertie. Or perhaps point of view necessarily limits information, making judgment a difficult task. Dangerous, unstable, and at times inhuman, Cullingworth seems to hold an attraction for Munro that he does not hold for Bertie (and perhaps readers). Munro is bright, educated, scientific, and articulate, yet Doyle

128   represents the difficulties of knowing through Bertie's point of view and through Munro's own doubts about Cullingworth.

Although doubtful, Munro is evidently taken with Cullingworth. For example, Cullingworth adheres to beliefs about the healthiness of "open-air life" that nearly freeze his wife to death, yet Munro remains at least partly convinced (13). Cullingworth's experiments with waxy livers fail, but Munro remains confident of Cullingworth's genius (15). Later, Munro abandons his secure assistantship in Yorkshire with kindly Dr. Horton to join Cullingworth's practice based on Cullingworth's promise of three hundred pounds a year (118). Munro says, "[M]aking every allowance for Cullingworth's inflated way of talking, there must be something at the back of it" (129). On his arrival at Cullingworth's house, Munro notes that something seems amiss: the bedrooms are barely furnished, but the dining room is lavish (130). Even as Cullingworth boasts of his expensive, new dining-room chairs, a tradesman appears at the door demanding payment. Munro accepts Cullingworth's explanation that he purposely toys with this man as revenge for some previous misconduct, but readers must question Cullingworth's honesty and Munro's judgment (137). When Cullingworth explains his invention of a new magnet to deflect naval shells, Munro right away objects that such a magnet will also attract the ship's own nails, screws, and shells, but he nevertheless seems sure that Cullingworth is brilliant rather than foolish, claiming, "[T]here can be no doubt that he has in some inexplicable way made a tremendous hit" (144). Again and again, Munro notes and dismisses Cullingworth's failures and deceptions: "I think him thoroughly unscrupulous, and full of very sinister traits. I am much mistaken, however, if he has not a fine strata in his nature" (149). Is Cullingworth a fraud or a genius? Is he a trustworthy eccentric or a dangerous fool?

Cullingworth's medical practice, like his naval inventions, also arouses Munro's admiration and skepticism. Munro notes from the start that his position with Cullingworth may become "untenable," but he wishes for a "fair trial" before abandoning it (163). During their joint practice, Cullingworth schools Munro about how to handle patients using deception and pretense: "[Y]ou must never let them see that you want them. It should be pure condescension on your part seeing them at all. . . . Break your patients in early and keep them well to heel. Never make the fatal mistake of being polite to them" (152). When Munro objects, Cullingworth explains that an offended patient is "the finest advertisement in the world" (153) and reassures Munro, saying, in reference to his patients, "I cure them" (154). Munro says that Cullingworth's practice is a mix of "poisoning" and "personal magnetism" (183). He asserts that Cullingworth's practice "may smell of quackery, but it is exceedingly useful to the patient" (184). Nevertheless, Munro repeatedly questions Cullingworth's methods. Munro describes Cullingworth's "quickness of diagnosis," "scientific insight," and "daring and unconventional use of drugs" (156), but he is uncomfortable with diagnoses such as too much tea and too much sleep. He would not go so far as to label Cullingworth a charlatan, however: "Indeed, 'charlatanism' is a misapplied word in this connection; for it would describe the doctor who puts on an artificial and conventional manner with his patients, rather than one who is absolutely frank and true to his own extraordinary nature" (156). When Munro replaces Cullingworth during the latter's rheumatic fever, Munro concludes, "I held the thing together as best I could, and I don't think that he found the practice much the worse when he was able to take it over. I could not descend to what I thought was unprofessional, but I did my very best to keep the wheels turning" (225). Munro's experience with Cullingworth may be, as Rodin and Key suggest, a contrast between an orthodox physician and a quack, and as readers, we may deplore Munro's naïveté and pity his foolishness. However, Doyle uses Munro's doubts to raise questions about the nature of illusion in medical practice: When is the appearance of wealth a sham and when is it respectability? Is Munro foolish, or are his doubts symptomatic of genuine ambiguity in medical standards with regard to truth-telling in patient care? When should patient care involve deception, and when does deceiving patients become charlatanism? What is the difference between unprofessionalism and "keeping the wheels turning"?

The conflict between polite fiction and dangerous quackery was significant during the 1880s and 1890s, when Doyle studied and practiced medicine. Lilian Furst identifies the late nineteenth century as a period in which the status of the physician was in flux. According to Furst, patient-physician communication depends on a contract in which both parties ask questions and demand truthful answers, since physicians rely on patient history for diagnosis and patients may choose to seek alternative advice and to refuse treatment.[24] Furst describes doctors' "readiness to bow to the will of patients" in diagnosis and treatment early in the nineteenth century; however, in the later decades of the century, Furst claims, technological advances encouraged physician-determined methods of diagnosis and treatment.[25] In the jargon-filled language of

scientific medicine, Furst finds "barely-repressed aggression against patients who are seen as challenges or even threats to the physician's rule.
The subtext is one of discord between doctor and patient in which the
doctor has to fight to maintain sovereignty."[26] In this context, Munro's
doubts seem indicative of genuine ambiguity regarding truth-telling in
patient care because the power dynamics of physician-patient relations
are quite complex. In her discussion of chloroform, Mary Poovey suggests that the medical establishment displayed anxiety about patient demand for anesthesia in childbirth and concealed facts in order to restrict
public debate, lest "the entire issue get out of its hands."[27] Conversely,
Ian A. Burney notes widespread frustration among scientific-minded
public health officers with the long-standing practice of falsifying death
certificates to spare family feelings in cases of shameful death involving,
for example, syphilis, alcohol, or suicide.[28] The conflict between polite
fiction and sinister deception appears in more commonplace circumstances as well. For example, in 1880, a physician wrote to the *Lancet* to
clarify whether a rival practitioner was correctly using the title "Doctor"
instead of "Mister," to which the letter-writer believed him entitled, only
to be told that while the College of Physicians did not condone using
the title without a university degree, they would not interfere in such
cases.[29] In one respect, this is a trivial matter of etiquette, an innocent
business ploy, yet the letter-writer was correct in assuming that his rival's
pretense might have real financial effects on his own practice and on
patient trust, if it truly deceived patients as to this practitioner's qualifi-
cations. The letter also raised the specter of quackery in that it depicted
a physician pretending, whether through ignorance or craft, to qualifi-
cations that he did not possess. Another letter to the *Lancet* complains
about established practitioners who underbid young practitioners:
"Under the cloak of charity it is a lever to try to starve a new man and
give vent to their professional jealousy."[30] Here, charitable treatment
covers sharp business practices that damage the profession as a whole;
"The poverty of the profession flourishes on the jealous suicidal policy
of its members."[31] Yet another brief article describes the peculiar trust
placed in medical practitioners such that they were often approached
for advice about nonmedical matters: "[A]t such times, as inevitable as
they are undesired, a judicious mind and a careful tongue are far more
to their owner than an accurate knowledge of medicine. It is the possession of these and similar elements of character, as much as technical
training, which have earned for family practitioners that reputation for

wisdom and integrity which we would in no boastful spirit acknowledge   131
as an honour conferred on the profession as a whole."[32] In this article,
patient confidence appears to be a sacred trust, yet the article advocates
cultivating a "reputation" through strategic silence rather than frankly
confessing one's unwillingness, inexperience, or unfamiliarity with the
nonmedical issue at hand, a pretense that may be viewed either as genteel propriety or selfish fraud. In this context, Munro's difficulty in discriminating between the illusions of genteel practice and the illusions of
quackery become understandable.

While at first glance Munro appears to be an honorable physician
and Cullingworth a quack, Doyle troubles these too-easy categories
in several ways: by depicting Munro's doubts about and admiration
of Cullingworth (as discussed), by bookending their shared practice
with Munro's experiences as an independent practitioner, and by con-
trasting Munro's philosophies with his experience in daily life. First,
Munro's conduct prior to joining with Cullingworth complicates the
notion that illusions such as Cullingworth's are altogether undesirable
in medical practice. For example, before joining Cullingworth, Munro
exploits professional visits to flirt with a patient's daughter. Disaster
strikes when Munro mistakes the mother for the daughter and attempts
to kiss her: he is both shamed and booted out of the house. This is a violation of the Hippocratic injunction to avoid sexual liaisons with any
member of the patient's household. While Munro dismisses it as a "silly
ill-timed boyish joke," his father, also a physician, views it as a "shocking breach of professional honour" (66). Subsequently, Munro is hired
as live-in care for a wealthy young lunatic. Munro loses this job by
vigorously propounding his agnostic views at the dinner table, where
he offends his patient's Tory mother. In his next job in Yorkshire with
the kindly Dr. Horton, Munro mistakes a wealthy master for a poor
clubman laborer and embarrasses his employer by addressing the man
inappropriately. In these instances, Doyle illuminates the value of illusion in medical practice; despite his religious doubts, Munro perhaps
should have hidden his views from his patient's mother, as he should
have concealed his attraction to his patient's daughter and maintained
decorum before the wealthy master. While Cullingworth's deception
may be easily classified as charlatanism, Munro's frankness in avowing
his opinions and in following his impulses is also unprofessional (hence
his dismissals and disgrace). At the same time, because of incomplete
information, Munro genuinely cannot tell a mother from a daughter

or a clubman from a master. Given that medical practice is inescapably fraught with such uncertainty, it seems to demand some measure of pretense. Perhaps Munro's admiration of Cullingworth's charisma with patients is unsurprising, since successful medical practice seems to require a certain level of disingenuousness. In this sense, Doyle complicates medical orthodoxy by pointing out that transparency and honesty may be as undesirable in daily medical practice as manipulation and dishonesty, practices that are often labeled quackery but that seem at times invaluable.

Second, Doyle troubles orthodoxy and quackery by exploring the gap between ideals and everyday practice. Munro often sends Bertie long passages of metaphysical speculation, but, far from helping in daily life, Munro's theories often leave him open to fraud and manipulation. For example, Munro believes that humans are by nature unstable and ambiguous; "That a man's individuality swings round from pole to pole, and yet that one life should contain these two contradictory possibilities—is it not a wondrous thing?" (69). Munro critiques organized religion for its failure to progress and its intolerance of uncertainty. Unlike astronomy or invention, religion, Munro claims, is nonprogressive, so "the truly inspired priest is the man or woman with the big brain" (24). He argues that one should develop an ethic of "toleration," since "faith is not a virtue but a vice" (19). At the same time, Munro trusts that Providence guides humanity. He writes, "For *all* is good, if understood, / (Ah, could we understand!)" (113 [original italics]). His bracketed comment indicates that he believes uncertainty to be humanity's normal state, but the italicized word *all* indicates that Munro also believes that good may come from apparent evil, even if we do not see it. Looking at the stars, Munro concludes, "But there's order in it, Bertie, there's order! And where there is order there must be mind, and where there is mind there must be [a] sense of Justice" (171). In this way, Munro can account for infant deaths, heart disease, plague, drunkenness, and other ailments that appear to inflict undeserved misery. While theoretically satisfying, these ideas in some measure explain Munro's failure to recognize Cullingworth's charlatanism. He is not willing to call Cullingworth a quack because he tolerates ambiguity and realizes that human nature is inconsistent and changeable. Munro wants to explore Cullingworth's practice fully before condemning his methods, and his view of Providence leads Munro to assume that Cullingworth's medical treatment will eventually work toward good, even if he cannot see that end. In this sense, Doyle shows the limitations of logic and consistency, since Munro's ideas render him peculiarly vulnerable to Cullingworth's manipulation.

Rodin and Key note that Munro's philosophical ideas have long been viewed as Doyle's own; however, Munro's ideas are often undermined by his daily experience, indicating a gap between author and character.[33] For example, Munro speculates that Providence prevents cruelty between humans: "It may be that Providence is not only not cruel itself, but will not allow man to be cruel either" (175). But as he writes, Munro notes that he has been (rather comically) shot in the finger by Cullingworth, who was trying to display a new invention, and his finger is festering painfully. On a more serious note, Munro expounds upon his hopes for humanity's mastery of air and water, development of education and preventative medicine, and elimination of war and crime (328). Munro writes, "I am ready to adapt myself to whatever the great Designer's secret plan may be" (326). Speaking of his married and professional life, Munro expresses his hopes to Bertie:

> We are both in our twenty-fifth year, and I suppose that without presumption we can reckon that thirty-five more years lie in front of us. I can foresee the gradually increasing routine of work, the wider circle of friends, the identification with this or that local movement, with perhaps a seat on the Bench, or at least in the Municipal Council in my later years. It's not a very startling programme, is it? But it lies to my hand, and I see no other. I should dearly love that the world should be ever so little better for my presence. (383)

His joyous belief in Providence and happy visions of the future are shockingly undermined by a bracketed comment from Bertie shortly afterward:

> This is the last letter which I was destined to receive from my poor friend. He started to spend the Christmas of that year (1884) with his people, and on the journey was involved in the fatal railroad accident at Sittingfleet, where the express ran into a freight train which was standing in the depot. Dr. and Mrs. Munro were the only occupants of the car next [to] the locomotive, and were killed instantly, as were the brakesman [sic] and one other passenger. (384)

134   Bertie assures readers that this is the death the newly married Munros would have chosen: quick and united (384); however, it is horrifying to readers, whose belief in kindly Providence is shaken.

Another of Munro's theories leaves him vulnerable to Mrs. Cullingworth's manipulation and hostility. Munro believes that women are less insightful than men because "men are following their reason, and women their emotion" (197). Munro depicts his mother as one of these women because, although admirable and honorable, she is proud of her Plantagenet blood and very traditional in her ideas. His mother advises him to break with Cullingworth because of the latter's "unscrupulous character and doubtful antecedents," and she writes a "pretty violent letter" abusing Cullingworth (200–201). Munro dismisses his mother's opinion and hopes that she will "cool down" and take a "more reasonable view" (201). Because Munro lauds the scientific ideals of detachment and reason, his mother seems irrational and reactionary to him. Ironically, Mrs. Munro's old-fashioned and nonprogressive view is quickly proven correct. Even as Munro rejects his mother's opinion, he notices a change in the Cullingworths. Mrs. Cullingworth shoots him "malignant" looks and displays "hardness" of conduct (202), while Cullingworth appears too friendly: Cullingworth "almost overdoes it, and I find myself wondering whether he is not acting" (203). Munro wonders, "[W]hat possible object could his wife and he [Cullingworth] have in pretending to be amiable, if they did not really feel so?" (203). Munro learns too late that Mrs. Cullingworth has been reading his mother's letters and informing her husband about Mrs. Munro's hostility. Under the show of friendliness, Cullingworth offers Munro a pound a week to leave the practice, and only after he informs Cullingworth that he has signed a lease in a new city does Munro realize that no money is coming (299). Munro laments, "I for the first time felt something like fear as I thought of Cullingworth. It was as though in the guise and dress of a man I had caught a sudden glimpse of something sub-human—of something so outside my own range of thought that I was powerless against it" (302). In this instance, Munro's theory and experience are wildly different. Munro had viewed Mrs. Cullingworth as a weakling, "like a child repeating a lesson" (138), but she is a very formidable opponent who compounds pills in her husband's practice, provides a newspaper clipping describing Cullingworth's heroism on the very evening Cullingworth mentions it, and reads and replaces Mrs. Munro's letters. His own mother is both quick-witted and far-sighted, despite his view of her as irrational and backward. In Mrs. Cullingworth and Mrs. Munro, Doyle points to the gap between theory and experience and to the limitations of rationality in understanding human experience. Ironically, Munro's philosophical ideals make him more vulnerable, not less, to quackery and fraud, since they blind him to the power of the irrational, the cruel, and the old-fashioned.

Despite their split, Cullingworth reappears briefly near the end of the novel on his way to South America, and during this visit Munro sees clearly that Cullingworth is a fraud and possibly a madman: "I tried to think that Cullingworth's treatment of me had been pathological— the result of a diseased brain" (378). Cullingworth plans to go to South America and become an itinerant eye specialist, because a series of inquests has damaged his earlier practice: "I work a town at a time. I send on an agent to the next to say that I am coming. 'Here's the chance of a lifetime,' says he, 'no need to go back to Europe. Here's Europe come to you. Squints, cataracts, iritis, refractions, what you like; here's the great Signor Cullingworth, right up to date and ready for anything!'" (380). Notably, Munro predicted much earlier that coroners' inquests might ruin Cullingworth's practice (183). By calling Cullingworth "signor" and by depicting him as an itinerant eye doctor, Doyle draws upon classic hallmarks of quackery, including foreignness, itinerancy, advertising, and hyperbolic showmanship.[34] Cullingworth had always engaged with the two latter activities, and with the addition of the former two qualities, he appears finally to Munro as a recognizable quack. Yet Munro is still impressed by Cullingworth's chicanery: "Of course it sounded absurd as he put it but I could soon see that he had worked out his details, and that there was a very practical side to his visions" (380). Rather than showing Munro learning a simple lesson about quackery, Doyle depicts quackery as an ever-present temptation, which works on Munro even after his experience with Cullingworth's chicanery.

Finally, Doyle complicates the nature of medical illusion by depicting Munro's utilization of and victimization by pretense, impersonation, and deception after his break with Cullingworth. Once in his own practice in Birchespool, Munro employs many of Cullingworth's tricks, just as Doyle borrowed from George T. Budd. Munro borrows Cullingworth's idea that patient care is a matter of belief, not medical skill and training: "My experience with Cullingworth had taught me one thing at least,— that patients care nothing about your house if they only think that you can cure them. Once get that idea into their heads, and you may live

136   in a vacant stall in a stable and write your prescriptions on the manger"
(267). Munro affirms that what patients "think" is more important than
actual practices or scientific theories. In addition, Munro manipulates
his public image: he chooses showy premises and attire (236), maps
out which streets to walk in order to garner attention (249), and even
grows a beard to look older (349). Munro advises Bertie that scientific
knowledge is not as important as image in practice: "Be friendly, genial,
convivial—what you will—but preserve the tone and bearing of a gentleman. If you can make yourself respected and liked you will find every
club and society that you join a fresh introduction to practice" (344).
Like Cullingworth, Munro uses every opportunity to get publicity: "You
may believe that I saw my chance, bustled in, treated the man, concili-
ated the wife, tickled the child, and gained over the whole household"
(321), and he even reports his own activities to the newspaper:

> [I] ran down to the newspaper office on each occasion, and had
> the gratification of seeing in the evening edition that "the driv-
> er, though much shaken, is pronounced by Dr. Stark Munro, of
> Oakley Villa, to have suffered no serious injury." As Cullingworth
> used to say, it is hard enough for the young doctor to push his
> name into any publicity, and he must take what little chances he
> has. Perhaps the fathers of the profession would shake their heads
> over such a proceeding in a little provincial journal; but I was
> never able to see that any of them were very averse from seeing
> their own names appended to the bulletin of some sick statesman
> in The Times. (321)

Munro's practice after his break with Cullingworth shows that Munro
has learned the value of illusion, even if that illusion may be viewed as
quackery by the heads of the profession, who are here charged with
practicing the very conduct they condemn in theory. In this depiction
of Munro's solo practice, Doyle asserts the importance of illusion in
medicine, despite the view of the "fathers of the profession" that medicine is precise and scientific.

At the same time, Munro retains some of his pre-Cullingworth
traits. For example, he offends the local clergyman with his agnosti-
cism despite the obvious detrimental effects on his practice, just as he
offended his lunatic's Tory mother earlier. Munro also rejects his uncle's
letter of introduction to the local Wesleyan minister, for "it seemed to

me that it would be playing it rather low down to use a religious organisation to my own advantage, when I condemned them in the abstract. It was a sore temptation, but I destroyed the letter" (320). In this case, Munro deliberately chooses to reject material benefit for theoretical consistency. Unlike Cullingworth, Munro shows compassion toward others by treating some poor gypsies for free, then offering them his change (297). Most significantly, Munro is defrauded a second time by his housekeeper, Miss Wotton. Munro hires a single lady, Miss Wotton, as his housekeeper and then allows her sister to share her room; however, he learns later that the two women are impostors: "She [Miss Wotton] had passed as a miss, because she thought I was more likely to take a housekeeper without encumbrances. Her husband had come home unexpectedly from a long voyage, and had returned last night. And then—plot within plot—the other woman was not her sister, but a friend, whose name was Miss Williams. She thought I was more likely to take two sisters than two friends" (334). The supposed Miss Wotton turns out to be an alcoholic who drinks Munro's only keg of beer before he can fire her, but he harnesses Miss Williams's housekeeping skills and deceptive talents, just as Cullingworth harnessed his wife's. Miss Williams invents fictions about the practice to impress patients: "She seems in these interviews to inspire them with a kind of hushed feeling of awe, as if they had found their way into some holy of holies. My own actual appearance is quite an anti-climax after the introduction by Miss Williams" (346). In depicting Munro as a victim of a second fraud, Doyle underscores the danger of illusion: Munro suffers far less from this fraud than from Cullingworth's, but it is a betrayal of trust nevertheless and harms his meager finances. At the same time, Munro exploits Miss Williams's deceptive talent, just as he exploits Cullingworth's methods. Although Munro learns the value of illusion in medical practice, Doyle displays the tension between illusion as necessary to medical success and the ever-present dangers of fraud.

Rather than simply contrast a quack and an orthodox physician, *The Stark Munro Letters* explores the nature of illusion in medical practice. Medicine may laud truth as an ideal, but it exploits practices labeled as quack, even as it deplores them. Doyle shows physicians as peculiarly vulnerable to imposture, given the necessity of pretense in the face of incomplete and ambiguous information. Moreover, scientific training's rational and progressive ideals hinder rather than help Munro spot quackery and fraud. Whereas his mother immediately realized

138   Cullingworth's dishonor, Munro's theories about progress and evolution make him less able to comprehend and to judge the irrational. Throughout the story, Munro learns that a little quackish conduct is desirable because everyday practice cannot reach the realm of theoretical truth and knowledge, but Doyle shows that illusion is not harmless. Munro suffers when he fails to discriminate between the sweetheart and her mother, when he mistakes the mill owner and the clubman at Dr. Horton's Yorkshire practice, in his experience with Miss Wotton, and most significantly in his experience with the Cullingworths. Munro's repeated mistakes imply that no amount of experience can protect individuals from the dangers of ambiguity and its attendant potential for misconduct. In *The Stark Munro Letters*, medicine is not a matter of scientific certainty, precision, and progress, but an ambiguous, idiosyncratic occupation. While quacks such as Signor Cullingworth may perhaps eventually be identified, the uncertain nature of medical life makes quack practices both the basis of successful medical practice and its greatest danger.

The Quackery of Sherlock Holmes

The short story "The Adventure of the Speckled Band" appears in the 1892 collection *The Adventures of Sherlock Holmes*, dedicated to Doyle's medical school professor, Joseph Bell. In this story, as in *The Stark Munro Letters*, illusion is both necessary and dangerous to scientific inquiry. The plot begins with Holmes and Watson summoned by bride-to-be Helen Stoner to the country house of her stepfather, Dr. Roylott, where her sister, Julia, died mysteriously several years earlier crying, "The speckled band!"[35] When Dr. Roylott forces Helen to move into her dead sister's bedroom, Helen consults Holmes, who travels to Roylott's house to investigate the suspicious room, uncover the meaning of Julia's last words, determine whether Roylott poisoned Julia, and preserve Helen's life until her forthcoming marriage. In her reading of "The Speckled Band," Susan Cannon Harris notes that there is some overlap between Holmes and the evil Dr. Roylott, but Harris argues that Doyle discriminates between Roylott the poisoner and Holmes the physician, who is capable of bringing "organic toxins out of the toxicologies and into the pharmacopeia."[36] As Harris notes, discriminating between proper and improper medicine is central to this story; however, as in *The Stark Munro Letters*, Doyle depicts orthodoxy and quackery as deeply intertwined and difficult, even undesirable, to separate. On one hand, Holmes and Watson embody an idealized medical professionalism that contrasts sharply with Roylott's irrationality and crime. For example, Watson frames Helen's story by referring to his casebook, which contains over seventy unusual cases and strongly resembles a medical student's casebook such as Doyle kept under Dr. Bell (165).[37] In this frame, it is apparent that Watson dislikes inaccuracy and values precision, since he claims that he is telling Helen's story because he wants to reveal the "true facts" of Dr. Roylott's death (189), to place events "upon record," and to squash "rumours as to the death of Dr. Grimesby Roylott which tend to make the matter even more terrible than the truth" (165). Just as Watson values precision, reason, and logic in the frame, so too does he value it in the main narrative. Whereas Watson describes Helen Stoner in a "pitiable state of agitation" and "with restless, frightened eyes, like those of some hunted animal" (166), Holmes offers "professional investigations" on a "logical basis" using "rapid deductions" (166). Clearly, Helen earns Watson's pity, but Holmes demands his admiration. This is highlighted during Holmes and Helen's first meeting, when Holmes impressively identifies Helen's route by train and dogcart using splatters of mud on her sleeve and a mark in her glove in his trademark exhibition of observation and analysis. In contrast, Dr. Grimesby Roylott, whose clothes are "a peculiar mixture of the professional and of the agricultural," is neither precise nor logical despite his medical training (176). Roylott's "thousand wrinkles," "deep-set, bile-shot eyes," and "high thin fleshless nose" make him appear a "fierce old bird of prey" who is "marked with every evil passion" (176). Roylott "screamed . . . furiously" and "snarled" at Holmes, calling him "scoundrel," "busybody," "meddler," and "jack-in-office" (176). Roylott even threatens Holmes, bends a fire-place poker, and throws it into the fireplace (176). Whereas Helen's animal qualities earn pity, Roylott's earn contempt, because his bestial qualities are associated not with terror but with violence that is inappropriate in a medical man. As Harris suggests, Roylott, Holmes, and Watson's shared medical background seems to highlight Watson and Holmes's professionalism and Roylott's criminality. Similarly, Paula J. Reiter argues that although Holmes may mirror the malefactor at times, "Holmes solves the mystery and the problem of resemblance [to the malefactor] through the display of specifically professional characteristics: superior training, discretion, status, and disinterested service."[38] Holmes certainly displays tact and discretion in this instance, for as Roylott screams and threatens, Holmes quietly smiles and then unbends the poker after Roylott has gone. In

140   Roylott, Holmes, and Watson, Doyle seems to contrast the logic and
precision of orthodox medical practitioners with the unseemly violence
and irrationality of the unorthodox, hinting that unorthodoxy slides
easily down a slippery slope from irrationality to violence to crime.
     On the other hand, perhaps the relationship between Holmes,
Watson, and Roylott is, like the relationship between Cullingworth and
Munro, more complex. Thomas A. Sebeok and Jean Umiker-Sebeok
note that Holmes explicitly praises deduction but that his style of
questioning resembles a medical examination, which relies on hidden
guesswork and is, in some measure, theatrical.[39] Like physicians, Holmes
asks a series of seemingly unrelated questions designed to confirm a
hypothesis already in his mind, a process that Sebeok and Umiker-
Sebeok consider one of medicine's (and Holmes's) "tricks."[40] In questioning Helen Stoner, Holmes uses theatrics to startle and impress her: she
gives a "violent start" when he describes her route by dogcart and train
(167), and she "coloured deeply" when he reveals the bruises Dr. Roylott
left on her arm (174). Neither detail serves a purpose in the case beyond bolstering Holmes's image. Like Roylott's theatrical bending of the
poker, Holmes's questions are not entirely logical analysis (as Watson
assumes) but medico-scientific theater designed to arouse Helen's and,
to a lesser extent, Watson's awe. If so, Holmes is resorting to medicine-
show methods to bolster his reputation for scientific investigation.[41]
     Similarly, Doyle complicates Holmes's trademark deductive method
in the collection's opening story, "A Scandal in Bohemia." Like "The
Speckled Band," this story begins with Watson's panegyric upon Holmes's
rationality: "Grit in a sensitive instrument, or a crack in one of his own
high-power lenses, would not be more disturbing than a strong emotion in a nature such as his."[42] Watson views Holmes as a scientific instrument, like a microscope or a telescope, and Holmes also lectures
Watson on his own scientific acumen: "It is a capital mistake to theorize
before one has data. Insensibly one begins to twist facts to suit theories, instead of theories to suit facts."[43] But Holmes's and Watson's views
should not be mistaken for Doyle's. The same conversation describes
Holmes's addiction to narcotics, his desire for his "Boswell," Watson's
attention, and his hope of "money in this case." In these details, Doyle
complicates Watson's view (and Holmes's own view) of Holmes as logical, discreet, emotionless, and disinterested by providing Holmes with
qualities such as pride, covetousness, and gluttony. In this presentation,
as in the questioning of Helen in "The Speckled Band," Doyle depicts

Holmes's methods as Pasquale Accardo describes medicine: "part art, part craft, and part social activity."[45] Although Holmes may be based on Joseph Bell, Accardo suggests that Holmes might also be influenced by the American physician Oliver Wendell Holmes Sr., whom Doyle admired and whose name Sherlock shares: "As a professional medical educator, [Oliver Wendell] Holmes was committed to the scientific method and was a harsh critic of the many forms of imposture prevalent in the medicine of his day."[46] At the same time, Accardo claims that Oliver Wendell Holmes "combined a belief in the necessity of a scientific approach with a certain skepticism with regard to the physician's ability to consistently distinguish science fact from personal opinion."[47] According to Accardo, Oliver Wendell Holmes provided Doyle with a model that both embraces science and acknowledges the difficulty of translating scientific ideals into daily practice. As a result, Accardo believes that readers should view Holmes skeptically: "The exaggeration of Holmes's deductive powers frequently borders on absurdity. Doyle corrects this impression by documenting many false trails followed, missed clues, premature hypotheses, and erroneous conclusions."[48] If Roylott's clothes symbolize his mixture of the professional and the agricultural, perhaps Holmes should be viewed as a mixture also because medicine, the field from which he draws his methods, is itself a mixture of facts and illusion, logic and manipulation.

As Munro learns from Cullingworth, a little theatricality is a necessary part of daily medical practice, and Holmes's famous equanimity serves him well in "The Speckled Band." Holmes is often very reticent with Helen: he stares at the fire, asks questions, and murmurs vague comments such as "this is very deep business" (174). Only after she leaves does he explain to Watson that he concurs with Helen's theory that gypsies may be involved in Julia's death; "I think there is good ground to think the mystery may be cleared along those lines" (175). When he arrives at Roylott's house, Holmes examines Julia's window and confesses to Watson with some "perplexity" that his "theory certainly presents some difficulties" (180). As before, Helen has already left before he voices his doubts. Similarly, Holmes murmurs "very strange" as he examines the floor, walls, ventilator, and bell-pull in Julia's room (181). Only after Helen's departure does Holmes explain to Watson that he expected to see a ventilator (184). Holmes then examines Roylott's room, leaves with a "grim" face, paces the lawn, and advises Helen to leave, deflecting her questions by demanding "clearer proof" before speaking (182–83). Is Holmes's emotionless façade genuine or an act designed to impress clients, such as Helen, but dropped before his colleague, Watson? Doyle provides hints that this may be the case when the two men are alone in Julia's room. They are startled by the appearance of Dr. Roylott's baboon, and Watson writes, "Holmes was for the moment as startled as I. His hand closed like a vice upon my wrist in his agitation" (186). It is possible that Holmes wears a cloak of certitude but that he is, as in the instance with the baboon, more emotional than he appears, indeed, more emotional than Watson, whose hand he grasps for comfort. This is magnified by Holmes's confession at the end of the case about his failure to follow his own method of scientific deduction: "I had . . . come to an erroneous conclusion which shows, my dear Watson, how dangerous it always is to reason from insufficient data" (189). Holmes confesses that he accepted Helen's theory about the gypsies without evidence, and he revised it only when he found the bed, bell-pull, and ventilator in Julia's room. John A. Hodgson notes that "The Speckled Band" is one of the perennially favorite Holmes stories but that it is famously also one of the more irrational, given the factual errors in Doyle's representation of the snake.[49] Holmes's cloak of certitude blinds Helen, Watson, and perhaps readers to his errors: while Watson and some readers see that Holmes fails to employ strict logic in solving the case, Helen and other readers do not.

If Holmes reaps the benefits of wearing a "cloak of certitude" in his dealings with Helen, Dr. Roylott shows the undesirable consequences of openly following one's impulses, just as Munro displays the undesirable consequences of honesty and impulsiveness in *The Stark Munro Letters*. Helen describes Roylott's longstanding social isolation and professional failure: "Violence of temper approaching to mania has been hereditary in the men of the family, but in my stepfather's case it had, I believe, been intensified by his long residence in the tropics" (169).[50] Helen explains that Roylott was imprisoned in Calcutta for murdering his butler in a fit of rage (168), and in Britain, he "hurled" a blacksmith over a cliff, to the horror of the previously friendly villagers (169). Unable to sustain propriety's genteel fictions, Roylott displays a "passion" for the "wandering gipsies" who live on his property and for Indian animals, including a cheetah, a baboon, and (unbeknownst to Helen) a snake (169). At the same time, Doyle reminds readers that dishonesty may also be a sinister trait. Cullingworth's and Miss Wotton's deceits cause Munro financial hardship and hurt feelings, but Roylott's conduct

enacts an even worse sort of deception. Having released the poisonous snake into Julia's bed by means of the ventilator and dummy bell-
pull, Roylott proceeds to treat the unconscious Julia with brandy, then
sends for more aid in a show of medical and fatherly care. His pretense
is partially successful: Helen reveals that he was the prime suspect at
the time but neither poison nor violence could be proven against him.
Similarly, his show of concern for Helen manipulates her into sleeping
in Julia's room despite her conviction that he murdered Julia. In Roylott,
Doyle asserts the dangers of both extreme impulsiveness and extreme
deception: the former results in the murder of Roylott's butler and the
attempted murder of the blacksmith, and the latter facilitates the murder
of Julia and the attempted murder of Helen.

Paula J. Reiter notes this problematic overlap between medical professionals and criminals in her examination of the Thomas Neill Cream
trial. Reiter argues that the trial of physician-poisoner Cream "effaced
distinctions between the delinquent and the professional" and that
Holmes reestablishes these distinctions.[51] Yet in "The Speckled Band,"
Doyle repeatedly emphasizes the overlap between Holmes, Watson, and
Roylott.[52] In the opening scene, Roylott bends an iron bar and Holmes
unbends it. At first glance, this symbolizes Holmes's undoing of Roylott's mischief; however, the incident also implies that both men share
qualities such as physical strength and showmanship, since Watson is
the audience for both. Hodgson argues that this moment is evidence
of the story's ambiguity, simultaneously serving as both a red herring
(Roylott does not kill by violence but through medicine) and a clue
(Holmes will not undo Roylott's crime but repeat it).[53] When Helen says
that Roylott is "so cunning," Holmes replies, "[H]e may find that there is
someone more cunning than himself upon his track" (179). In this case,
Holmes applies the same word to himself, Watson, and Roylott, implying that all three are clever, educated, and devious. Medical knowledge
is particularly singled out as a shared field. Holmes tells Watson, "When
a doctor does go wrong he is the first of criminals. He has nerve and he
has knowledge. Palmer and Pritchard were among the heads of their
profession. This man strikes even deeper, but I think, Watson, that we
shall be able to strike deeper still" (185). In this speech, Holmes places
himself, Watson, Roylott, Palmer, and Pritchard on a continuum, with
Watson and Holmes as the deepest of the lot. Holmes laments, "Ah, me!
It's a wicked world, and when a clever man turns his brain to crime it is
the worst of all" (182). Although Reiter views Holmes as the opposite

144   of the physician-poisoner, Doyle seems repeatedly to draw parallels between Roylott, Holmes, and Watson and, indeed, between his fictional
medical men and real physician-murderers.

In allusions to notorious physician-poisoners of the late Victorian
period, Doyle most strongly depicts medicine's tricky position with regard to illusion; if too much frankness is undesirable because it leads to
unprofessionalism, too much deception is similarly undesirable, since
deception may lead to exploitation, crime, and even death. In his discussion of physician-poisoner Thomas Neill Cream, Angus McLaren
notes that Cream's conduct was an extreme version of deceptive practices common in medicine at the time. For example, McLaren asserts
that many physicians considered lying to patients not simply acceptable but even beneficial and that "medical men felt they had a right to
lie."[54] McLaren describes the practice of dispensing candy pills to preg-
nant women requesting an abortifacient rather than refusing them outright, to prevent such women from seeking other avenues. For McLaren,
"What is really germane was how symbolically important it was that
the doctor alone determined what to give his patient while keeping her
in ignorance of its effects."[55] In place of candy, Cream dispensed poison to women seeking an abortifacient, on the grounds that their moral
character excused his own wrongdoing. Thus, McLaren's assessment of
Cream, like Doyle's depiction of Roylott, Watson, and Holmes, places
the physician-poisoner on a continuum with rather than in opposition to
orthodox practice. Similarly, McLaren notes that poisoner Dr. Pritchard
exploited accepted medical deception when he poisoned his wife and
mother-in-law with antimony in 1865, then filled out their death certificates himself, an impropriety other physicians routinely overlooked
through collegial etiquette.[56] Judith R. Walkowitz describes popular
anxiety about the ways in which routine medical activity became misconduct and exploitation in social movements against private asylums
and against the Contagious Disease Act, which enforced mandatory
examination of suspected prostitutes. Walkowitz notes that medical examination of prostitutes created a view of doctors as sexually suspect
and dangerous characters, and private asylums made physicians appear
greedy and manipulative.[57] Walkowitz connects physicians' dark reputation for coercion, deception, and antifeminist, sexual violation to the
development of a popular theory that Jack the Ripper was a physician.[58]
In contrast, Susan Sontag describes well-intentioned nineteenth- and
early twentieth-century practices in which physicians deceived patients

by hiding diagnoses such as tuberculosis and cancer to lessen patients' fear.[59] But Keith Allan and Kate Burridge note the multivalent nature of such omissions, because naming a disease may provide comfort, generate superstitious fear, or create suffering through suggestion.[60] Similarly, Doyle depicts the tricky nature of well-intended deception throughout *The Adventures of Sherlock Holmes*. In "The Speckled Band," Holmes hides information from Helen, which seems fairly harmless or even beneficial as Holmes allays Helen's distress. In "A Case of Identity," Holmes does not tell his client the fate of her missing fiancé, leaving her at the mercy of her cruel and manipulative family. In "The Five Orange Pips," Holmes does not explain the meaning of the letters KKK to his client, waiting, as he does in "The Speckled Band," until the client has gone before sharing information with Watson. The ill-informed client is then murdered by the KKK on his way home.[61] In these omissions, Doyle asserts the dangers of even well-intentioned deception, because it may result in unfortunate outcomes.

The dangers of orthodox quackery are most evident when Holmes inadvertently causes Roylott's death. Holmes says of Roylott, "The idea of using a form of poison which could not possibly be discovered by any chemical test was just such a one as would occur to a clever and ruthless man who had an Eastern training" (189). Indeed, Holmes might be describing himself, since he immediately thinks of snake poison upon finding the dummy bell-pull and the ventilator. When Holmes spies the actual snake on the bell-pull, he lashes "savagely" and "furiously" at it, "filled with horror and loathing" (187). The violence of Holmes's response, like his fear of the baboon earlier, shows the strong emotion beneath Holmes's apparent equanimity. When the angry snake returns to Roylott's room, Watson and Holmes hear a "most horrible cry" of "pain and fear and anger all mingled in the one dreadful shriek" before finding Roylott dead and encircled by the adder (188). Looking at the body, Holmes repeats Julia's dying words: "The band! The speckled band!" (188). The utterance momentarily fuses Holmes with the victim, Julia, and the murderer, Roylott, who heard Julia's screams after driving the snake through the ventilator just as Watson and Holmes heard his. Holmes concludes, "In this way, I am no doubt indirectly responsible for Dr. Grimesby Roylott's death, and I cannot say that it is likely to weigh very heavily upon my conscience" (190). Replace Roylott's name with Julia's and the confession may be Roylott's rather than Holmes's. Readers may accept Holmes's claims about science and equanimity at

146   face value, but readers also see Holmes use a violent attack on a snake and the snake's own poison to kill Roylott, just as Roylott was suspected of using violence or poison to kill Julia. One might argue that Roylott deserved death; however, Holmes's conduct is neither professional nor logical and scientific, and his unconcern for the result of his investigation seems quite as chilling as Roylott's initial crime. In addition, Holmes's manslaughter does not bring the truth about Julia's or Roylott's deaths to light but clouds it further, a cloud Watson expressly attempts to clear in the frame story years after Helen's death.

Considered thus, "The Speckled Band" deploys Doyle's medical background not to defend order and science but to undermine the view of medicine as scientific and progressive. While Holmes is famous for his philosophy of deductive reasoning, perhaps his philosophy, like Munro's, often fails in daily practice. Indeed, a little chicanery helps both Holmes and Munro in their day-to-day work, and transparency seems, as Osler says, an impossible way to practice medicine. While physicians such as Roylott and Cullingworth may appear to be quacks in the sense that they are greedy, selfish, dishonest, violent, and immoral, both are educated and certified practitioners. At the same time, genteel physicians such as Munro, Watson, and Holmes often betray motives and engage in activities similar to those of their quackish counterparts. If a quack is expelled at the end of "The Speckled Band" and *The Stark Munro Letters*, quackery itself remains ensconced in the very midst of orthodox practice. In this sense, Arthur Conan Doyle offers a unique and interesting view of quackery. Doyle encourages readers to reexamine medicine not as a field of scientific certitude but as a field particularly invested in practices it theoretically deplores. Because of the ambiguous aspects of medicine, illusion and deception are requirements for successful practice, but Doyle also realizes the dangers of illusion, because even well-intentioned illusion may lead down a slippery slope ending in manipulation, imposture, fraud, and even murder. In Doyle's medicine, readers see the difficulties of discriminating between quacks and physicians because of many shared behaviors. Orthodoxy and quackery appear so tightly intertwined that separating the two becomes very difficult: what is most radical about Doyle's view of medicine is his suggestion that, despite the dangers of illusion, it might be undesirable to even try.

Conclusion

The In-Laws
Orthodoxy and Quackery in Vernon Galbray

> Quack politicians, quack divines, quack lawyers, and
> quack players,
>
> Quack ladies too, whose varnish'd charms are giddy
> youth's betrayers;
>
> There's quack philanthropy, quack love, quack
> friendship, and quack trade, sirs,
>
> In short—_except my customers_—the world's in masquerade, sirs.
>
> —Jack Ketch (the hangman) in John Corry, "Quack
> Doctors Dissected," 1805.

_T_he anonymous novel _Vernon Galbray; or, The Empiric: The History of a Quack Dentist_ (1875) describes the career of Samuel Moses, a part-English, part-Dutch, Jewish dentist from Rotterdam. Moses changes his name to Vernon Galbray and moves to England because of the "gullibility, the ease with which money could be made there, and how readily they were imposed upon by a specious address or a plausible announcement."[1] Under his new name, Galbray establishes a dental practice (complete with a sign claiming the practice is forty years old) and buys silver plate and London suits. He then advertises heavily, dwelling on the dangers of poor dentistry and unqualified practitioners. Of course, Galbray is himself unskilled, and his abused assistant, Spyk, crafts the very dentures that Galbray can barely put in. His advertisements are written by an alcoholic Englishman who later becomes another so-called assistant. In this manner, Galbray quickly becomes a

148   wealthy, socially prominent, middle-class, English professional. Aside
      from his workplace shenanigans, Vernon Galbray and his beleaguered
      wife neglect their lovely daughter, Adele. But Galbray fatally overreaches
      when he takes on an apprentice, Rivington, for an exorbitant fee. The
      son of a vicar, Rivington diligently studies dentistry (guided by Spyk),
      befriends Spyk, converts Adele to Anglicanism, and proposes to her
      after her mother runs away with another man and Galbray loses his
      practice in a fire, a fact that concerns Galbray far more than the death
      of Spyk in the fire. In the end, a trustworthy Anglo-Jewish lawyer helps
      Rivington unmask Galbray and drive him out of business.

      The author of *Vernon Galbray* begins with seemingly clear boundaries
      between orthodoxy and quackery. The novel's double subtitle makes it
      doubly plain that this is the history of a *quack* dentist who is an *empiric*. As
      we have seen in earlier chapters, quackery is often described according
      to behaviors such as empiricism, itinerancy, advertising, self-promotion,
      and trickery and qualities such as greed, foreignness, lack of skill, and
      lack of faith (Galbray is both Dutch and Jewish). By embodying many
      of these qualities and behaviors in Galbray, the author encourages read-
      ers to view quackery as an external force that can be recognized and
      eliminated. Like Mrs. Sweeney's Indian shawl in *Villette* or Cullingworth's
      posh dining room in *The Stark Munro Letters*, Galbray's London suits, plate,
      and premises allow him to mask his blatant self-promotion, incompe-
      tence, foreignness, immorality, and greed, but in the end, he is identi-
      fied, categorized, and eliminated. Just as Galbray appears to embody
      quackery, so too does Rivington appear to embody dental orthodoxy
      through his competence, manners, Anglicanism, and Englishness. In this
      desire for clear boundaries between orthodoxy and quackery and for es-
      sentialized hallmarks of each, the author of *Vernon Galbray* resembles
      several of the writers, legislators, physicians, and others cited through-
      out this book who imagined an end to quackery through professional
      and legal maneuverings. Indeed, the novel's publication coincided with
      the beginning of a campaign by the Dental Reform Committee, later
      the British Dental Association, to professionalize dentistry. In the same
      way that Rivington joins with a lawyer to cast out Galbray, dentists of
      the 1870s appealed to legislators to stem the perceived tide of malprac-
      tice as dentistry expanded to include rising numbers of practitioners.[2]
      Founded in 1880, the British Dental Association apparently devoted
      much of its energy to prosecuting unqualified dentists. This is not to say
      that the development of professional standards is unnecessary for both

practitioner security and public safety; rather, *Vernon Galbray* presents an   149
oversimplified view of legal and professional reform as a relatively easy
and effective remedy for quackery in which quackery originates in an
unqualified, immoral outsider who can be identified by given hallmarks
and cast out.

In fact, as with Rochester's Italian cordial in *Jane Eyre*, the apparently clear boundaries between orthodoxy and quackery are difficult to
maintain, even in this most polemical of novels. What about Spyk? The
secondary subtitle of the novel, *History of a Quack Dentist*, might easily
describe him as well as Galbray since he bears many of the same essentialized hallmarks, such as foreignness and Jewishness. Spyk works
for Galbray and thus may be seen as a supporter of quackery, but he is
hardworking and competent. Moreover, he teaches Rivington dentistry,
so he may be seen as more professional and more knowledgeable than
his Christian, English pupil. His self-sacrifice in helping Rivington and
Adele, despite his own feelings for her, appears as noble as Dr. Woodcourt's in *Bleak House*. With Galbray's disappearance and Spyk's death,
all hallmarks of quackery seem to be eradicated along with quackery's
undesirable social and moral traits in a triumphant fantasy in which
English Christianity marches hand-in-hand with professionalism. Yet
the fact remains that Rivington learned his trade in Galbray's shop, from
a man, Spyk, bearing some of the hallmarks of quackery despite being
competent and moral. In addition, Galbray's disappearance at the end of
the novel leaves us to wonder when and where he might reappear in a
new guise. How will we recognize him in this new guise, if his shop contains honorable and competent men such as Spyk and Rivington, who
share his workplace and, in the case of Spyk, his faith and his ethnicity?
Spyk's convenient death in the fire leaves Rivington free to marry and to
set up a new dental practice, but what are readers to make of Rivington's
union with Galbray's daughter and the fact that dental orthodoxy, as
embodied in Rivington, learned its trade in the very shop of quackery,
just as Stark Munro learned his trade in Cullingworth's? Will Rivington
employ some of Galbray's tactics in his new office, just as Munro employed Cullingworth's and Doyle himself employed Budd's?

This novel seems a good place to end this study because it handily
summarizes the essentialized hallmarks of nineteenth-century quackery
and the hopes of legislators, professionals, and members of the public
that medico-legal discourse might end what they perceived to be bla-
tant quackery. Despite the widely recognized difficulties of stemming

150   quackery in medicine and pharmacy, the author of *Vernon Galbray* implies that dentistry can successfully address quackery through legislation and professional association. This novel does not encourage readers, as Brontë's does, to question the way the boundaries of orthodoxy are generated and maintained, although the contrasts between Jewishness and Christianity and between Rotterdam and London recall Lucy Snowe's nationalist binaries. *Vernon Galbray* seems to lack Brontë's radical skepticism about narrative and about the supposedly stable binaries that structure culture. Nor does this author seem to encourage us to question the overlap between Christianity and professionalism. If Rivington's virtues recall the vocation-based physicians of *Bleak House* and *Little Dorrit*, the novel betrays no hint of the difficulties Dickens presents with such an identity, notably, the intraprofessional rivalry and the problems with crafting a modern, professional identity from traditional, Christian virtue. Adele certainly has no role in the healing arts, so the novel avoids questions about female practitioners and amateurs, which are so prevalent in *Bleak House* and *Little Dorrit*. Despite aiding her husband in various ways, Galbray's wife is no Mrs. Oldershaw or Lydia from *Armadale*, and she is only too eager to abandon business when the opportunity arises. *Vernon Galbray* seems to be a tale of quackery unmasked, unaware that it is repeating earlier attempts to identify, unmask, and eliminate quackery using these same strategies. Instead of persuading us that quackery may be unmasked, this repetitiveness highlights the foolishness of believing that any legislation, professional association, or social movement can unmask and eradicate quackery. This is not to say that legal or professional standards are useless or misguided; on the contrary, they are very valuable in many ways, but they are not panaceas. Even in this rather heavy-handed novel, quackery and orthodoxy are slippery entities that are always in conversation, two sides of a continually flipping coin. Rivington and Galbray only appear to be opposites, but they are, by the end of the novel, in-laws.

The Specter of Quackery

Although *Vernon Galbray* depicts the eradication of quackery through medico-legal discourse, we have found that this is a tricky task because both orthodoxy and quackery rely on language and language resists medico-legal attempts to determine meaning. As we have seen, the language of orthodoxy may perpetuate the very quackery it seeks to eliminate. For example, the word *anatomy* slips in meaning from the queen of the medical sciences to a necessary but inhumane practice to a crime to vainglorious boasting to a mask for incompetence. Indeed, anatomy is an excellent example of quackery's ability to imaginatively haunt medicine through language. In novels throughout the Victorian period, anatomy, body snatching, and burking may be used individually or in combination to connote medical greed, selfishness, and crime, long after the actual practice of body snatching had ceased and despite the relative rarity of burking. In Harriet Martineau's *Deerbrook* (1839), for example, Dr. Hope is young, attractive and modern, so the conservative, aging population spread stories about his quackery and body snatching, although he engages in neither. In Charles Dickens's *Our Mutual Friend* (1864), poor Betty distrusts the middle-class ladies who want to help her for fear that they will send her to a workhouse where they will let her die (or burke her?) so that they can have her body for dissection. In George Eliot's *Middlemarch* (1872), Dr. Lydgate opts for new scientific techniques rather than traditional remedies and is subject to rumors of quackery, body snatching, and even murder. Robert Louis Stevenson's *Strange Case of Dr. Jekyll and Mr. Hyde* (1886) introduces Jekyll as the owner of a laboratory that is a converted dissecting theater, instantly signifying to readers his immorality and selfishness and foreshadowing his complicity in Hyde's crimes, just as anatomists were considered morally culpable for body snatching and burking. Drs. Hope, Lydgate, and Jekyll (and presumably the philanthropic ladies in *Our Mutual Friend*) do not engage in actual body snatching or burking. On the one hand, Hope, Lydgate, and Jekyll exploit anatomy's connotations of science and progress, but on the other hand, these novels deploy the negative connotations of early nineteenth-century anatomy to articulate distrust of medical practitioners throughout the century because of anatomy's residual connotations of cruelty, immorality, and crime. The persistence of anatomy in literature does not fit with the notion that the Anatomy Act of 1832 quashed anatomy's negative connotations; rather, these novels testify to the limits of medico-legal discourse in controlling orthodoxy or quackery, because connotations continued to circulate in imagination long after the material practices had disappeared. At first glance, these novels may appear to depict simply aspects of contemporary medical practice as part of the verisimilitude common in Victorian literature; however, these texts do more: they test, challenge, and undermine configurations of orthodoxy using the cast-off, the repressed, the disavowed, and the quack.

Although Vernon Galbray is identifiable as a quack because of his constellation of moral failures and professional incompetence, orthodoxy often proves more difficult to define. This is not to suggest that there is no mainstream or dominant medical viewpoint at a given time; instead, we should consider that medicine is not a unified field, and many of the practices that exist under the wide medical umbrella might generate uncertainty or even bear the charge of quackery despite their employment by licensed and trained practitioners. For example, physicians such as Dr. John in *Villette* and Stark Munro in *The Stark Munro Letters* often confuse the boundary between the social niceties (without which medical practice cannot succeed) and inappropriate or quackish deception and self-indulgence. John's flirtations and humoring of his child-patients appear at first glance harmless, even kind; however, in retrospect they are first steps down a slippery slope toward serious misconduct. The first two novellas in the Sherlock Holmes series, *A Study in Scarlet* and *The Sign of Four*, exemplify the conflicted and changing configurations of orthodoxy. In the former, Holmes is a rather frightful if cutting-edge scientist: he describes beating a corpse to study postmortem bruising and is suspected of testing opium on his fellow students. In the latter, Holmes appears wielding the latest medical technology, the hypodermic injection, and the latest pharmaceutical, cocaine. Holmes takes his syringe down from the mantel, adjusts the needle, rolls back his shirtsleeve, displays a forearm scarred with injection marks, and injects cocaine under Watson's disapproving gaze. At the time, injections connoted medical innovation and progress. In his 1885 address to the British Medical Association, for example, Dr. Talfourd Jones describes his favorite syringe design in detail, calling it a "pocket-companion," and he encourages his audience to perform proper maintenance on their syringes, listing joint adjustments and graduation markings as particular trouble spots.[3] Jones also describes the difficulty of getting needles and bottles that fit together well, a necessity if the needle is to reach the bottom of the bottle without grating, and because many syringe users, like Jones, designed and maintained their own syringes, Holmes's skill with the tricky apparatus testifies to his scientific prowess.

However, Holmes uses his syringe to inject morphine and cocaine, two drugs that generated controversy during this period. While the dangers of morphine were clear by the 1880s, the later years of the 1880s and early 1890s witnessed increasing concern about cocaine. One account in the *Lancet* describes a death from cocaine overdose, but the author suggests that the solution may have been adulterated.[4] Conversely, accounts of morphine deaths blame the toxic nature of the drug and encourage dispensaries to warn patients about overdosing and to prevent dispensing errors, even though the word *poison* appeared on morphine labels.[5] Although some attached culpability only to morphine, one American writer in the late 1880s strenuously objected to the lackadaisical handling of cocaine. Dr. Mattison denied the popular view that cocaine is not addictive and warned against accepting evidence from doctors who used the drug themselves: "[T]he testimony of an intoxicated person respecting his experience while intoxicated [is] . . . proverbially untrustworthy."[6] Moreover, he called cocaine "more dangerous than alcohol or opium" and the "most fascinating, seductive, dangerous and destructive drug extant" and "insist[ed] on the great danger of self-injecting, a course almost certain to entail added ill."[7] Holmes relies on cocaine injections for mental stimulation and as a reward when the case is solved, but Watson views morphine *and* cocaine injections as dangerous. Given that injections and cocaine were generally regarded as cutting-edge discoveries during this period, Holmes's use of injectable cocaine adds dramatically to the scientific prowess of his character, but in Watson's disapproval, Doyle represents fissures in medical orthodoxy itself. In depicting injectable cocaine, Doyle was at the forefront of medical innovation, although his description of Holmes's scarred arm bolsters Watson's view that the drug is as dangerous as it is progressive. Watson's point of view would eventually become dominant and cause Doyle to drop Holmes's drug habit from later stories. Even Doyle, himself a medical practitioner, could not foresee which view would eventually become dominant in the medical community; thus, Doyle included cocaine in the early novels, then downplayed Holmes's habit in later novels after cocaine's connotations had become increasingly negative. In the depiction of cocaine injections in *The Sign of Four* and in Doyle's suppression of Holmes's drug use, we are reminded that the dominant, mainstream, conventional, what I have called orthodox, viewpoint is not always clear, that it changes over time, and that standards of medical competence and conduct are often tricky when set amid a field of uncertainty.

Medicine and the Professions

If Vernon Galbray might be banished, quackery is a concept that resists banishment because it draws upon and sometimes originates from

154   within orthodoxy itself, as in the case of Rivington and Stark Munro, both of whose training occurred in quack shops. Orthodoxy expends a great deal of energy combating quackery, and Victorian professionals championed legislation including the Anatomy Act of 1832, the Arsenic Act of 1851, the Poisons Act of 1857, the Chemists and Druggists Bill of 1865, and the Pharmacy Act of 1868, among others. Although quackery may be external to the accepted professional associations and colleges and uninformed about given techniques or facts, it may also emerge from orthodoxy's own ranks. As Arthur Conan Doyle brilliantly shows, a licensed physician such as Roylott in "The Adventure of the Speckled Band" might be a poisoner, and a young physician such as Stark Munro may benefit from a little chicanery. In earlier chapters, advertising by college members is discussed as a sign of professional quackery, regardless of education or registration. Quackery is the fissure within a college or a professional association, but it also exhibits fissures between various medical professions, between medicine and bourgeois consumers, and between professions, from whom one might expect accord rather than discord. To druggists, shopkeepers were engaged in quackery, even though the substances in question, such as arsenic, had been traditionally sold freely in shops and were widely accepted as proper in that context. To some practitioners, patients themselves were quacks in need of professional supervision, a view hotly contested by patients who demanded a free marketplace and home remedies without prescription. As we have seen, some lay commentators called colleges and professional associations quackish because of their demands for ever-increasing control of the medical market at the expense of patients and amateurs. Although physicians such as Richard Quain, whose speech opens this book, chart medical orthodoxy using scientific breakthroughs, physicians often deployed the language of nationalism and Christianity to forge their professional identity. For example, Christianity pervaded medical journals and commentary throughout the mid-Victorian period and wrestled prestige away from other professional groups. Medicine seems to have carved its professional space not merely from the turf formerly occupied by amateurs (or quacks?) but from other professional fields, such as business, trade, the army, the government, and the church. This complicates the notion not only of a unified medical establishment or orthodoxy but also of a united professional class.

    In literature such as Richard Quain's Harveian Oration, there is an emphasis on science, because science is prestigious and indeed profoundly

affects medical practice in many ways. However, significant differences 155
between laboratory activity and medical practice can be seen even in
today's culture. How do we evaluate practitioner competence, emerging
professions, drug marketing, patient advocacy, and government regulation? How are we influenced by our cultural biases about the role of
women in society, the status of foreigners, the power of religious beliefs,
the influence of nationalism, the independence of individual consumers,
and the authority of government? Should drugs be marketed directly to
the public? Should dietary supplements be regulated? How are health-
science graduates of foreign schools to be licensed? Ought practitioners
to be able to refuse procedures and patients based on their personal
convictions, or is this unprofessional and an infringement on patient autonomy? We answer these questions not merely through scientific criteria but through moral, social, religious, environmental, racial, gendered,
and even celebrity discourse. The latter is especially powerful given that
we live in a world of television commercials, billboards, and magazines
featuring hospitals, nursing homes, physicians, surgeons, doulas, and
others touting their own services as the most convenient, best quality,
and safest. We are inundated with advertisements promising weight loss,
beauty, and youth. As medical consumers, we are challenged to balance
personal autonomy, scientific knowledge, government regulation, and
free-market forces. We realize that questions of orthodoxy and quackery
challenge us as surely as they did the Victorians and that such questions
are astonishingly familiar and still remarkably relevant.

Notes

Introduction: False Professions

Epigraphs: William H. Helfand, *Quack, Quack, Quack: The Sellers of Nostrums in Prints, Posters, Ephemera and Books* (New York: Grolier, 2002), 11; "The Profession and Its Dignity," *Lancet*, March 27, 1858, 318–19.

1. Charlotte Brontë, *Jane Eyre* (New York: Random House, 1943), 160 (chap. 20).

2. Richard Quain, "History and Progress of Medicine," *British Medical Journal*, October 24, 1885, 775.

3. Ibid.

4. Ibid., 776.

5. Ibid., 780.

6. Peter Stallybrass and Allon White, *The Politics and Poetics of Transgression* (Ithaca, NY: Cornell University Press, 1986), 5.

7. Ibid., 21.

8. Roger Cooter, introduction to *Studies in the History of Alternative Medicine*, ed. Roger Cooter (New York: St. Martin's Press, 1988), xiv. Similarly, Christopher Lawrence and George Weisz explore nineteenth-century movements within the mainstream that celebrate a holistic approach to the body, ranging from the Arts and Crafts movement to the work of William Osler in "Medical Holism: The Context," in *Greater than the Parts: Holism in Biomedicine, 1920–1950*, ed. Christopher Lawrence and George Weisz (Oxford: Oxford University Press, 1998), 4, 11. James Bradley and Marguerite Dupree describe hydropathy's overlap with orthodoxy in its qualified practitioners and in its theoretical understanding of disease in "A Shadow of Orthodoxy? An Epistemology of British Hydropathy, 1840–1858," *Medical History* 47 (2003): 173–94.

9. Lilian R. Furst, ed., *Medical Progress and Social Reality: A Reader in Nineteenth-Century Medicine and Literature* (Albany: State University of New York Press, 2000), 4, 21. Similarly, Solomon Posen reads literary doctors as scientific and prestigious "during different periods," a role that "seem[s] unaffected by time, place or the changing social status of medical practitioners." This figure is "usually a male, tends to be arrogant and paternalistic. He is a man of action rather than contemplations. He works hard but he is not a good family man. He is aggressively irreligious, though he has his own ethical standards." Posen, *The Doctor in Literature: Satisfaction or Resentment?* (Oxford: Radcliffe, 2005), 2–3. What, then, are we to make of surgeon Carter's situation and Quain's complaints about medicine's poor status and rampant quackery?

158   10. Quain, "History and Progress," 776–77.

11. Additionally, as Roy Porter notes, quackery is particularly difficult to identify given the widespread use of the word and our inability to evaluate competence and integrity at a distance, leaving us in danger of "becoming way-laid with superficial characteristics." Porter, "Before the Fringe: 'Quackery' and the Eighteenth-Century Medical Market," in *Studies in the History of Alternative Medicine*, ed. Roger Cooter (New York: St. Martin's Press, 1988), 2.

12. As Mary E. Fissell notes, there is a "tendency in cultural history to-ward fetishizing the marginal." Fissell, "Making Meaning from the Margins: The New Cultural History of Medicine," in *Locating Medical History: The Stories and Their Meaning*, ed. Frank Husman and John Harley Warner (Baltimore, MD: Johns Hopkins University Press, 2004), 364. I hope to show that quack-ery is not about fringe practices but central to the understanding of ortho-doxy itself.

13. Edward Schiappa, *Defining Reality: Definitions and the Politics of Meaning* (Carbondale: Southern Illinois University Press, 2003), 7. Similarly, Charles E. Rosenberg and Janet Golden argue that "a disease does not exist as a social phenomenon until we agree that it does—until it is named." Rosenberg and Golden, introduction to *Framing Disease: Studies in Cultural History*, ed. Rosenberg and Golden (New Brunswick, NJ: Rutgers University Press, 1992), xiii.

14. Schiappa, *Defining Reality*, 82.

15. Thomas F. Gieryn, *Cultural Boundaries of Science: Credibility on the Line* (Chi-cago: University of Chicago Press, 1999), 1.

16. Ibid., 13. According to Gieryn, there are three types of contest: expul-sion (seeking to banish an incompatible authority), expansion (seeking author-ity in a field in which one was not an authority previously), and autonomy (claiming science's superiority to and independence from other activities such as commerce or politics) (*Cultural Boundaries of Science*, 16–18).

17. Ibid., 27.

18. Ibid., 3. W. F. Bynum examines the role of science in the eighteenth and early nineteenth century and argues that science mattered a great deal, even if it sometimes was ignored by individual doctors and despite the persistence of unscientific practices. Bynum, *Science and the Practice of Medicine in the Nineteenth Century* (Cambridge: Cambridge University Press, 1994), 219. Christopher Lawrence argues that the medical elite capitalized on science's prestige to bring the profession "in line with the rest of the Victorian establishment." Lawrence, *Medicine in the Making of Modern Britain, 1700–1920* (London: Routledge, 1994), 57. Conversely, in another work, Christopher Lawrence finds both deployment of scientific rhetoric and deliberate erasure of scientific language, especially by those protecting the high-status, patronage-based consultant system in London. Lawrence, "Incommunicable Knowledge: Science, Technology, and the Clinical Art in Britain, 1850–1914," *Journal of Contemporary History* 20, no. 4 (1985): 503–20.

19. Jacques Derrida, "Plato's Pharmacy," in *Dissemination*, by Jacques Derrida, trans. Barbara Johnson (Chicago: University of Chicago Press, 1981), 99. Original italics.

20. Raymond Williams, *Marxism and Literature* (Oxford: Oxford University Press, 1977), 165.

21. Ibid., 166–67.

22. W. F. Bynum and Roy Porter, eds., *Medical Fringe and Medical Orthodoxy, 1750–1850* (London: Croom Helm, 1987), 2.

23. Roy Porter, *Disease, Medicine, and Society in England, 1550–1860,* 2nd ed. (Cambridge: Cambridge University Press, 1995), 48. Christopher Lawrence also recognizes the Medical Act of 1858's failure to organize education and licensure (*Medicine in the Making*, 58). Irvine Loudon notes the failure of legislation alone to alter the medical landscape when he describes the failure of the Apothecaries Act of 1815 to curb so-called quackery by druggists. Loudon, "'The Vile Race of Quacks with Which This Country Is Infested,'" in *Medical Fringe and Medical Orthodoxy, 1750–1850,* ed. W. F. Bynum and Roy Porter (London: Croom Helm, 1987), 120. M. Jeanne Peterson concurs that quackery remained prominent after 1858, although she accounts for this by linking quacks to poor patients and orthodoxy to wealthier patients. Peterson, *The Medical Profession in Mid-Victorian London* (Berkeley: University of California Press, 1978), 38.

24. Smiles's *Self-Help* (1859) embraces a philosophy of "energetic individualism," which includes "action, conduct, self-culture, self-control . . . a kind of education not to be learned from books, or acquired by any amount of mere literary training." Smiles hails this philosophy as particularly English and classless, and he praises John Keats and Sir Humphrey Davy for rising from their low rank as apothecaries and Lord Denman for rising from the lowly rank of physician's son, a sign of medicine's status during the first half of the nineteenth century (25). Samuel Smiles, *Self-Help, with Illustrations of Character, Conduct, and Perseverance,* ed. Peter W. Sinnema (Oxford: World's Classics, 2002), 20.

25. Michael Neve, "Orthodoxy and Fringe: Medicine in Late Georgian Bristol," in Bynum and Porter, *Medical Fringe,* 50.

26. John Chapman, "Medical Despotism," *Westminster Review,* April 1856, 295.

27. Bynum and Porter similarly argue in their introduction to *Medical Fringe and Medical Orthodoxy* that the public could "vote with its feet" in matters of quackery (3).

28. Despite the social power of the gentleman-physician, Flannery notes that patients sometimes viewed them as out-of-touch, greedy, and elitist. Flannery focuses on the American context. Michael Flannery, introduction to *The English Physician,* by Nicholas Culpeper, ed. Michael A. Flannery (Tuscaloosa: University of Alabama Press, 2007), 22.

29. P. S. Brown, "Social Context and Medical Theory in the Demarcation of Nineteenth-Century Boundaries," in Bynum and Porter, *Medical Fringe,* 217.

160   30. Ibid. Helfand likewise finds that treatments offered by so-called quacks and by regular practitioners were often very similar, at least until the mid-nineteenth century (*Quack, Quack, Quack*, 14).

31. P. S. Brown, "Social Context," 230. In *Medical Fringe and Medical Orthodoxy*, Bynum and Porter foreground the difficulties of examining quackery in the public sphere, because "one age's quackery has often become another's orthodoxy, or vice versa" (1).

32. K. Codell Carter, "The Concept of Quackery in Early Nineteenth Century British Medical Periodicals," *Journal of Medical Humanities* 14, no. 2 (1993): 91.

33. Helfand, *Quack, Quack, Quack*, 11.

34. Ibid., 13.

35. Loudon, "Vile Race of Quacks," 107.

36. Helfand defines eighteenth-century quackery by practices including itinerancy, advertising, publishing (often testimonials supposedly by famous or royal patients), hyperbolic storytelling, and showmanship (*Quack, Quack, Quack*, 17–19).

37. Roy Porter, *Quacks: Fakers and Charlatans in Medicine* (Stroud, Gloucestershire: Tempus, 2003), 12.

38. George Eliot, *Middlemarch* (Harmondsworth, UK: Penguin, 1985), 117.

39. Self-Respect, "Social Position of the Profession," *Lancet*, October 2, 1858, 365.

40. David E. Shuttleton, *Smallpox and the Literary Imagination, 1660–1820* (Cambridge: Cambridge University Press, 2007), 3. In this, Shuttleton seems to depart from a methodology best summarized by Lilian Furst when she claims that literature gives "flesh" to the bare bones of medical history. Furst, *Between Doctors and Patients: The Changing Balance of Power* (Charlottesville: University of Virginia Press, 1988), x. Recent criticism that engages more fully with literature includes Miriam Bailin, *The Sickroom in Victorian Fiction: The Art of Being Ill* and Janis McLarren Caldwell, *Literature and Medicine in Nineteenth-Century Britain: From Mary Shelley to George Eliot*. Gillian Beer's landmark *Darwin's Plots: Evolutionary Narrative in Darwin, George Eliot and Nineteenth-Century Fiction*, while not recent or focused on medicine, explores the relationship between Darwinian thought and novels in a rich and fruitful way.

41. In *Discipline and Punish*, for example, Foucault introduces the panopticon as an image of state control over the individual through the power of the gaze. Medicine is endowed with similar power in *The Birth of the Clinic* and *The History of Sexuality*, both of which position medicine as a means of official control and allow little room for individual will or for social development and change, as other scholars have ably argued. D. A. Miller's *The Novel and the Police* (Berkeley: University of California Press, 1988) and Lawrence Rothfield's *Vital Signs: Medical Realism in Nineteenth-Century Fiction* (Princeton: Princeton University Press, 1992) describe a stable, hegemonic, medical orthodoxy.

42. Mary Poovey, *Uneven Developments: The Ideological Work of Gender in Mid-Victorian England* (Chicago: University of Chicago Press, 1988), 34. In contrast, Kristine Swenson's *Medical Women and Victorian Fiction* (Columbia: University of Missouri Press, 2005) questions this view of women practitioners but posits a stable medical orthodoxy nonetheless. See also Susan Wells, *Out of the Dead House: Nineteenth-Century Women Physicians and the Writing of Medicine* (Madison: University of Wisconsin Press, 2001). In contrast, studies of women consumers recognize female agency (although often without explicit attention to the medical marketplace). See Lori Anne Loeb, *Consuming Angels: Advertising and Victorian Women* (Oxford: Oxford University Press, 1994) and Erika Diane Rappaport, *Shopping for Pleasure: Women in the Making of London's West End* (Princeton: Princeton University Press, 2000).

43. Poovey, *Uneven Developments*, 166.

44. David Glover, *Vampires, Mummies, and Liberals: Bram Stoker and the Politics of Popular Fictions* (Durham, NC: Duke University Press, 1996), 9. Similar studies grounding literature in medical discourses include Robert Mighall, *A Geography of Victorian Gothic Fiction: Mapping History's Nightmares* (Oxford: Oxford University Press, 2003); Stephen Arata, *Fictions of Loss in the Victorian Fin de Siècle: Identity and Empire* (Cambridge: Cambridge University Press, 1996); and Nicholas Daly, *Modernism, Romance and the Fin de Siècle: Popular Fiction and British Culture* (Cambridge: Cambridge University Press, 1999). These insightful studies connect late Victorian texts with medical discourses such as sexology, criminal anthropology, and eugenics, although without, I assert, enough attention to the status of medical subfields in Victorian medicine or society.

45. George Weisz, *Divide and Conquer: A Comparative History of Medical Specialization* (Oxford: Oxford University Press, 2006), xix.

46. Ibid., 27–28.

47. Ibid., 27.

48. Notable studies of professionalism include Jennifer Ruth, *Novel Professions: Interested Disinterest and the Making of the Professional in the Victorian Novel* (Columbus: Ohio State University Press, 2006); Bruce Robbins, *Secular Vocations: Intellectuals, Professionalism, Culture* (London: Verso, 1993); and Susan E. Colón, *The Professional Ideal in the Victorian Novel: The Works of Disraeli, Trollope, Gaskell, and Eliot* (New York: Palgrave-Macmillan, 2007).

49. For some discussion of medical or quasi-medical fraud in the Victorian period, see Ian A. Burney, *Poison, Detection, and the Victorian Imagination* (Manchester: Manchester University Press, 2006) and Rebecca Stern, *Home Economics: Domestic Fraud in Victorian England* (Columbus: Ohio State University Press, 2008), which examines the pervasive nature of fraud in the domestic sphere, including in matters of adulterated food and legislation designed to ensure purity.

50. Amanda Anderson, *The Powers of Distance: Cosmopolitanism and the Cultivation of Detachment* (Princeton: Princeton University Press, 2001), 7.

51. Ibid., 4.

162   52. Elaine Scarry, *The Body in Pain: The Making and Unmaking of the World* (Oxford: Oxford University Press, 1985), 7.

Chapter 1: Orthodoxy or Quackery? Anatomy in *Frankenstein*

Epigraphs: "Regulation of Anatomy," *Westminster Review*, April 1832, 485; Select Committee on Anatomy, "Report from the Select Committee on Anatomy," HC (1828) 568 (1–150), 18 (in-text references are to this report).

1. Select Committee on Anatomy, "Report," 14.

2. In 1752, Parliament passed the Murder Act, which sentenced murderers not simply to death by public hanging but to dissection postmortem. Before it was repealed in 1832, the Murder Act provided the only legal method of obtaining anatomical specimens, and its connection between anatomy and punishment is often cited as the cause of anatomy's unpopularity, although the practice of anatomizing a few felons per year dates from the reign of Henry VIII. Douglas Hay explores the spectacle of the eighteenth-century public hanging as a complex event that delicately balanced majesty, justice, cruelty, and mercy and provided spectacular terror but was also keenly sensitive to public opinion. Hay, "Property, Authority and the Criminal Law," in Hay et al., *Albion's Fatal Tree: Crime and Society in Eighteenth-Century England* (New York: Pantheon, 1975), 18, 29, 43.

3. The Select Committee on Anatomy's report cites the 1788 *Rex vs. Lynn* case as the precedent that made possession of a snatched body a misdemeanor: "It is stated that there is scarcely a student or teacher of Anatomy in England, who under the law, if truly thus interpreted, is not indictable for a misdemeanor" (6).

4. Ludmilla Jordanova, "Melancholy Reflection: Constructing an Identity for Unveilers of Nature," in *Frankenstein: Creation and Monstrosity*, ed. Stephen Bann (London: Reaktion, 1994), 60. Maurice Hindle explores the novel in terms of early nineteenth-century sciences in general, particularly chemistry, and in terms of Coleridge's influence, as an artist and amateur man of science, on Mary Shelley. Hindle, "Vital Matters: Mary Shelley's *Frankenstein* and Romantic Science," *Critical Survey* 2, no. 1 (1990): 29–35. Similarly, Fred Botting argues that Shelley does not advocate a simple split between science and humanism but contends that Shelley's allusions to alchemy, chemistry, and physics imply that science fulfills humanism's aims, although "when science's technical power is allied with a human quest for authority the results are catastrophic." Botting, "Frankenstein and the Art of Science," in *Making Monstrous: Frankenstein, Criticism, Theory*, by Botting (Manchester: Manchester University Press, 1991), 176. Lester D. Friedman argues that Shelley does not condemn science so much as exhibit the interplay between scientific and social responsibilities. Friedman, "Sporting with Life: *Frankenstein* and the Responsibility of Scientific Research," *Medical Heritage* 1, no. 3 (1985): 181–85. In contrast, Alan Rauch argues that "there is little in the novel that actually describes Frankenstein's scientific

activity, much less his scientific context." Rauch, "The Monstrous Body of   163
Knowledge in Mary Shelley's *Frankenstein*," *Studies in Romanticism* 34 (1995): 228.

5. Jordanova, "Melancholy Reflection," 74, 60–61.

6. Ibid., 63.

7. Ibid., 72, 65.

8. Ibid., 65.

9. *Oxford English Dictionary*, s.v. "anatomy," online edition, http://www.oed.com.

10. Other subdefinitions of *anatomy* include dissection of a living body (definition II.b) and anatomy as a logical exercise (definition III). *Oxford English Dictionary*, s.v. "anatomy."

11. Of course, the belief in a "proper" burial can be seen even in antiquity, for example, in *The Iliad*, with its funeral games, and in *The Odyssey* when Odysseus meets the restless ghost of one of his men, who fell off a roof and died. The sailor begs Odysseus to bury him so he may enter Hades, which Odysseus does.

12. Ruth Richardson, *Death, Dissection and the Destitute* (London: Routledge, 1987), 266.

13. Ibid., 130.

14. Ibid.

15. For further discussion of this issue, see Hugh Douglas, *Burke and Hare: The True Story* (London: Hale, 1993); Brian Bailey, *The Resurrection Men: A History of the Trade in Corpses* (London: Macdonald, 1991); Suzanne M. Shultz, *Body Snatching: The Robbing of Graves for the Education of Physicians* (Jefferson, NC: McFarland, 1992); Tim Marshall, *Murdering to Dissect: Grave-Robbing, Frankenstein and the Anatomy Literature* (Manchester: Manchester University Press, 1995); and Mary Roach, *Stiff: The Curious Lives of Human Cadavers* (New York: Norton, 2003).

16. Bailey, *Resurrection Men*, 149.

17. Douglas, *Burke and Hare*, 155.

18. Richardson mentions supposedly lost folk practices such as washing the dead, using shrouds, and watching the corpse still occurring in the 1980s. Richardson, *Death*, 19, 21, 22.

19. Overviews of nineteenth-century medicine share this approach; for example, Lawrence Rothfield examines anatomy as a Foucaultian mode of social discipline. Rothfield, *Vital Signs: Medical Realism in Nineteenth-Century Fiction* (Princeton: Princeton University Press, 1992).

20. W. F. Bynum and Roy Porter, *William Hunter and the Eighteenth-Century Medical World* (Cambridge: Cambridge University Press, 1985), 2.

21. Roy Porter, "William Hunter: A Surgeon and a Gentleman," in *William Hunter and the Eighteenth-Century Medical World*, ed. W. F. Bynum and Roy Porter (Cambridge: Cambridge University Press, 1985), 22.

22. W. F. Bynum, *Science and the Practice of Medicine in the Nineteenth Century* (Cambridge: Cambridge University Press, 1994), 12.

23. Mary Shelley, *Frankenstein*, ed. Johanna M. Smith, 2nd ed. (Boston: Bedford/St. Martin's, 2000), 54. All in-text references are to this edition.

164   24. Samuel Holmes Vasbinder identifies the contemporary research to which Waldman refers in this speech, including anatomy. Vasbinder addresses anatomy as a medical science and mentions the difficulties anatomists had in obtaining bodies for dissection. Vasbinder, *Scientific Attitudes in Mary Shelley's Frankenstein* (Ann Arbor, MI: UMI Research Press, 1984), 75. In this chapter, I attempt to show that despite celebrated discoveries by Bichat, Harvey, and others, anatomy's scientific prestige was contested.

25. Crosbie Smith argues that Victor Frankenstein is not an orthodox scientist but an unbalanced creature tending toward genius and enthusiasm. Smith views Waldman's speech as a contrast between a true "man of science" and a "petty experimentalist." Smith, "*Frankenstein* and Natural Magic," in *Frankenstein, Creation, and Monstrosity*, ed. Stephen Bann (London: Reaktion, 1994), 51.

26. Judith Pike examines the female body in *Frankenstein* as fetish and argues that corpses in the novel should be read as corpses rather than as mere symbols. Pike, "Resurrection of the Fetish in *Gradiva, Frankenstein*, and *Wuthering Heights*," in *Romantic Women Writers: Voices and Countervoices*, ed. Paula R. Feldman and Theresa M. Kelly (Hanover, NH: University Press of New England, 1995). For discussion of the maternal body as symbol, see Barbara Johnson, "My Monster/My Self," *Diacritics* 12 (1982): 2–10; Mary Poovey, *The Proper Lady and the Woman Writer* (Chicago: University of Chicago Press, 1984); and Sandra Gilbert and Susan Gubar, *The Madwoman in the Attic: The Woman Writer and the Nineteenth-Century Literary Imagination* (New Haven, CT: Yale University Press, 1979).

27. Ellen Moers claims that the Gothic is always about fear and the body: "Its glands, muscles, epidermis, and circulatory system, quickly arousing and quickly allaying the physiological reactions to fear." Moers, "Female Gothic," in *The Endurance of Frankenstein: Essays on Mary Shelley's Novel*, ed. George Levine and U. C. Knoepflmacher (Berkeley: University of California Press, 1974), 77.

28. Judith Pike, in "Resurrection," calls the transformation of Elizabeth into Mrs. Frankenstein's corpse "a critical response to the idealization and fetishization of the exquisite corpse" (155). David Ketterer reads the scene in terms of Oedipal desire in *Frankenstein's Creation: The Book, the Monster, and Human Reality* (Victoria: University of Victoria Press, 1979). Anne K. Mellor does not explicitly address anatomy, but she points to Victor's use of bodies from churchyards as a violation of the "rhythms of nature." Mellor, *Mary Shelley: Her Life, Her Fiction, Her Monsters* (New York: Routledge, 1988), 101. Mellor argues that Walton and Victor view nature as "something separate from themselves, as passive and even dead matter" (110) and view human and animal bodies as "tools of [their] trade" (112). To Mellor, the female monster is particularly female rather than a dead body (or pieces of dead bodies) (119), and Victor's desire for his dead bride is also symbolic of necrophilia and incestuous desire for the mother rather than a dead body that he literally holds in his arms (121).

29. Pike, "Resurrection," 157.

30. Victor himself speaks of his creation as a Gothic double: "I considered the being whom I had cast among mankind . . . nearly in the light of my own vampire, my own spirit let loose from the grave, and forced to destroy all that was dear to me" (*Frankenstein*, 76). Christopher P. Toumey also notes the Gothic doubling of Victor and the creature in "The Moral Character of Mad Scientists: A Cultural Critique of Science," *Science, Technology and Human Values* 17, no. 4 (1992): 424. Ketterer discusses the doppelgänger motif at length in *Frankenstein's Creation*.

31. There might have been an appeal to nationalism in this report, because it repeatedly compares England unfavorably to continental Europe.

32. Mellor points to Shelley's concern with holism when she describes the overlap between Victor and the creature as both solitary and wretched. Mellor concludes that "organic modes of production and reproduction" will "protect and nurture all the products of nature—the old, the sick, the handicapped, the freaks—with love and compassion." Mellor, *Mary Shelley*, 135–37. In this chapter, I find Shelley using anatomy to extend an argument for holism into even scientific modes of inquiry.

33. Using Thomas S. Kuhn's well-known model of scientific paradigm shifts (Kuhn, *The Structure of Scientific Revolutions* [Chicago: University of Chicago Press, 1962]), Johanna M. Smith argues that Victor's conflict between alchemy and chemistry represents an incomplete paradigm shift because Paracelsus and Agrippa, Victor's first icons, were "also physicians and thus scientists" and "cannot simply be dismissed as nonscientists." Smith argues that "the pertinent distinction is not between false science (alchemy or natural magic) and true science (chemistry) but between a discredited form of science and a newly dominant scientific paradigm." Thus, Smith views Victor's laboratory as a multivalent space. Smith, "'Cooped Up' with 'Sad Trash': Domesticity and the Sciences in *Frankenstein*," in *Frankenstein*, ed. Johanna M. Smith (Boston: Bedford/St. Martin, 2000), 325–27.

34. Rauch, "Monstrous Body," 235. Challenging critics such as James Reiger and others, Vasbinder argues that Victor is not an alchemist and does not believe in the occult until after his breakdown. Vasbinder, *Scientific Attitudes*, 59, 54.

35. Rauch, "Monstrous Body," 235.

36. Ibid., 238–39, 246. Ketterer (in *Frankenstein's Creation*, 78) and Vasbinder (*Scientific Attitudes*, 79–80) likewise connect the creature's formation to electrical and galvanic experiments, including Darwin's with vermicelli and Aldini's with corpses, although Vasbinder does not stress the medical application as strongly as Rauch. Mellor mentions Galvani's experiments with executed corpses and Aldini's 1803 experiments with the hanged British felon Thomas Forster (*Mary Shelley*, 105).

37. Rauch, "Monstrous Body," 243. Friedman views the monster as proof of Victor's scientific success and argues that Victor's failures are social and ethical, not scientific ("Sporting with Life," 182).

166   38. Rauch, "Monstrous Body," 249. Rauch discusses patient frustration with deaths in childbirth during this period because of medicine's lack of knowledge, a topic surely familiar to Mary Shelley.

39. Marilyn Butler, "*Frankenstein* and Radical Science," in *Frankenstein*, ed. J. Paul Hunter (New York: Norton, 1996), 307.

40. Toumey ("Moral Character," 414) argues that the omission of scientific detail originates in antirationalism. Warren Montag argues that Shelley enacts a series of omissions in which scientific detail is suppressed, notably at the birth of the monster, and that this suppresses any reference to the material conditions of industrial culture of which the monster comes to be symbolic. Montag, "'The Workshop of Filthy Creation': A Marxist Reading of *Frankenstein*," in *Frankenstein*, ed. Johanna M. Smith (Boston: Bedford/St. Martin's, 2000), 392, 394. Marilyn Butler views the novel in the context of "evolutionary science," particularly the 1818 edition's allusions to the Abernethy and Lawrence debates at the Royal College of Surgeons, which she claims "opened up the way anatomy and physiology were taught to London medical students in the second decade of the century." Butler, "*Frankenstein* and Radical Science," 303–5.

41. Butler, "*Frankenstein* and Radical Science," 313.

42. Shelley's 1831 preface famously asserts that she "changed no portion of the story, nor introduced any new ideas or circumstances" (*Frankenstein*, 25); however, it is a critical commonplace to question this. For a brilliant discussion of these changes, see Mellor, *Mary Shelley.*

43. *Oxford English Dictionary*, s.v. "unhallowed," online edition, http://www.oed.com.

44. Peter Linebaugh, "The Tyburn Riot against the Surgeons," in Douglas Hay et al., *Albion's Fatal Tree: Crime and Society in Eighteenth-Century England* (New York: Pantheon, 1975), 65–117.

45. Anatomist James Somerville, in his testimony before the Select Committee on Anatomy, asserts that resurrection men drove up prices through fraudulent means: "The resurrection men are fully aware, that when the pupils first come to town, they are very anxious to proceed with their dissection, accordingly they create difficulties, in order to enhance the price" (48).

46. "Resurrection Men Have Lately Hit upon a New Mode of Getting Possession of Prey without the Trouble and Hazard," *Times* (London), September 27, 1823, available online at http://infotrac.galegroup.com.

47. "Extraordinary Attempt to Steal a Dead Body," *Times* (London), April 7, 1827, available online at http://infotrac.galegroup.com.

48. Ketterer examines questions of guilt, innocence, and justice when he notes the series of unfair trials in the novel and questions Victor's responsibility for the murders of William, Justine, Henry, and Elizabeth (*Frankenstein's Creation*, 101).

49. Moers, "Female Gothic," 80. Emphasis added.

50. Ibid., 83. Emphasis added.

51. Mellor, *Mary Shelley*, 122–23.   167

52. Ibid., 124. Quotation of Mary Shelley.

53. For a discussion of Victor's usurpation of female reproduction, see references in note 26.

54. "Anatomy," *Westminster Review*, January 1829, 129.

55. *Oxford English Dictionary*, s.v. "burke," online edition, http://www.oed.com.

56. Richardson, *Death*, 132. For Richardson, Robert Knox exemplifies anatomy's complicity in crime and anatomists' privilege as members of the middle class, in contrast to the poor, who expressed their discontent with his conduct through folk punishments such as effigy abuse and "skimmington" (mob harassment by loud music and jeering). She calls this "symbolic punishment" that shows "popular disgust towards Knox" and "a thorough disgust of the legal process" (138).

57. Ibid., 140.

58. [David] Paterson, "Letter to the Lord Advocate, disclosing the accomplices, secrets and other facts relative to the Late Murders; with a correct account of the manner in which the anatomical schools are supplied with subjects" [1829], in *Burke and Hare: The Resurrection Men*, ed. Jacques Barzun (Metuchen, NJ: Scarecrow, 1974).

59. Shultz, *Body Snatching*, 70.

60. Paterson, "Letter," 257.

61. "What Is Our Land Come To?" in Barzun, *Burke and Hare*, 345.

62. *History of the London Burkers* (London, 1832), 365. A burking incident involving the notorious Bishop and Williams occurred in London in 1831, just prior to the passage of the Anatomy Act, but the medical men in this case informed police.

63. Ibid., 6.

64. Ibid., 332. This quotation also addresses other surgeons involved in burking cases, notably, the London Burkers.

65. *Deadly Adulteration and Slow Poisoning Unmasked* (London, 1839), 155.

66. MacGregor's text is the sole source for the "William Burke" entry in the 1911 *Encyclopedia Britannica*. See George MacGregor, *The History of Burke and Hare and of the Resurrectionist Times* (Glasgow, 1884).

67. "An Expostulation," in MacGregor, *History of Burke and Hare*, 288–89.

68. "William Burke," in ibid., 291.

69. Ibid., 291.

70. "Regulation of Anatomy," *Westminster Review*, 491.

71. "The Philosophy of Burking," *Fraser's Magazine*, February 1832, 52–55. In this version of events, Dr. Knox is not told of the method of procuring specimens, since "he is, in all probability, labouring under the same superstitious prejudices as the rest of the public." Yet the commentary notes the irony of Burke and Hare's arrest in terms that could easily apply to Knox: "[T]hese distinguished individuals, whose minds were unweariedly [sic] directed to protect their countrymen

168   from *murders* at the hands of ignorant physicians and surgeons . . . were charged with being themselves guilty of *murder*" (56–58). Original italics.

Chapter 2: Doctoring in *Little Dorrit* and *Bleak House*

Epigraphs: "Quackery on Its Death-Bed," *Lancet*, October 16, 1858, 405; "Important Educational Changes," *Lancet*, June 12, 1858, 586.

    1. *Oxford English Dictionary*, s.v. "doctor," online edition, http://www.oed.com. Definitions 2a, b for *doctor* as verb.

    2. Ibid., definition 3.

    3. Concern about authenticity appears in many novels during the mid-Victorian period, not exclusively in the medical context. The forged document, the stolen inheritance, and the assumed identity feature in novels such as Charlotte Brontë's *Jane Eyre* (1847), Wilkie Collins's *The Woman in White* (1860), Charles Dickens's *Great Expectations* (1861), Mary Elizabeth Braddon's *Lady Audley's Secret* (1862), and Anthony Trollope's *The Way We Live Now* (1875).

    4. Richard D. Mallen, "George Eliot and the Precious Mettle of Trust," *Victorian Studies* 44 (2001): 60.

    5. In his examination of blackmail in George Eliot's novels, Alexander Welsh describes a paradox in which modern systems such the credit economy create the need for privacy and trust and also open the door to blackmail, since blackmail is only possible in societies that value privacy and trust. Welsh, *George Eliot and Blackmail* (Cambridge, MA: Harvard University Press, 1985).

    6. In her examination of professionalism, Jennifer Ruth examines the "double discourse of value" in which finance offers one sort of value and culture another. For Ruth, the Victorian professional is "inside and outside the market—at once complicit and transcendent—is not a counterfeit but a dialectic—that is, a position that works both ways, enabling but also destabilizing the system within which it functions." Ruth, *Novel Professions: Interested Disinterest and the Making of the Professional in the Victorian Novel* (Columbus: Ohio State University Press, 2006), 22.

    7. Patrick Brantlinger examines the connection between money and fiction, both of which rely on "credit." Brantlinger, *Fictions of State: Culture and Credit in Britain, 1694–1994* (Ithaca, NY: Cornell University Press, 1996), 144. Daniel Hack's reading of *Bleak House* focuses on the "materiality of documents and the interpretation of that materiality," and Hack argues that spontaneous combustion is a vital element of the book because of its symbolic troubling of material bodies and texts. Hack, *The Material Interests of the Victorian Novel* (Charlottesville: University of Virginia Press, 2005), 38.

    8. Charles Dickens, preface to *Bleak House* (New York: Bantam, 1992), xxvii.

    9. Ibid.

    10. Authenticity was a concern prior to the Victorian period (for example, the eighteenth-century epistolary novel routinely masquerades as personal

correspondence); however, the mid-Victorian defense of avowedly *fictional*   169
characters and events as authentic implies a deep concern with issues of textual authenticity and authority. Wilkie Collins's sensation novel *The Woman in
White* includes a preface claiming fictional authenticity in response to charges
of improbable plot points and characters, and indeed Collins claims that he
used real people as models for Count Fosco so as to render the Count "as true
to nature as I have tried to make him." Collins, *The Woman in White* (Oxford:
World's Classics, 1999), 645. Similarly, George Eliot's "Prelude" to *Middlemarch*
pleads for Dorothea's plausibility by comparing her to St. Theresa of Avila.
Eliot, *Middlemarch* (Harmondsworth, UK: Penguin, 1985), 26. Aside from his
medical authenticity, Dickens defends his representation of the Chancery suit,
Jarndyce and Jarndyce, as "substantially true and within the truth." Dickens,
preface to *Bleak House*, xxvi.

11. Chapter 1 examines Sir Astley Cooper's claim that dissection formed
the basis for surgery's prestige because of its scientific nature (grounding that
which can be inauthentic [prestige] in that which is [considered] authentic and
verifiable [science]). Richard Quain's Harveian Oration similarly cites scientific breakthroughs to bolster medical prestige. Quain, "History and Progress
of Medicine," *British Medical Journal*, October 24, 1885, 775–81.

12. Roy Porter argues that a practitioner's conduct mattered greatly because of the power of patients, Poor Law boards, and Friendly Societies to
discard an unpopular practitioner in an overcrowded profession. Porter, *Disease, Medicine, and Society in England, 1550–1860*, 2nd ed. (Cambridge: Cambridge
University Press, 1995), 51. Similarly, M. Jeanne Peterson argues that science
was less important practically than a practitioner's social position (*The Medical Profession in Mid-Victorian London* [Berkeley: University of California Press,
1978], 47), and Lawrence Rothfield finds charisma to be a key component in
medical professionalization (*Vital Signs: Medical Realism in Nineteenth-Century Fiction* [Princeton: Princeton University Press, 1992], 47). Lilian Furst notes that
Victorian practitioners failed to implement scientific advances, as in the case
of the stethoscope, which took at least thirty years to become commonplace.
Furst, *Medical Progress and Social Reality: A Reader in Nineteenth-Century Medicine and
Literature* (Albany: State University of New York Press, 2000), 2. In contrast,
W. F. Bynum contends that "science did matter to doctors collectively, even if
it could be neglected by them individually" (*Science and the Practice of Medicine in
the Nineteenth Century* [Cambridge: Cambridge University Press, 1994], 219), and
Christopher Lawrence argues that "science was projected into an ever more
prominent position" (*Medicine in the Making of Modern Britain, 1700–1920* [London:
Routledge, 1994], 34).

13. Bynum, *Science*, 109.

14. Janis McLarren Caldwell, *Literature and Medicine in Nineteenth-Century Britain: From Mary Shelley to George Eliot* (Cambridge: Cambridge University Press,
2004), 8.

170   15. Porter, *Disease, Medicine, and Society*, 48.

16. A Surgeon, "The Police and the Medical Profession," *Times* (London), March 7, 1850. Michel Foucault's *The Birth of the Clinic* connects the medical gaze of the teaching hospital with disciplinary power, but this physician clearly discriminates between his duty as a medical practitioner and the policeman's duty as the agent of the law.

17. Self-Respect, "Social Position of the Profession," *Lancet*, October 2, 1858, 365.

18. Quid Pro Quo, "The Cholera and the Poor Law Medical Officers," *Times* (London), September 3, 1850.

19. Ernest Hart, "The Condition of Our State Hospitals," *Fortnightly Review*, December 1, 1865, 222.

20. J. G. Wood, "Inner Life of a Hospital," *Cornhill*, April 1862, 463.

21. "Quackery on Its Death-Bed," *Lancet*, 405.

22. "Important Educational Changes," *Lancet*, 586.

23. Quain, "History and Progress," 775.

24. Miriam Bailin, *The Sickroom in Victorian Fiction: The Art of Being Ill* (Cambridge: Cambridge University Press, 1994), 79.

25. Ibid., 81.

26. Charles Dickens, *Little Dorrit*, ed. Stephen Wall and Helen Small (London: Penguin, 2003), 672. All in-text references to *Little Dorrit* are to this edition.

27. Mallen, "George Eliot," 43.

28. There are two even more minor medical men in this novel, the surgeon who treats John Baptist and the doctor in the Marshalsea who delivers Amy.

29. Amanda Anderson, *The Powers of Distance: Cosmopolitanism and the Cultivation of Detachment* (Princeton: Princeton University Press, 2001), 76. In Anderson's reading, Merdle signals the dangers of global capitalism (*Powers of Distance*, 88). Similarly, Patrick Brantlinger argues that Merdle's suicide illustrates the dangers of the investment system, although the novel defends banking in general (*Fictions of State*, 160). Audrey Jaffe calls Merdle "a personification of every character's inner speculator" who signals an internalization of the "drama of the stock market." Jaffe, *The Affective Life of the Average Man: The Victorian Novel and the Stock-Market Graph* (Columbus: Ohio State University Press, 2010), 58.

30. Avrom Fleishman notes the anti-Semitic nature of the Victorian Jewish financier, such as Melmotte in Trollope's *The Way We Live Now*. Fleishman, *Fiction and the Ways of Knowing: Essays on British Novels* (Austin: University of Texas Press, 1978).

31. Jeff Nunokawa, *The Afterlife of Property: Domestic Security and the Victorian Novel* (Princeton: Princeton University Press, 1994), 8.

32. Christopher Herbert, "Filthy Lucre: Victorian Ideas of Money," *Victorian Studies* 44 (2002): 191.

33. Monica F. Cohen, *Professional Domesticity in the Victorian Novel: Women, Work and Home* (Cambridge: Cambridge University Press, 1998), 115–16.

34. In her reading of the sickroom in Dickens's fiction, Miriam Bailin (*Sick-* room *in Victorian Fiction*, 89) notes the dangerous nature of the sickroom, which offers both to restore identity and to arrest its development, as in Maggy's case.

35. Ruth, *Novel Professions*, 17.

36. Jeff Nunokawa describes a disjuncture between acquiring wealth and owning it (*Afterlife of Property*, 24–28); however, Dorrit's blindness to affective economy is not simply psychological distance of the marketplace but fraud: his erasures of his own methods of acquisition are part of a larger pattern of deception and misrepresentation that inflicts damage on both his own psyche and Amy.

37. To Amanda Anderson, Arthur Clennam's guilt about his business is a symptom of larger imperialist guilt (*Powers of Distance*, 72). To Jeff Nunokawa, Clennam's guilt is accumulation of wealth at all, since in Nunokawa's reading all wealth must circulate, inevitably leaving the purchaser "as night follows day" (*Afterlife of Property*, 22).

38. Cohen, *Professional Domesticity*, 124.

39. Ibid., 118. In contrast, Amanda Anderson examines Daniel Doyce as a representative of vocation, a "nationalistic vocationalism," because of his dedication to craftsmanship, but Doyce suffers from a narrow view, an inability to interpret society, and an incapacity for detachment (*Powers of Distance*, 84–85).

40. Several critics interpret Arthur Clennam and Amy's marriage in the Marshalsea as a reconciliation or negotiation. Dianne F. Sadoff reads Arthur's marriage to Amy, the "redeeming daughter," as a way to "heal the wounds" his search for his own origins has opened. Sadoff, *Monsters of Affection: Dickens, Eliot, and Brontë on Fatherhood* (Baltimore, MD: Johns Hopkins University Press, 1982), 57. The identification of Clennam as "wounded" seems to allude to, if not explicitly address, illness in the novel. John Kucich identifies Amy and Arthur's language at the end as mediating between self-destruction and power. John Kucich, *Repression in Victorian Fiction: Charlotte Brontë, George Eliot, and Charles Dickens* (Berkeley: University of California Press, 1987). Jeff Nunokawa reads the scene as Clennam's possession of Amy Dorrit, where marriage stabilizes property (*Afterlife of Property*, 30).

41. Ruth, *Novel Professions*, 19.

42. Examining *Bleak House*, Laura Fasick argues that disease in Dickens's novels is a "marker of social wrong" and observes that diseases that spread from the poor to the wealthy allow Dickens to advocate personal responsibility and systemic reform simultaneously. In *Little Dorrit*, Merdle's complaint spreads from the wealthy to the poor, and so complicates this circulation. Fasick, "Dickens and the Diseased Body in *Bleak House*," *Dickens Studies Annual* 24 (1996): 140.

43. Jeremy Tambling speculates that in *Bleak House*'s Woodcourt and in *Little Dorrit*'s Physician, Dickens's analysis "goes soft." Tambling, introduction to *Bleak House: Charles Dickens*, ed. Jeremy Tambling (New York: St. Martin's, 1998), 12. For a discussion of Woodcourt as an undeveloped or clichéd character, see

172   Bruce Robbins, "Telescopic Philanthropy: Professionalism and Responsibility in *Bleak House*," in Tambling, *Bleak House: Charles Dickens;* and Lauren M. E. Goodlad, *Victorian Literature and the Victorian State: Character and Governance in a Liberal Society* (Baltimore, MD: Johns Hopkins University Press, 2003).

44. John Kucich identifies a tension in Dickens's work between "wishing to annihilate the self, but also to conserve it at the same time"; thus, self-promotion is the "chief sin" of Dickens's characters, so successful characters must seek "self-circumscribing forms of desire" to avoid becoming "martyrs" or "ascetics." Kucich, *Repression in Victorian Fiction*, 207–8.

45. Robbins, "Telescopic Philanthropy," 143.

46. Ibid., 154.

47. Charles Dickens, *Bleak House* (New York: Bantam, 1992), 129. All in-text references to *Bleak House* are to this edition.

48. In this respect, Vholes is a kind of sinister Wemmick from *Great Expectations.*

49. Chancery's anxiety over textual authenticity mirrors Dickens's own anxiety that the text of this novel be considered authentic, despite its rather far-fetched plot points involving coincidence and spontaneous combustion. William F. Axton examines the language of science and of Providence in the novel ("Religious and Scientific Imagery in *Bleak House*," *Nineteenth-Century Fiction* 22, no. 4 [1968]: 349–59), and Daniel Hack in *Material Interests of the Victorian Novel* examines the relationship between material writing and character.

50. Richard's failure to progress in his medical training is significant: when he abandons medicine for Chancery, Esther and readers feel he has chosen the wrong path (*Bleak House*, 156).

51. F. S. Schwarzbach argues that there is a parallel between Woodcourt and Dickens; both enter the dark, diseased, miasmic courts of London and cleanse them by letting in air and light, Woodcourt literally as a physician and Dickens metaphorically as a novelist. Schwarzbach, "*Bleak House*: The Social Pathology of English Life," *Literature and Medicine* 9 (1990): 98.

52. Goodlad argues that the midcentury period witnessed the decline of the "middle-class hero-expert" who pioneered sanitary reform, in favor of a more gentlemanly model (*Victorian Literature*, 102).

53. Eric G. Lorentzen argues that *Bleak House* critiques imperial philanthropy since Woodcourt's absence allows the outbreak of domestic disease: "As a physician, only by treating domestic illness can Woodcourt help to improve the salubrity of home; as a charitable philanthropist, only by concentrating on the domestic malaise can Woodcourt improve the social ills." Lorentzen, "'Obligations of Home': Colonialism, Contamination, and Revolt in *Bleak House*," *Dickens Studies Annual* 34 (2004): 170.

54. Schwarzbach argues that Dickens critiques the social systems that allowed diseased slums to fester in the heart of London. Woodcourt's retreat to the "improbably pastoral" Yorkshire symbolizes, for Schwarzbach, the role of

the physician in Dickensian reform: "In that struggle he saw the selfless work 173
of humble and self-sacrificing physicians as a model worthy not only of respect
but of profound emulation as well" ("Bleak House," 102).

55. "Important Educational Changes," Lancet, 586.

56. "Of the Three Learned Professions," Times (London), January 25, 1856.

57. Ibid.

58. Quid Pro Quo, "The Cholera and the Poor Law Medical Officers,"
Times (London), September 3, 1850.

59. W.T.M., "The Medical Staff in the Crimea," Times (London), November
24, 1854.

60. "Lord Palmerston's Declaration on Medical Reform," Lancet, July 9,
1853, 36.

61. Eric G. Lorentzen notes the connection between imperial concerns
and domestic dirt and disease in the disordered home of the Jellybys, arguing that imperial concerns generate domestic disease. He also notes that such
enterprises degrade the Pardiggle children to a state of savagery. Lorentzen,
"'Obligations of Home.'" For a discussion of the antifeminism of these portray-
als, see Goodlad, Victorian Literature.

62. Lorentzen, "'Obligations of Home,'" 163.

63. In D. A. Miller's The Novel and the Police, knowledge and power together
inform the detective as an agent of control. Similarly, Lauren Goodlad argues
that Bucket displays "charismatic authority" as he supports the status quo (Victorian Literature, 98). In contrast, in "Bleak House: The Social Pathology of English
Life," Schwarzbach argues that Dickens both enacts and critiques medical discourse and its associated middle-class reform.

64. Welsh, George Eliot and Blackmail, 16.

65. According to Bruce Robbins, Dr. Woodcourt is a "thin character," so
much so that Esther marries his "profession" rather than himself because of his
"limited but systematic professional action" ("Telescopic Philanthropy," 145). She
does indeed, although not quite in the spirit Robbins implies, given the resonances of Woodcourt's profession in the novel. Schwarzbach argues that Dickens
is keenly aware of the affinities between reformers and the systems in need of
reforming; however, he asserts that "Dickens cannot fault the men who practice
it" ("Bleak House," 101).

66. Sadoff, Monsters of Affection, 59. Miriam Bailin reads Esther's two illnesses
as a separation from her identity, an "inability to reconcile past and present
selves" (Sickroom in Victorian Fiction, 87). Laura Fasick argues that Esther's scarring
and her continued beauty in the eyes of Jarndyce and Woodcourt reveal the
bodilessness of the middle-class heroine, whose affect trumps her physicality.
Fasick sees this as Dickens's privileging of personal virtue over systemic reform
("Dickens and the Diseased Body," 142).

67. Michael S. Gurney, "Disease as Device: The Role of Smallpox in
Bleak House," Literature and Medicine 9 (1990): 86. Gurney argues that Esther and

174   Woodcourt's marriage embodies the human bonds that are broken by others in this diseased society ("Disease as Device," 142).

Chapter 3: Legerdemain and the Physician in Charlotte Brontë's *Villette*

Epigraph: Robert M. Glover, "Lectures on the Philosophy of Medicine: Lecture VI," *Lancet*, January 11, 1851, 35.

1. Miriam Bailin argues that Victorian novels turn "social pathologies into bodily ailment." Bailin, *The Sickroom in Victorian Fiction: The Art of Being Ill* (Cambridge: Cambridge University Press, 1994), 5. For an examination of Lucy's illness as madness, see Sandra Gilbert and Susan Gubar, *The Madwoman in the Attic: The Woman Writer and the Nineteenth-Century Literary Imagination* (New Haven, CT: Yale University Press, 1979). Conversely, Philip Rogers argues that the "Faubourg Clotilde" chapter alludes to an eighteenth-century hoax involving poetry supposedly written by a medieval woman, Clothilde. Rogers, "Fraudulent Closure in *Villette's* 'Faubourg Clotilde,'" *Brontë Studies* 30 (2005): 125–30.

2. Athena Vrettos, "From Neurosis to Narrative: The Private Life of the Nerves in *Villette* and *Daniel Deronda*," *Victorian Studies* 33, no. 4 (1990): 556.

3. Ibid., 563, 566. Vrettos argues that the ending of the novel, and Lucy's supposed cure, is held in abeyance by the ambiguous closure (576).

4. Sally Shuttleworth, "'The Surveillance of the Sleepless Eye': The Constitution of Neurosis in *Villette*," in *One Culture: Essays in Science and Literature*, ed. George Levine (Madison: University of Wisconsin Press, 1987), 313.

5. Nicholas Dames, "The Clinical Novel: Phrenology and *Villette*," *Novel* 29, no. 3 (Spring 1996): 367. Dames draws upon Foucault's concept of the clinical gaze, which penetrates and normalizes its subject matter. Margaret L. Shaw similarly views this novel as a model of contemporary hermeneutics: "Brontë's method of reading seems to repeat paradigms of meaning/making already existing in the phrenological and physiognomic readings of contemporary alienists." Shaw, "Narrative Surveillance and Social Control in *Villette*," *SEL* 34, no. 4 (1994): 820.

6. Following Lucy's lead, critics tend to view John's lapses in conduct as accidental or innocuous. Amanda Anderson calls John "a model of professional discretion and genuine altruism." Anderson, *The Powers of Distance: Cosmopolitanism and the Cultivation of Detachment* (Princeton: Princeton University Press, 2001), 60. Nicholas Dames calls John a "true doctor" in a "world of amateur physicians and psychologists" ("Clinical Novel," 381). Monica F. Cohen argues that John is a "transgressor" when playing the lover but not when acting as a doctor. Cohen, *Professional Domesticity in the Victorian Novel: Women, Work and Home* (Cambridge: Cambridge University Press, 1998), 56.

7. "Quackery on Its Death-Bed," *Lancet*, October 16, 1858, 405. The 1858 Medical Act created a register of licensed practitioners and was hailed as the

defeat of quackery; however, according to Roy Porter, the *Lancet*'s antiquackery   175
campaign dates from the 1820s. Porter, *Quacks: Fakers and Charlatans in Medicine*
(Stroud, Gloucestershire: Tempus, 2003), 310.

8. "The First of October," *British Medical Journal*, September 25, 1858, 811.

9. Homeopathy reasons that if a compound can cause certain symptoms
then a diluted version of the compound may cure these symptoms because the
dilutions increase the potency of the original compound. Hydropathy involves
bathing in and/or ingesting water. Several of these beliefs have long histories,
both before and after the mid-Victorian period.

10. Glover, "Lectures," 35.

11. *Oxford English Dictionary*, s.v. "legerdemain," online edition, http://www
.oed.com. *Legerdemain* is here italicized to emphasize its foreign origin and its
relative unpopularity today. Literary usages from the *OED* date from the six-
teenth century and include authors such as Spencer, Beaumont and Fletcher,
and Coleridge.

12. Glover, "Lectures," 36.

13. Thomas F. Gieryn, *Cultural Boundaries of Science: Credibility on the Line* (Chicago: University of Chicago Press, 1999), 181.

14. Ibid. In Gieryn's view, phrenology was recognized as quackery in the
1830s, but in Shuttleworth's and Dames's articles phrenology was equated with
orthodoxy in the 1850s.

15. William H. Helfand argues that "hard and fast lines" between quackery
and orthodoxy have always been "difficult, if not impossible, to draw." Helfand, *Quack, Quack, Quack: The Sellers of Nostrums in Prints, Posters, Ephemera and Books*
(New York: Grolier, 2002), 25. Similarly, W. F. Bynum and Roy Porter recognize quackery's persistence and malleability in observing that "one age's quackery has often become another's orthodoxy, or vice versa." Bynum and Porter,
Medical Fringe and Medical Orthodoxy, 1750–1850 (London: Croom Helm, 1987), 1.

16. Porter, *Quacks*, 321.

17. "British College of Health," *Times* (London), April 18, 1848; "Works of
James Morrison," *Times* (London), June 25, 1861. A single snake coils around
the staff of Asclepius. The caduceus is a winged staff encircled by two snakes
and represents Hermes (the trickster god). Hygeia is the daughter of Asclepius
and the goddess of health: her symbol is a bowl with a serpent drinking from it.

18. Helfand, *Quack, Quack, Quack*, 43; Porter, *Quacks*, 318.

19. "Hygiean System of Medicine," *Times* (London), March 24, 1856.

20. "Morison versus Moat," *Lancet*, December 20, 1851, 586.

21. Glover, "Lectures," 35.

22. "Quacks and Their Impostures," *Lancet*, December 24, 1853, 604.

23. Christopher Lawrence, *Medicine in the Making of Modern Britain, 1700–1920*
(London: Routledge, 1994), 34.

24. "The Profession and Its Dignity," *Lancet*, March 27, 1858, 318. Original
italics.

176   25. Helfand, *Quack, Quack, Quack*, 32.

26. Porter, *Quacks*, 306.

27. Ibid., 310. As Roy Porter argues, mesmerists, hydropathists, homeopaths, and other fringe practitioners may have genuinely believed that their system was superior to orthodox medicine (*Quacks*, 319). Wakley's crusade against quackery raises similar issues of belief and self-interest, because his crusade (earnest as it was) also benefited his business enterprise. Helfand asserts that Victorian culture was skeptical of any heated rhetoric in medicine, viewing it as "the chatter of the quack" (*Quack, Quack, Quack*, 14).

28. Helfand, *Quack, Quack, Quack*, 17.

29. Ibid., 37.

30. "Medical Quackery and Mr. John St. John Long," *Fraser's Magazine*, October 1830, 265.

31. Ibid., 264.

32. "On Quackery, Twaddle, and Other Offences," *Fraser's Magazine*, April 1831, 371. While "Medical Quackery" treats testimonials as genuine documents written by dupes, "On Quackery" implies that testimonials were written by quacks themselves or by professional writers. Helfand discourages the division of quacks into sincere and insincere, because such matters are difficult, or even impossible, to settle (*Quack, Quack, Quack*, 15).

33. [G. H. Lewes,] "Physicians and Quacks," *Blackwood's Magazine*, February 1862, 167.

34. Ibid., 165.

35. Benjamin Brodie, "Homoeopathy," *Fraser's Magazine*, September 1861, 340.

36. Helfand, *Quack, Quack, Quack*, 16, 27. Roy Porter also addresses issues of scapegoating of quacks through such epithets (*Quacks*, 29). Of course, Victorians did not believe that all quacks were actually foreign. On the contrary, a medical commentator in the *Lancet* bewailed the fact that "[q]uackery flourishes right heartily in the United Kingdom, and its votaries discover in it a product and congenial soil." "Scandalous Proceedings of the Advertising Quacks," *Lancet*, November 19, 1853, 489. Michael A. Flannery also identifies exotic ingredients in orthodox prescriptions, such as plants from the East Indies and ground mummy, presumably from Egypt. Flannery, introduction to *The English Physician*, by Nicholas Culpeper, ed. Flannery (Tuscaloosa: University of Alabama Press, 2007), 16.

37. "Quackery and the Quacked," *Fraser's Magazine*, June 1848, 652.

38. Ibid., 649.

39. Helfand, *Quack, Quack, Quack*, 33.

40. "Avis Tres Important! [sic]," *Times* (London), June 24, 1842.

41. "Certificate Written by His Highness the Prince," *Times* (London), July 28, 1836.

42. K. Codell Carter, "The Concept of Quackery in Early Nineteenth Century British Medical Periodicals," *Journal of Medical Humanities* 14, no. 2 (1993): 92.

43. Ibid., 93–94.

44. Charlotte Brontë, *Villette* (New York: Signet-Penguin, 1987), 3. All in-text references in this chapter refer to this edition. Monica F. Cohen in *Professional Domesticity in the Victorian Novel: Women, Work and Home* and Amanda Anderson in *The Powers of Distance: Cosmopolitanism and the Cultivation of Detachment* point to the importance of homes and homelessness in the novel.

45. Cohen, *Professional Domesticity*, 56.

46. Anderson, *Powers of Distance*, 61.

47. Rogers, "Fraudulent Closure," 128; Dames, "Clinical Novel," 374.

48. Glover, "Lectures," 35.

49. F. J. Brown, "Quackery in Opposition to Truth," *British Medical Journal*, October 30, 1858, 916.

50. Ibid.

51. Amanda Anderson views Mme. Beck's power as "negative and as culturally alien" because it is lacking in privacy and affect (*Powers of Distance*, 49).

52. Hippocrates, "Greek Medicine: The Hippocratic Oath," www.mlm.mih.gov /hmd/greek/greek_oath.html.

53. Lucy states that many girls claim "having received an admiring beam from our young doctor's blue eyes" (*Villette*, 103). Cohen asserts that John "functions as an agent of romance" (*Professional Domesticity*, 62).

54. Monica F. Cohen explains John's contradictory behavior according to place: John appears "noble" and "philanthropic" in public but "insensitive" and "vain" at home, which is the privileged site of authenticity (*Professional Domesticity*, 61). Does medicine complicate the home/away division, since its work takes place in private spaces (the patients' homes)?

55. *Oxford English Dictionary*, s.v. "rogue," online edition, http://www.oed.com.

56. "Quacks and Their Impostures," *Lancet*, December 24, 1853, 604.

57. "The First of October," *British Medical Journal*, September 25, 1858, 812.

58. Nicholas Dames argues that Rosine's sexual overtures to John are a mask for Lucy's own desire, which Lucy masks by describing Rosine in phrenological terms ("Clinical Novel," 372).

59. John Kucich, *Repression in Victorian Fiction: Charlotte Brontë, George Eliot, and Charles Dickens* (Berkeley: University of California Press, 1987), 47.

60. "I'll never be the wife of a bourgeois" (my translation).

61. Monica F. Cohen points to the importance of retrospection in this novel. Cohen argues that the domestic is privileged as the more truthful but relies upon retrospection, since private knowledge "is not privileged by any virtue proper to itself but derives its value from its relationship to what has already been seen from the outside" (*Professional Domesticity*, 61).

62. Dianne F. Sadoff argues that the play shows the pleasure in enacting desire. Sadoff, *Monsters of Affection: Dickens, Eliot, and Brontë on Fatherhood* (Baltimore, MD: Johns Hopkins University Press, 1982), 161. Kucich recognizes important similarities between John, Ginevra, and Lucy: "The three figures

178   are finally so complicated in their jealousies and triumphs—as the dizzying role reversals of the vaudeville suggest in a nutshell—that they manifest endless permutations of rivalry without finally fixing it" (*Repression in Victorian Fiction*, 108).

63. As Nicholas Dames shows, Brontë uses the language of phrenology throughout the novel, such as when Paul advises Mme. Beck to hire Lucy. In this instance, phrenology offers only commonsense advice: Paul admits that either good or evil may come of hiring Lucy ("Clinical Novel," 61). Simply to contrast phrenology and orthodox medicine misses Brontë's examination of the ways such categories are constructed.

64. Like John, many critics view the nun as a manifestation of Lucy's psyche. Cohen claims that medicine "materializes" Lucy's "inner life," including her loneliness and lovesickness (*Professional Domesticity*, 55). To Kucich, the nun is a symbol not merely of simple repression but of performance as well, the performance of repression (*Repression in Victorian Fiction*, 69). Sadoff argues that the nun is a symbol of repression and of desire, Lucy's "desire to put aside her desire" (*Monsters of Affection*, 153).

65. Shuttleworth, "Surveillance," 314–15.

66. "Quacks and Their Impostures," *Lancet*, December 24, 1853, 605.

67. "Quackery and the Quacked," *Fraser's Magazine*, June 1848, 650.

68. Nicholas Dames reads Lucy's quarrel with Graham as her assertion of phrenological knowledge; based on this, Dames argues that Lucy and her readers enact a dance of "clinical desire" and "hide and seek" ("Clinical Novel," 388). In contrast, Margaret L. Shaw argues that Brontë was "distrustful of outward behavior" although Shaw contends that Brontë portrays contemporary male doctors attempting to inscribe women into conventional femininity using outward appearance as a tool (Shaw, "Narrative Surveillance," 822, 825). In "The Surveillance of the Sleepless Eye," Shuttleworth likewise argues that Lucy resists John's diagnosis.

69. Lawrence, *Medicine in the Making*, 68. Roy Porter also asserts the relative power of Victorian patients and the physician's need to "please his patients" to survive in the competitive medical marketplace. Porter, *Disease, Medicine, and Society in England, 1550–1860* (Cambridge: Cambridge University. Press, 1995), 51.

70. Lucy excuses John from deliberately manipulating her affection, however, believing that his kindness to her is "the honey of his temper," which he bestows, "like a flower, on any passing bee" (*Villette*, 341). Lucy calls his conduct toward her a "misapprehension," saying, "[H]e did not at all guess what I felt" (298). Should readers take Lucy's view at face value?

71. Shuttleworth traces Lucy's use of diagnostic terms and the ways in which she draws upon recognized medical language ("Surveillance," 323–26).

72. Sadoff reads Graham's relationship with Polly as the usurpation of the power of the father, whom Graham will eventually supplant (*Monsters of Affection*, 138).

73. Kucich views Polly's letters as an example of the disruption of the pas-   179
sion-repression concept in which repression is "the expressive sign of desire's
potency" (*Repression in Victorian Fiction*, 50). Thus, Kucich argues that John and
Paulina's marriage is something of a let-down.

74. Cohen claims that the novel foregrounds storytelling as a game in
order to display the power of "nonpersonal sociability" (*Professional Domesticity*,
69). In Anderson's reading, John is a model of professionalism, if an undesirable
one, but Lucy's narrative breaks down the opposition between home and away
(*Powers of Distance*, 51, 61). Kucich recognizes the considerable power of Lucy's
position as confidante (*Repression in Victorian Fiction*, 82). Shuttleworth claims
that Lucy's narrative shows the "tenuous process of negotiation" between inner
and outer life ("Surveillance," 332).

75. Lucy comments on representation in art at a gallery, when she claims
that "an original and good picture was just as scarce as an original and good
book" (*Villette*, 187), and at the play, where she is moved by the genuine power
of Vashti's acting but withholds Vashti's real name.

76. Kucich, *Repression in Victorian Fiction*, 70.

77. *Fraser's Magazine*, "Medical Quackery," 265; "On Quackery," 371; and
"Quackery and the Quacked," 652.

78. In *Professional Domesticity*, Cohen describes Mme. Beck's school as an
inauthentic home and John as part of a false romance plot. To Shaw, foreign is a
"deprivileged term," and she argues that Brontë uses "foreign characters as types
or emblems of what Lucy is not" ("Narrative Surveillance," 827–28).

79. "I've lied many times" (my translation).

Chapter 4: Poisons and the Poisonous in Wilkie Collins's *Armadale*

Epigraphs: Alfred Swaine Taylor before the Select Committee of the
Chemists and Druggists Bill, in "Special Report from the Select Committee
of the Chemists and Druggists Bill, and Chemists and Druggists (No. 2) Bill;
Together with the Proceedings of the Committee, Minutes of Evidence, and
Appendix" (1865) 381 (1–46), 4; "What Is a 'Noxious Thing'?" *British Medical
Journal*, March 13, 1880, 407.

1. *Dorland's Pocket Medical Dictionary*, 24th ed., s.v. "Poison."

2. *Oxford English Dictionary*, s.v. "Poison," online edition, http://www.oed
.com, definition 1a.

3. Ibid., definitions 1b, 2, 3a.

4. Mary E. Fissell, "Making Meaning from the Margins: The New Cultural
History of Medicine," in *Locating Medical History: The Stories and Their Meaning*,
ed. Frank Husman and John Harley Warner (Baltimore, MD: Johns Hopkins
University Press, 2004), 377.

5. Jacques Derrida, "Plato's Pharmacy," in *Dissemination*, by Derrida, trans.
Barbara Johnson (Chicago: University of Chicago Press, 1981), 63–171.

180   6. Judith Knelman, *Twisting in the Wind: The Murderess and the English Press* (Toronto: University of Toronto Press, 1998), 53.

7. Ibid.

8. Peter W. J. Bartrip, "How Green Was My Valence? Environmental Arsenic Poisoning and the Victorian Domestic Ideal," *English Historical Review* 109, no. 433 (September 1994): 893. The Pharmaceutical Society (now Royal Pharmaceutical Society) was founded in 1841. The 1852 Pharmacy Act created a register of chemists and druggists, and the 1868 Pharmacy Act mandated registration and exams for those calling themselves chemists, druggists, or pharmaceutical chemists.

9. Rebecca Stern, *Home Economics: Domestic Fraud in Victorian England* (Columbus: Ohio State University Press, 2008), 91.

10. Ibid., 94. In food adulteration, any foreign substance is undesirable but not necessarily poisonous.

11. Although Pamela K. Gilbert asserts that "identity is fluid and multiple, and resists naming," in Gilbert's work (as in Stern's) poison's identity seems stable. Gilbert, *Disease, Desire, and the Body in Victorian Women's Popular Novels* (Cambridge: Cambridge University Press, 1997), 1.

12. Wilkie Collins, *Armadale*, ed. John Sutherland (London: Penguin Classics, 2004). All in-text references to *Armadale* are to this edition. Lyn Pykett addresses the sensation novel (into which category *Armadale* falls) as a genre that transgresses categories, although not medical ones. Although Pykett finds a "gap between the domestic ideology and social practice," she asserts that the role of women is defined by discourses such as medicine and is "continually in the process of construction." Pykett, *The "Improper" Feminine: The Women's Sensation Novel and the New Woman Writing* (London: Routledge: 1992), 13. Pykett refers to the work of theorists such as William Acton and Henry Maudsley and thus tends to grant medicine exaggerated and monolithic power.

13. Piya Pal-Lapinski, "Chemical Seductions: Exoticism, Toxicology, and the Female Poisoner in *Armadale* and *The Legacy of Cain*," in *Reality's Dark Light: The Sensational Wilkie Collins*, ed. Maria K. Bachman and Don Richard Cox (Knoxville: University of Tennessee Press, 2003), 95.

14. Ibid., 100. Pal-Lapinski connects the borderland of poisons to that of racial otherness in the characters Lydia Gwilt and Ozias Midwinter. For a discussion of gender and imperialism, see also Monica M. Young-Zook, "Wilkie Collins's Gwilt-y Conscience: Gender and Colonialism in *Armadale*," in *Victorian Sensations: Essays on a Scandalous Genre*, ed. Kimberley Harrison and Richard Fantina (Columbus: Ohio State University Press, 2006), 234–46.

15. According to the Arsenic Act of 1851, arsenic was to be dyed blue or black for easy identification, but many witnesses before the select committees in 1857 and in 1865 reported that coloring was unreliable, and Taylor testified that chemists could separate the color from the arsenic. Alfred Swaine Taylor before the Select Committee on the Sale of Poisons, "Report from the Select

Committee of the House of Lords on the Sale of Poisons, &c. Bill Together 181 with the Proceedings of the Committee, Minutes of Evidence and Index," HL (1857) 294 (3–133).

16. Tanya Pollard, "Beauty's Poisonous Properties," *Shakespeare Studies* 27 (1998): 188.

17. Select Committee on the Sale of Poisons, "Report" (1857), 31.

18. Ibid., 113.

19. Ibid., 117, 50, 53.

20. Ibid., 25.

21. John Sutherland, introduction to *Armadale*, by Wilkie Collins (London: Penguin Classics, 2004), ix.

22. Select Committee on the Sale of Poisons, "Report" (1857), 130.

23. Select Committee of the Chemists and Druggists Bill, "Special Report" (1865), 4.

24. Robert Christison, "The Address in Therapeutics," *British Medical Journal*, August 14, 1858, 672.

25. Ibid., 674. What is here called hydrocyanated volatile oil is popularly called cyanide.

26. Ibid. This is a variety of hemlock plant, well known to be poisonous. Anecdotally, the roots are said to have been mistaken for parsnips, with fatal results.

27. Ibid.

28. Ibid.

29. Sutherland, introduction to *Armadale*, xvi. Sutherland also claims that Collins was influenced by the Yelverton bigamy case and the Tichborne impersonation case (x).

30. Knelman points to Victorian concern over a supposed rash of domestic poisoning by women during the 1840s, and she mentions the cases of poisoners Betty Eccles (1843), Sarah Dazely (1843), Eliza Joyce (1844), Sarah Freeman (1845), Mary Ann Milner (1847), Mary May (1848), Mary Ann Geering (1849), Rebecca Smith (1849), and Sarah Chesham (1851), all of whom were hanged as poisoners (*Twisting in the Wind*, 55).

31. Ibid., 62, 64.

32. Mary S. Hartman, *Victorian Murderesses: A True History of Thirteen Respectable French and English Women Accused of Unspeakable Crimes* (New York: Shocken, 1977), 131.

33. Hartman contends that stereotypes could harm or help a woman accused of poisoning. Ibid., 41, 158.

34. Karin Jacobson, "Plain Faces, Weird Cases: Domesticating the Law in Collins's *The Law and the Lady* and the Trial of Madeleine Smith" in *Reality's Dark Light: The Sensational Wilkie Collins*, ed. Maria K. Bachman and Don Richard Cox (Knoxville: University of Tennessee Press, 2003), 283.

35. In his 1895 *The Female Offender* (trans. William Ferrero [Littleton, CO: Rothman, 1980]), Cesare Lombroso calls female poisoners "monsters" (147).

182

36. I.114 Parl. Deb. (3d ser.) (1851), 1300.

37. Ibid., 422.

38. Select Committee on the Sale of Poisons, "Report" (1857), 97.

39. Ibid., 22, 9. This discussion focuses on white powder arsenic, although accidental poisonings from other arsenic-containing products, such as wallpapers, were well-known. For a discussion of environmental poisoning with arsenic, see Bartrip, "How Green."

40. Select Committee on the Sale of Poisons, "Report," (1857), 9.

41. Select Committee of the Chemists and Druggists Bill, "Special Report" (1865), 6.

42. Ibid., 10.

43. "Alcohol a Poison," *Twice a Week: An Illustrated London Journal of Entertaining Literature and Useful Information*, May 1862, 64.

44. Michael Diamond, *Victorian Sensation; Or, the Spectacular, the Shocking and the Scandalous in Nineteenth-Century Britain* (London: Anthem, 2003), 176; Bartrip, "How Green," 894.

45. Select Committee on the Sale of Poisons, "Report" (1857), 13.

46. Ibid.

47. "Arsenic-Eating and Arsenic Poisoning," *Chamber's Journal of Popular Literature, Science, and Arts*, August 1861, 117, 115.

48. Select Committee of the Chemists and Druggists Bill, "Special Report" (1865), 15.

49. Sutherland in his introduction to *Armadale* and Diamond in *Victorian Sensation* connect Collins's Oldershaw with real-life cosmetics quack and fraud artist Madame Rachel, who was eventually imprisoned. Tammy A. Whitlock connects the Madame Rachel trial with anxiety about women as consumers in the public sphere and about consumer culture. Whitlock, "'Taint upon Them': The Madame Rachel Case, Fraud, and Retail Trade in Nineteenth-Century England," *Victorian Review* 24 (1998): 29–51.

50. As Lyn Pykett points out, 1857 was the date of the Matrimonial Causes Act and an important year in the agitation about prostitution and fallen women (*"Improper" Feminine*, 62).

51. Lilian R. Furst claims that medical women have been represented as quacks since the medieval period. She examines Victorian physician Sophia Jex-Blake's 1869 pamphlet, "Medicine as a Profession for Women," which explicitly attacks this stereotype. Furst, *Women Healers and Physicians: Climbing a Long Hill* (Lexington: University Press of Kentucky, 1997), 3–4. For a discussion of early modern women and pharmaceuticals, see Pollard, "Beauty's Poisonous Properties."

52. William H. Helfand, *Quack, Quack, Quack: The Sellers of Nostrums in Prints, Posters, Ephemera and Books* (New York: Grolier, 2002), 174–75.

53. Ibid., 165.

54. I.114 Parl. Deb. (3d ser.) (1851), 1300.

55. Select Committee on the Sale of Poisons, "Report" (1857), 44.

56. Thomas D. Mitchell, *Materia Medica and Therapeutics: Ample Illustrations of*   183
Practice in All the Departments of Medical Science and Very Copious Notes of Toxicology,
rev. ed. (Philadelphia: Lippincott, 1857), 65–69. Witnesses in the report by the
Select Committee on the Sale of Poisons also referred to oil of bitter almonds,
which contains prussic acid.

57. Mitchell, *Materia Medica*, 767, 772.

58. Ibid., 725.

59. Ibid., 736.

60. Select Committee on the Sale of Poisons, "Report" (1857), 34.

61. Ibid., 59.

62. Select Committee of the Chemists and Druggists Bill, "Special Report"
(1865), 15.

63. Diamond, *Victorian Sensation*, 207. The *London Review*'s review of *Armadale*
complains that Lydia is a sensation novel cliché and that her "changes of mood
are always such as is easy to detect and represent." Review of *Armadale* by Wilkie
Collins, *London Review of Politics, Society, Literature, Art, and Science*, June 16, 1866,
681. The *Reader*'s review says that Lydia "is always in a most degraded state of
heart and mind" but picks up on Collins's medical theme: "[W]e are not inclined
to quarrel with the author for the extraordinary ability with which he dissects
evil minds, any more than we should find fault with the first practitioner of the
age for having performed a successful operation." Review of *Armadale* by Wilkie
Collins, *Reader*, June 2, 1866, 538.

64. Select Committee on the Sale of Poisons, "Report" (1857), 94.

65. Mitchell, *Materia Medica*, 630.

66. Select Committee on the Sale of Poisons, "Report" (1857), 49.

67. Ibid., 64.

68. "Coleridge and Opium-Eating," *Blackwoods Edinburgh Magazine*, January
1845, 130.

69. "Opium Traffic," *Dublin University Magazine*, July 1857, 60.

70. Ibid.

71. Diamond, *Victorian Sensation*, 166.

72. Ibid., 167.

73. Ibid., 168.

74. Select Committee on the Sale of Poisons, "Report" (1857), 137. In
"How Green Was My Valence," Bartrip also notes the ongoing issue of commercial poisoning throughout the nineteenth century.

75. Select Committee of the Chemists and Druggists Bill, "Special Report"
(1865), 1.

76. "Popular Poisons," *Sharpe's London Magazine of Entertainment and Instruction*,
November 1864, 257–60. In "Poisonous Plots: Women Sensation Novelists and
Murderesses of the Victorian Period" (*Victorian Review* 21, no. 2 [Winter 1995]),
Randa Helfield similarly compares female poisoners and female authors of sen-
sation novels in light of contemporary views of femininity.

184   77. "Popular Poisons," 258.

78. Ibid., 259.

79. Pykett, *"Improper" Feminine*, 47. Pamela K. Gilbert argues that sensation fiction is about transgression, the "violation of the domestic body, with class and gender transgression, and most importantly, with the violation of the privileged space of the reader/voyeur, with the text's reaching out to touch the reader's body" (*Disease, Desire*, 4). Nick Rance contends that Collins, like Henry Mayhew, complicates the middle-class ideology of propriety and self-help through characters such as Anne Catherick, who display the "immorality of conventional morality." Rance, "Wilkie Collins in the 1860s: The Sensation Novel and Self-Help," in *Nineteenth-Century Suspense: From Poe to Conan Doyle*, ed. Clive Bloom, Brian Docherty, Jane Gibb, and Keith Shand (New York: St. Martin's, 1988), 56. Winifred Hughes's *The Maniac in the Cellar: Sensation Novels of the 1860s* (Princeton: Princeton University Press, 1980) also explores issues of gender and transgression in sensation fiction.

80. Ann French Dalke, "The Shameless Woman Is the Worst of Men: Sexual Aggression in Nineteenth Century Sensation Novels," *Studies in the Novel* 18, no. 3 (1986): 299.

81. Ibid.

Chapter 5: The Quackery of Arthur Conan Doyle

Epigraphs: C. S. Hall, "Abstract of an Address: The Aspects of Medicine as a Profession, and on the Training and Work of Medical Men," *British Medical Journal*, July 18, 1885, 94; William Osler, "Aequanimitas," in *Aequanimitas with Other Addresses to Medical Students, Nurses and Practitioners of Medicine* (1904), available online at http://mcgovern.library.tmc.edu/data/www/html/people/osler /AQ/AQ.htm; Pasquale Accardo, *Diagnosis and Detection: The Medical Iconography of Sherlock Holmes* (Cranbury, NJ: Associated University Presses, 1987), 13.

1. Ely Liebow, *Dr. Joe Bell: Model for Sherlock Holmes* (Bowling Green, OH: Bowling Green University Press, 1982), 172–74. For additional material on the Bell-Holmes connection, see also Accardo, *Diagnosis and Detection*; Paula J. Reiter, "Doctors, Detectives, and the Professional Ideal: The Trial of Thomas Neill Cream and the Mastery of Sherlock Holmes," *College Literature* 35, no. 3 (Summer 2008): 57–95; Martin Booth, *The Doctor and the Detective: A Biography of Sir Arthur Conan Doyle* (New York: Thomas Dunne/St. Martin's, 2000); Daniel Stashower, *Teller of Tales: The Life of Arthur Conan Doyle* (New York: Holt, 1999); and Alvin E. Rodin and Jack D. Key, *Medical Casebook of Doctor Arthur Conan Doyle: From Practitioner to Sherlock Holmes and Beyond* (Malabar, FL: Krieger, 1984).

2. Susan Cannon Harris, "Pathological Possibilities: Contagion and Empire in the Sherlock Holmes Stories," *Victorian Literature and Culture* 31, no. 2 (2003): 459. According to Harris, Holmes's medicine has imperialist implications. Through Holmes, she argues, Doyle "demonstrates his fidelity to the ideologies

of racial difference and moral supremacy that sustained the British Empire and   185
the public support without which it could not survive" (457).

3. Ibid., 459.

4. Ibid., 461.

5. Reiter, "Doctors, Detectives," 74. Original italics.

6. Ibid., 87.

7. Ibid.

8. Maria Cairney, "The Healing Art of Detection: Sherlock Holmes and the Disease of Crime in the *Strand* Magazine," *Clues: A Journal of Detection* 26, no. 1 (Fall 2007): 63.

9. Holmes critics sometimes abbreviate "The Adventure of the Speckled Band" as SPEC; however, in this chapter the abbreviated title "The Speckled Band" is preferred.

10. Rodin and Key, *Medical Casebook*, 160. Daniel Stashower in *Teller of Tales* similarly views incidents in *The Stark Munro Letters* as autobiographical, even putting Mrs. Munro's statement about Cullingworth's "doubtful antecedents" into the chapter title describing Doyle and his mother's conflict over George T. Budd (43).

11. Rodin and Key, *Medical Casebook*, 26–27.

12. Booth, *Doctor and the Detective*, 78, 81–82.

13. Ibid., 79, 81.

14. Booth, *Doctor and the Detective*, 83; Rodin and Key, *Medical Casebook*, 28.

15. Rodin and Key, *Medical Casebook*, 29.

16. Ibid., 36–38.

17. Ibid., 38.

18. Booth, *Doctor and the Detective*, 89, 96. Booth speculates that Doyle's appointment as an examiner for an insurance company may have been due to club connections (96) and that Doyle's membership in a scientific society "had not only intellectual advantage but a social and professional one as well" (97).

19. Ibid., 87.

20. Rodin and Key show that Doyle's medical writing offered a very nuanced view of medical breakthroughs, viewing medical progress as "sometimes real and sometimes illusionary" (*Medical Casebook*, 105).

21. This device appears in novels by authors from Jonathan Swift and Daniel Defoe to Wilkie Collins and Bram Stoker.

22. Arthur Conan Doyle, *The Stark Munro Letters*, reprint of the 1895 edition by Appleton, http://etext.lib.virginia.edu/toc/modeng/public/DoyStar.html. All in-text references are to this edition.

23. Cullingworth's comparison to lower animals and to demons anticipates *Dracula*, which is often read as a specter of degeneration. For a discussion of degeneration, see Daniel Pick, *Faces of Degeneration: A European Disorder, 1848–1918* (Cambridge: Cambridge University Press, 1989); and Stephen Jay Gould, *Ever Since Darwin: Reflections in Natural History* (New York: Norton, 1992).

186   24. Lilian R. Furst, *Between Doctors and Patients: The Changing Balance of Power* (Charlottesville: University of Virginia Press, 1988), 2.

25. Ibid., 56, 179.

26. Ibid., 206.

27. Mary Poovey, *Uneven Developments: The Ideological Work of Gender in Mid-Victorian England* (Chicago: University of Chicago Press, 1988), 47.

28. Ian A. Burney, *Bodies of Evidence: Medicine and the Politics of the English Inquest, 1830–1926* (Baltimore, MD: Johns Hopkins University Press, 2000), 70.

29. "The Title of 'Doctor,'" *Lancet*, May 29, 1880, 862.

30. "Provident Dispensaries Suicidal to the Profession," *Lancet*, February 12, 1887, 351.

31. Ibid.

32. "The 'Doctor,'" *Lancet*, April 16, 1887, 791.

33. Rodin and Key, *Medical Casebook*, 160.

34. For a discussion of the traditional epithets of quackery, see William H. Helfand, *Quack, Quack, Quack: The Sellers of Nostrums in Prints, Posters, Ephemera and Books* (New York: Grolier, 2002), 17–19, and the introduction to this volume.

35. "The Adventure of the Speckled Band," in *The Adventures of Sherlock Holmes*, by Arthur Conan Doyle (Harmondsworth, UK: Penguin, 1981), 172. All in-text references are to this edition.

36. Harris, "Pathological Possibilities," 460.

37. In "Sherlock Holmes and Clinical Reasoning" (in *Teaching Literature and Medicine*, ed. Anne Hunsaker Hawkins and Marilyn Chandler McEntyre [New York: MLA, 2000]), Kathryn Montgomery draws parallels between Watson's casebook and her own medical students' casebooks as part of a course designed to explore clinical reasoning in the Holmes stories. Montgomery identifies both the logic and the illogic of Holmes and Watson's methods.

38. Reiter, "Doctors, Detectives," 58.

39. Thomas A. Sebeok and Jean Umiker-Sebeok, "'You Know My Method': A Juxtaposition of Charles S. Peirce and Sherlock Holmes," in *The Sign of Three: Dupin, Holmes, Peirce*, ed. Umberto Eco and Thomas A. Sebeok, 11–54 (Bloomington: Indiana University Press, 1983). In "To Guess or not to Guess" (another chapter in Eco and Sebeok, *Sign of Three*), Massimo A. Bonfantini and Giampaolo Proni explore the interrelationship of logic and guesswork in *A Study in Scarlet*, identifying a complex mixture of deduction, induction, and abduction rather than the simple deduction Holmes describes (119–34). Agnès Botz argues that Holmes provides only the *"illusion of science"* because imagination is Holmes's (and Doyle's) strength. Botz, "'Cut the Poetry, Watson': Science and Fiction in the Sherlock Holmes Stories," *Cahiers Victoriens et Edouardiens* 46 (1997), 99. Original italics.

40. Sebeok and Umiker-Sebeok, "You Know My Method," 44.

41. Other stories have also been addressed in terms of a conflict between reason and irrationality. In "The Hound of the Baskervilles," for example, Jesse

Oak Taylor-Ide finds that Holmes occupies a liminal space between science and   187
irrationality; thus, Holmes is a paradox that allows "different epistemologies"
to coexist. Taylor-Ide, "Ritual and the Liminality of Sherlock Holmes and *The
Sign of Four*," *ELT: English Literature in Transition* 48, no. 1 (2005): 67. In "Degeneration," Nils Clausson argues that the "Hound of the Baskervilles" represents
two antithetical late nineteenth-century movements: the detective story, which
draws upon scientific positivism, and the Gothic story; thus, the plot works "to
create mystery and then to give the illusion—but only the illusion—of solving
it." Clausson, "Degeneration, Fin-de-Siècle Gothic, and the Science of Detection: Arthur Conan Doyle's *The Hound of the Baskervilles* and the Emergence of
the Modern Detective Story," *JNT: Journal of Narrative Theory* 35, no. 1 (Winter 2005): 78. In "The Case of the Anomalous Narrator," Clausson describes
the plot of "The Musgrave Ritual" as held in "tension between two contrary
pressures: the desire to dispel, or even explain away, mystery and the recognition that real mysteries can't be rationally explained." Clausson, "The Case of
the Anomalous Narrator: Gothic Surmise and Trigonometric Proof in Arthur
Conan Doyle's 'The Musgrave Ritual,'" *Victorian Newsletter* 107 (Spring 2005): 6.

   42. "A Scandal in Bohemia," in *The Adventures of Sherlock Holmes*, by Arthur
Conan Doyle (Harmondsworth, UK: Penguin, 1981), 9.

   43. Ibid., 12.

   44. Ibid., 13.

   45. Accardo, *Diagnosis and Detection*, 109.

   46. Ibid., 31. Oliver Wendell Holmes Sr. was the father of Oliver Wendell Holmes Jr., a well-known jurist. Joseph A. Kestner notes Doyle's interest
in America as a developing world power and claims that Doyle visited jurist
Oliver Wendell Holmes's grave. It may be that Doyle visited the grave of the
physician Oliver Wendell Holmes (the father), because Doyle predeceased the
son. Kestner, *Sherlock's Men: Masculinity, Conan Doyle, and Cultural History* (Aldershot, UK: Ashgate, 1997), 8.

   47. Accardo, *Diagnosis and Detection*, 32.

   48. Ibid., 39.

   49. John A. Hodgson, "The Recoil of 'The Speckled Band': Detective Story
and Detective Discourse," *Poetics Today* 13, no. 2 (Summer 1992): 310.

   50. Like Cullingworth, Roylott shows signs of degeneracy in his affinity for and resemblance to animals. Roylott's old family has sunk into poverty
through vice (Doyle, "The Speckled Band," 168), just as his manor house has
fallen into ruins (179).

   51. Reiter, "Doctors, Detectives," 58.

   52. In *Sherlock's Men*, Joseph A. Kestner argues that "The Speckled Band"
contrasts two forms of masculinity: "the colonial, eastern, aristocratic model
of Roylott, and the middle-class gentlemanly nature of Holmes and Watson,"
although this division is troubled by Holmes and Watson's secrecy, Helen's
early death, and the widespread threat of crime (91). Audrey Jaffe notes the

188   instability of gentlemanly and professional identity in "The Man with the Twisted Lip" and concludes that "truth matters less than the production and maintenance of the proper fiction." Jaffe, "Detecting the Beggar: Arthur Conan Doyle, Henry Mayhew, and the 'Man with the Twisted Lip,'" in "The Margins of Identity in Nineteenth-Century England," special issue, *Representations* 31 (Summer 1990): 108.

53. Hodgson, "Recoil of 'The Speckled Band,'" 316.

54. Angus McLaren, *A Prescription for Murder: The Victorian Serial Killings of Dr. Thomas Neill Cream* (Chicago: University of Chicago Press, 1993), 87.

55. Ibid., 87.

56. Ibid., 100.

57. Judith R. Walkowitz, *City of Dreadful Delight: Narratives of Sexual Danger in Late-Victorian London* (Chicago: University of Chicago Press, 1992), 99, 185.

58. Ibid., 210.

59. Susan Sontag, *Illness as Metaphor* (New York: Farrar, Straus, Giroux, 1978), 6.

60. Keith Allan and Kate Burridge, *Forbidden Words: Taboo and the Censoring of Language* (Cambridge: Cambridge University Press, 2006), 212.

61. Kestner addresses Holmes's failure to save his client in "The Five Orange Pips" in the context of anxiety about the power of American organizations and goes on to discuss the motif of failure in "A Scandal in Bohemia," "A Case of Identity," "The Copper Beeches," and "The Speckled Band," arguing that Holmes's defeat "reveals the fissure in the putative stability of Victorian conceptions about maleness" (*Sherlock's Men*, 13). These stories all appear in *The Adventures of Sherlock Holmes* alongside "The Speckled Band."

Conclusion: The In-Laws

Epigraph: John Corry, "Quack Doctors Dissected," in *Quack Doctors Dissected; or, A New, Cheap, and Improved Edition of Corry's Detector of Quackery* (Gloucester, UK, [1805?]), 37. Original italics.

1. *Vernon Galbray; or, The Empiric: The History of a Quack Dentist* (London, 1875), 9.

2. British Dental Association, "History of the BDA," British Dental Association website, http://www.bda.org/about-the-bda/history.aspx.

3. Talfourd Jones, "Hypodermic or Subcutaneous Medication," *British Medical Journal*, September 26, 1885, 582.

4. C. S. Kilham, "Case of Cocaine Poisoning," *Lancet*, January 1, 1887, 712.

5. "Three-Pennyworth of Morphine," *British Medical Journal*, June 12, 1886, 1121.

6. J. B. Mattison, "Cocaine Dosage and Cocaine Addiction," *Lancet*, May 21, 1887, 1025.

7. Ibid.

Accardo, Pasquale. *Diagnosis and Detection: The Medical Iconography of Sherlock Holmes.* Cranbury, NJ: Associated University Presses, 1987.

Ackerknecht, Erwin H. *A Short History of Medicine.* Revised Edition. Baltimore, MD: Johns Hopkins University Press, 1982. First published 1955.

Allan, Keith, and Kate Burridge. *Forbidden Words: Taboo and the Censoring of Language.* Cambridge: Cambridge University Press, 2006.

Anderson, Amanda. *The Powers of Distance: Cosmopolitanism and the Cultivation of Detachment.* Princeton: Princeton University Press, 2001.

Arata, Stephen. *Fictions of Loss in the Victorian Fin de Siècle: Identity and Empire.* Cambridge: Cambridge University Press, 1996.

Austin, J. L. *How to Do Things with Words.* Edited by J. O. Urmson and Marina Sbisà. 2nd ed. Cambridge, MA: Harvard University Press, 1975.

Axton, William F. "Religious and Scientific Imagery in *Bleak House.*" *Nineteenth-Century Fiction* 22, no. 4 (1968): 349–59.

Bailey, Brian. *The Resurrection Men: A History of the Trade in Corpses.* London: Macdonald, 1991.

Bailin, Miriam. *The Sickroom in Victorian Fiction: The Art of Being Ill.* Cambridge: Cambridge University Press, 1994.

Bartrip, Peter W. J. "How Green Was My Valence? Environmental Arsenic Poisoning and the Victorian Domestic Ideal." *English Historical Review* 109, no. 433 (September 1994): 891–913.

Barzun, Jacques, ed. *Burke and Hare: The Resurrection Men.* Metuchen, NJ: Scarecrow, 1974.

Beer, Gillian. *Darwin's Plots: Evolutionary Narrative in Darwin, George Eliot and Nineteenth-Century Fiction.* London: Routledge, 1983.

Blackwoods Edinburgh Magazine. "Coleridge and Opium-Eating." January 1845, 117–32.

British Dental Association. "History of the BDA." British Dental Association website, http://www.bda.org/about-the-bda/history.aspx.

Bonfantini, Massimo A., and Giampaolo Proni. "To Guess or not to Guess." In *The Sign of Three: Dupin, Holmes, Peirce,* edited by Umberto Eco and Thomas A. Sebeok, 119–34. Bloomington: Indiana University Press, 1983.

Booth, Martin. *The Doctor and the Detective: A Biography of Sir Arthur Conan Doyle.* New York: Thomas Dunne/St. Martin's, 2000. First published 1997 by Hodder and Stoughton as *The Doctor, the Detective and Arthur Conan Doyle: A Biography of Arthur Conan Doyle.*

190   Botting, Fred. "Frankenstein and the Art of Science." In *Making Monstrous: Frankenstein, Criticism, Theory*, by Botting, 164–85. Manchester: Manchester University Press, 1991.

Botz, Agnès. "'Cut the Poetry, Watson': Science and Fiction in the Sherlock Holmes Stories." *Cahiers Victoriens et Édouardiens* 46 (1997): 91–101.

Bradley, James, and Marguerite Dupree. "A Shadow of Orthodoxy? An Epistemology of British Hydropathy, 1840–1858." *Medical History* 47 (2003): 173–94.

Brantlinger, Patrick. *Fictions of State: Culture and Credit in Britain, 1694–1994.* Ithaca, NY: Cornell University Press, 1996.

British Medical Journal. "The First of October." September 25, 1858, 811–12.

———. "Three-Pennyworth of Morphine." June 12, 1886, 1120–21.

———. "What Is a 'Noxious Thing'?" March 13, 1880, 407–8.

Brodie, Benjamin. "Homoeopathy." *Fraser's Magazine*, September 1861, 337–40.

Brontë, Charlotte, *Jane Eyre.* New York: Random House, 1943. First published 1847.

———. *Villette.* New York: Signet-Penguin, 1987. First published 1853.

Brown, F. J. "Quackery in Opposition to Truth." *British Medical Journal*, October 30, 1858, 916.

Brown, P. S. "Social Context and Medical Theory in the Demarcation of Nineteenth-Century Boundaries." In Bynum and Porter, *Medical Fringe*, 216–33.

Burney, Ian A. *Bodies of Evidence: Medicine and the Politics of the English Inquest, 1830–1926.* Baltimore, MD: Johns Hopkins University Press, 2000.

———. *Poison, Detection, and the Victorian Imagination.* Manchester: Manchester University Press, 2006.

Butler, Marilyn. "*Frankenstein* and Radical Science." In *Frankenstein*, edited by J. Paul Hunter, 302–13. New York: Norton, 1996.

Bynum, W. F. *Science and the Practice of Medicine in the Nineteenth Century.* Cambridge: Cambridge University Press, 1994.

Bynum, W. F., and Roy Porter, eds. *Medical Fringe and Medical Orthodoxy, 1750–1850.* London: Croom Helm, 1987.

———. *William Hunter and the Eighteenth-Century Medical World.* Cambridge: Cambridge University Press, 1985.

Cairney, Maria. "The Healing Art of Detection: Sherlock Holmes and the Disease of Crime in the *Strand* Magazine." *Clues: A Journal of Detection* 26, no. 1 (Fall 2007): 62–74.

Caldwell, Janis McLarren. *Literature and Medicine in Nineteenth-Century Britain: From Mary Shelley to George Eliot.* Cambridge: Cambridge University Press, 2004.

Carter, K. Codell. "The Concept of Quackery in Early Nineteenth Century British Medical Periodicals." *Journal of Medical Humanities* 14, no. 2 (1993): 89–96.

Chamber's Journal of Popular Literature, Science, and Arts. "Arsenic-Eating and Arsenic Poisoning," August 1861, 115–17.

Chapman, John. "Medical Despotism." *Westminster Review*, April 1856, 292–309.   191
Christison, Robert. "The Address in Therapeutics." *British Medical Journal*, August 14, 1858, 671–75.
Clausson, Nils. "The Case of the Anomalous Narrator: Gothic Surmise and Trigonometric Proof in Arthur Conan Doyle's 'The Musgrave Ritual.'" *Victorian Newsletter* 107 (Spring 2005): 5–10.
———. "Degeneration, Fin-de-Siècle Gothic, and the Science of Detection: Arthur Conan Doyle's *The Hound of the Baskervilles* and the Emergence of the Modern Detective Story." *JNT: Journal of Narrative Theory* 35, no. 1 (Winter 2005): 60–87.
Cohen, Monica F. *Professional Domesticity in the Victorian Novel: Women, Work and Home*. Cambridge: Cambridge University Press, 1998.
Collins, Wilkie. *Armadale*. Edited by John Sutherland. London: Penguin Classics, 2004. First published 1866.
———. *The Woman in White*. Oxford: World's Classics, 1999. First published 1860.
Colón, Susan E. *The Professional Ideal in the Victorian Novel: The Works of Disraeli, Trollope, Gaskell, and Eliot*. New York: Palgrave-Macmillan, 2007.
Cooter, Roger. Introduction to *Studies in the History of Alternative Medicine*, edited by Roger Cooter, x–xx. New York: St. Martin's Press, 1988.
Corry, John. "Quack Doctors Dissected." In *Quack Doctors Dissected; or, A New, Cheap, and Improved Edition of Corry's Detector of Quackery*, 37. Gloucester, UK, [1805?].
Dalke, Anne French. "The Shameless Woman Is the Worst of Men: Sexual Aggression in Nineteenth Century Sensation Novels." *Studies in the Novel* 18, no. 3 (1986): 291–303.
Daly, Nicholas. *Modernism, Romance and the Fin de Siècle: Popular Fiction and British Culture*. Cambridge: Cambridge University Press, 1999.
Dames, Nicholas. "The Clinical Novel: Phrenology and *Villette*." *Novel* 29, no. 3 (Spring 1996): 367–90.
Deadly Adulteration and Slow Poisoning Unmasked. London, 1839.
Derrida, Jacques. "Plato's Pharmacy." In *Dissemination*, by Jacques Derrida, 63–171. Translated by Barbara Johnson. Chicago: University of Chicago Press, 1981. First published in *Tel Quel* nos. 32, 33 (1968).
Diamond, Michael. *Victorian Sensation; Or, the Spectacular, the Shocking and the Scandalous in Nineteenth-Century Britain*. London: Anthem, 2003.
Dickens, Charles. *Bleak House*. New York: Bantam, 1992. First published 1853.
———. Preface to the first edition of *Bleak House*, xxvi–xxvii. New York: Bantam, 1992. First published 1853.
———. *Little Dorrit*. Edited by Stephen Wall and Helen Small. Rev. ed. London: Penguin, 2003. First published 1857.
Douglas, Hugh. *Burke and Hare: The True Story*. London: Hale, 1993.
Doyle, Arthur Conan. "The Adventure of the Speckled Band." In *The Adventures of Sherlock Holmes*, by Arthur Conan Doyle, 165–90. Harmondsworth, UK: Penguin, 1981. First published 1892.

192 ————. "A Scandal in Bohemia." In *The Adventures of Sherlock Holmes*, by Arthur Conan Doyle, 9–32. Harmondsworth, UK: Penguin, 1981. First published 1892.

————. *The Stark Munro Letters*. Reprint of the 1895 edition by Appleton. Electronic Text Center, University of Virginia Library, 1995. http://etext.lib. virginia.edu/toc/modeng/public/DoyStar.html.

Dublin University Magazine. "Opium Traffic." July 1857, 59–66.

Eliot, George. *Middlemarch*. Harmondsworth, UK: Penguin, 1985. First published 1872.

"An Expostulation." In MacGregor, *History of Burke and Hare*, 288–89. First published 1828.

Fasick, Laura. "Dickens and the Diseased Body in *Bleak House*." *Dickens Studies Annual* 24 (1996): 135–51.

Fissell, Mary E. "Making Meaning from the Margins: The New Cultural History of Medicine." In *Locating Medical History: The Stories and Their Meaning*, edited by Frank Husman and John Harley Warner, 364–89. Baltimore, MD: Johns Hopkins University Press, 2004.

Flannery, Michael A. Introduction to *The English Physician*, by Nicholas Culpeper, 1–29. Edited by Michael A. Flannery. Tuscaloosa: University of Alabama Press, 2007.

Fleishman, Avrom. *Fiction and the Ways of Knowing: Essays on British Novels*. Austin: University of Texas Press, 1978.

Foucault, Michel. *Birth of the Clinic: An Archaeology of Medical Perception*. Translated by A. M. Sheridan Smith. New York: Vintage, 1994.

————. *Discipline and Punish: The Birth of the Prison*. Translated by Alan Sheridan. New York: Vintage, 1995.

————. *History of Sexuality: An Introduction, Volume 1*. Translated by Robert Hurley. New York: Vintage, 1990.

Fraser's Magazine. "Medical Quackery and Mr. John St. John Long." October 1830, 264–65.

————. "On Quackery, Twaddle, and Other Offences." April 1831, 368–75.

————. "The Philosophy of Burking." February 1832, 52–65.

————. "Quackery and the Quacked." June 1848, 645–57.

Friedman, Lester D. "Sporting with Life: *Frankenstein* and the Responsibility of Scientific Research." *Medical Heritage* 1, no. 3 (1985): 181–85.

Furst, Lilian R. *Between Doctors and Patients: The Changing Balance of Power*. Charlottesville: University of Virginia Press, 1988.

————. *Medical Progress and Social Reality: A Reader in Nineteenth-Century Medicine and Literature*. Albany: State University of New York Press, 2000.

————, ed. *Women Healers and Physicians: Climbing a Long Hill*. Lexington: University Press of Kentucky, 1997.

Gieryn, Thomas F. *Cultural Boundaries of Science: Credibility on the Line*. Chicago: University of Chicago Press, 1999.

Gilbert, Pamela K. *Disease, Desire, and the Body in Victorian Women's Popular Novels.*   193
Cambridge: Cambridge University Press, 1997.

Gilbert, Sandra, and Susan Gubar. *The Madwoman in the Attic: The Woman Writer and the Nineteenth-Century Literary Imagination.* New Haven, CT: Yale University Press, 1979.

Glover, David. *Vampires, Mummies, and Liberals: Bram Stoker and the Politics of Popular Fictions.* Durham, NC: Duke University Press, 1996.

Glover, Robert M. "Lectures on the Philosophy of Medicine: Lecture VI." *Lancet,* January 11, 1851, 35–38.

Goodlad, Lauren M. E. *Victorian Literature and the Victorian State: Character and Governance in a Liberal Society.* Baltimore, MD: Johns Hopkins University Press, 2003.

Gould, Stephen Jay. *Ever Since Darwin: Reflections in Natural History.* New York: Norton, 1992. First published 1977 by Norton.

Gurney, Michael S. "Disease as Device: The Role of Smallpox in *Bleak House.*" *Literature and Medicine* 9 (1990): 79–92.

Hack, Daniel. *The Material Interests of the Victorian Novel.* Charlottesville: University of Virginia Press, 2005.

Hall, C. S. "Abstract of an Address: The Aspects of Medicine as a Profession, and on the Training and Work of Medical Men." *British Medical Journal,* July 18, 1885, 94.

Harris, Susan Cannon. "Pathological Possibilities: Contagion and Empire in the Sherlock Holmes Stories." *Victorian Literature and Culture* 31, no. 2 (2003): 447–66.

Hart, Ernest. "The Condition of Our State Hospitals." *Fortnightly Review,* December 1, 1865, 217–26.

Hartman, Mary S. *Victorian Murderesses: A True History of Thirteen Respectable French and English Women Accused of Unspeakable Crimes.* New York: Shocken, 1977.

Hay, Douglas. "Property, Authority and the Criminal Law." In Douglas Hay, Peter Linebaugh, John G. Rule, E. P. Thompson, and Cal Winslow, *Albion's Fatal Tree: Crime and Society in Eighteenth-Century England,* 17–64. New York: Pantheon, 1975.

Helfand, William H. *Quack, Quack, Quack: The Sellers of Nostrums in Prints, Posters, Ephemera and Books.* Winterhouse edition. New York: Grolier, 2002.

Helfield, Randa. "Poisonous Plots: Women Sensation Novelists and Murderesses of the Victorian Period." *Victorian Review* 21, no. 2 (Winter 1995): 161–88.

Herbert, Christopher. "Filthy Lucre: Victorian Ideas of Money." *Victorian Studies* 44 (2002): 185–213.

Hindle, Maurice. "Vital Matters: Mary Shelley's *Frankenstein* and Romantic Science." *Critical Survey* 2, no. 1 (1990): 29–35.

Hippocrates. "Greek Medicine: The Hippocratic Oath." History of Medicine Division, National Library of Medicine, National Institutes of Health, Department of Health and Human Services, available online at http://www.mlm.mih.gov/hmd/greek/greek_oath.html.

194   *History of the London Burkers.* London, 1832.

Hodgson, John A. "The Recoil of 'The Speckled Band': Detective Story and Detective Discourse." *Poetics Today* 13, no. 2 (Summer 1992): 309–24.

Hughes, Winifred. *The Maniac in the Cellar: Sensation Novels of the 1860s.* Princeton: Princeton University Press, 1980.

Jacobson, Karin. "Plain Faces, Weird Cases: Domesticating the Law in Collins's *The Law and the Lady* and the Trial of Madeleine Smith." In *Reality's Dark Light: The Sensational Wilkie Collins,* edited by Maria K. Bachman and Don Richard Cox, 283–312. Knoxville: University of Tennessee Press, 2003.

Jaffe, Audrey. *The Affective Life of the Average Man: The Victorian Novel and the Stock-Market Graph.* Columbus: Ohio State University Press, 2010.

———. "Detecting the Beggar: Arthur Conan Doyle, Henry Mayhew, and 'The Man with the Twisted Lip.'" In "The Margins of Identity in Nineteenth-Century England," special issue, *Representations* 31 (Summer 1990): 96–117.

Johnson, Barbara. "My Monster/My Self." *Diacritics* 12 (1982): 2–10.

Jones, Talfourd. "Hypodermic or Subcutaneous Medication." *British Medical Journal,* September 26, 1885, 581–87.

Jordanova, Ludmilla. "Melancholy Reflection: Constructing an Identity for Unveilers of Nature." In *Frankenstein: Creation and Monstrosity,* edited by Stephen Bann, 60–76. London: Reaktion, 1994.

Kestner, Joseph A. *Sherlock's Men: Masculinity, Conan Doyle, and Cultural History.* Aldershot, UK: Ashgate, 1997.

Ketterer, David. *Frankenstein's Creation: The Book, the Monster, and Human Reality.* ELS Monograph Series. Victoria: University of Victoria Press, 1979.

Kilham, C. S. "Case of Cocaine Poisoning." *Lancet,* January 1, 1887, 712.

Knelman, Judith. *Twisting in the Wind: The Murderess and the English Press.* Toronto: University of Toronto Press, 1998.

Kucich, John. *Repression in Victorian Fiction: Charlotte Brontë, George Eliot, and Charles Dickens.* Berkeley: University of California Press, 1987.

Kuhn, Thomas S. *The Structure of Scientific Revolutions.* Chicago: University of Chicago Press, 1962.

Lancet. "The 'Doctor.'" April 16, 1887, 790–91.

———. "Important Educational Changes." June 12, 1858, 586.

———. "Lord Palmerston's Declaration on Medical Reform." July 9, 1853, 36–37.

———. "Morison versus Moat." December 20, 1851, 586.

———. "The Profession and Its Dignity." March 27, 1858, 318–19.

———. "Provident Dispensaries Suicidal to the Profession." February 12, 1887, 351.

———. "Quackery on Its Death-Bed." October 16, 1858, 405–6.

———. "Quacks and Their Impostures." December 24, 1853, 604–5.

———. "Scandalous Proceedings of the Advertising Quacks." November 19, 1853, 489–90.

———. "The Title of 'Doctor.'" May 29, 1880, 862.   195

Lawrence, Christopher. "Incommunicable Knowledge: Science, Technology, and the Clinical Art in Britain, 1850–1914." *Journal of Contemporary History* 20, no. 4 (1985): 503–20.

———. *Medicine in the Making of Modern Britain, 1700–1920.* London: Routledge, 1994.

Lawrence, Christopher, and George Weisz. "Medical Holism: The Context." In *Greater than the Parts: Holism in Biomedicine, 1920–1950,* edited by Christopher Lawrence and George Weisz, 1–24. Oxford: Oxford University Press, 1998.

[Lewes, G. H.] "Physicians and Quacks." *Blackwood's Magazine,* February 1862, 165–79.

Liebow, Ely. *Dr. Joe Bell: Model for Sherlock Holmes.* Bowling Green, OH: Bowling Green University Press, 1982.

Linebaugh, Peter. "The Tyburn Riot against the Surgeons." In Douglas Hay, Peter Linebaugh, John G. Rule, E. P. Thompson, and Cal Winslow, *Albion's Fatal Tree: Crime and Society in Eighteenth-Century England,* 65–117. New York: Pantheon, 1975.

Loeb, Lori Anne. *Consuming Angels: Advertising and Victorian Women.* Oxford: Oxford University Press, 1994.

Lombroso, Cesare. *The Female Offender.* Translated by William Ferrero. Littleton, CO: Rothman, 1980. First published 1895.

London Review of Politics, Society, Literature, Art, and Science. Review of *Armadale* by Wilkie Collins. June 16, 1866, 680–81.

Lorentzen, Eric G. "'Obligations of Home': Colonialism, Contamination, and Revolt in *Bleak House.*" *Dickens Studies Annual* 34 (2004): 155–84.

Loudon, Irvine. "'The Vile Race of Quacks with Which This Country Is Infested.'" In Bynum and Porter, *Medical Fringe and Medical Orthodoxy,* 106–28.

MacGregor, George. *The History of Burke and Hare and of the Resurrectionist Times.* Glasgow, 1884.

Mallen, Richard D. "George Eliot and the Precious Mettle of Trust." *Victorian Studies* 44 (2001): 41–75.

Marshall, Tim. *Murdering to Dissect: Grave-Robbing, Frankenstein and the Anatomy Literature.* Manchester: Manchester University Press, 1995.

Mattison, J. B. "Cocaine Dosage and Cocaine Addiction." *Lancet,* May 21, 1887, 1024–26.

McLaren, Angus. *A Prescription for Murder: The Victorian Serial Killings of Dr. Thomas Neill Cream.* Chicago: University of Chicago Press, 1993.

Mellor, Anne K. *Mary Shelley: Her Life, Her Fiction, Her Monsters.* New York: Routledge, 1988.

Mighall, Robert. *A Geography of Victorian Gothic Fiction: Mapping History's Nightmares.* Oxford: Oxford University Press, 2003.

Miller, D. A. *The Novel and the Police.* Berkeley: University of California Press, 1988.

196   Mitchell, Thomas D. *Materia Medica and Therapeutics: Ample Illustrations of Practice in All the Departments of Medical Science and Very Copious Notes of Toxicology.* Revised edition. Philadelphia: Lippincott, 1857.

Moers, Ellen. "Female Gothic." In *The Endurance of Frankenstein: Essays on Mary Shelley's Novel,* edited by George Levine and U. C. Knoepflmacher, 77–87. Berkeley: University of California Press, 1974.

Montag, Warren. "'The Workshop of Filthy Creation': A Marxist Reading of *Frankenstein.*" In *Frankenstein,* edited by Johanna M. Smith, 384–95. Boston: Bedford/St. Martin's, 2000.

Montgomery, Kathryn. "Sherlock Holmes and Clinical Reasoning." In *Teaching Literature and Medicine,* edited by Anne Hunsaker Hawkins and Marilyn Chandler McEntyre, 299–305. New York: MLA, 2000.

Neve, Michael. "Orthodoxy and Fringe: Medicine in Late Georgian Bristol." In Bynum and Porter, *Medical Fringe and Medical Orthodoxy,* 40–55.

Nunokawa, Jeff. *The Afterlife of Property: Domestic Security and the Victorian Novel.* Princeton: Princeton University Press, 1994.

Osler, William. "Aequanimitas." In *Aequanimitas with Other Addresses to Medical Students, Nurses and Practitioners of Medicine.* Facsimile of 1904 edition by H. K. Lewis. John P. McGovern Historical Collections and Research Center, Texas Medical Center Library. http://mcgovern.library.tmc.edu/data/www/html/people/osler/AQ/AQ.htm.

Pal-Lapinski, Piya. "Chemical Seductions: Exoticism, Toxicology, and the Female Poisoner in *Armadale* and *The Legacy of Cain.*" In *Reality's Dark Light: The Sensational Wilkie Collins,* edited by Maria K. Bachman and Don Richard Cox, 94–130. Knoxville: University of Tennessee Press, 2003.

[Paterson, David?]. "Letter to the Lord Advocate, disclosing the accomplices, secrets and other facts relative to the Late Murders; with a correct account of the manner in which the anatomical schools are supplied with subjects." In *Burke and Hare: The Resurrection Men,* edited by Jacques Barzun, 242–73. Metuchen, NJ: Scarecrow, 1974. First published 1829.

Peterson, M. Jeanne. *The Medical Profession in Mid-Victorian London.* Berkeley: University of California Press, 1978.

Pick, Daniel. *Faces of Degeneration: A European Disorder, 1848–1918.* Cambridge: Cambridge University Press, 1989.

Pike, Judith. "Resurrection of the Fetish in *Gradiva, Frankenstein,* and *Wuthering Heights.*" In *Romantic Women Writers: Voices and Countervoices,* edited by Paula R. Feldman and Theresa M. Kelly, 150–68. Hanover, NH: University Press of New England, 1995.

Pollard, Tanya. "Beauty's Poisonous Properties." *Shakespeare Studies* 27 (1998): 187–210.

Poovey, Mary. *The Proper Lady and the Woman Writer.* Chicago: University of Chicago Press, 1984.

———. *Uneven Developments: The Ideological Work of Gender in Mid-Victorian England.* Chicago: University of Chicago Press, 1988.

Porter, Roy. "Before the Fringe: 'Quackery' and the Eighteenth-Century Medi-   197
cal Market." In *Studies in the History of Alternative Medicine*, edited by Roger
Cooter, 1–27. New York: St. Martin's Press, 1988.

———. *Disease, Medicine, and Society in England, 1550–1860.* 2nd ed. Cambridge: Cambridge University Press, 1995. First edition published 1987 by Macmillan.

———. *Quacks: Fakers and Charlatans in Medicine.* Stroud, Gloucestershire: Tempus, 2003. First published 1989.

———. "William Hunter: A Surgeon and a Gentleman." In *William Hunter and
the Eighteenth-Century Medical World*, edited by W. F. Bynum and Roy Porter,
7–34. Cambridge: Cambridge University Press, 1985.

Posen, Solomon. *The Doctor in Literature: Satisfaction or Resentment?* Oxford: Radcliffe, 2005.

Pykett, Lyn. *The "Improper" Feminine: The Women's Sensation Novel and the New Woman
Writing.* London: Routledge, 1992.

Quain, Richard. "History and Progress of Medicine." *British Medical Journal*, October 24, 1885, 775–81.

Rance, Nick. "Wilkie Collins in the 1860s: The Sensation Novel and Self-
Help." In *Nineteenth-Century Suspense: From Poe to Conan Doyle*, edited by Clive
Bloom, Brian Docherty, Jane Gibb, and Keith Shand, 46–63. New York:
St. Martin's, 1988.

Rappaport, Erika Diane. *Shopping for Pleasure: Women in the Making of London's West
End.* Princeton: Princeton University Press, 2000.

Rauch, Alan. "The Monstrous Body of Knowledge in Mary Shelley's *Frankenstein*." *Studies in Romanticism* 34 (1995): 227–53.

Reader, The. Review of *Armadale* by Wilkie Collins. June 2, 1866, 538–39.

Reiter, Paula J. "Doctors, Detectives, and the Professional Ideal: The Trial of
Thomas Neill Cream and the Mastery of Sherlock Holmes." *College Literature* 35, no. 3 (Summer 2008): 57–95.

Richardson, Ruth. *Death, Dissection and the Destitute.* London: Routledge, 1987.

Roach, Mary. *Stiff: The Curious Lives of Human Cadavers.* New York: Norton, 2003.

Robbins, Bruce. *Secular Vocations: Intellectuals, Professionalism, Culture.* London:
Verso, 1993.

———. "Telescopic Philanthropy: Professionalism and Responsibility in *Bleak
House*." In *Bleak House: Charles Dickens*, edited by Jeremy Tambling, 139–62.
New York: St. Martin, 1998.

Rodin, Alvin E., and Jack D. Key. *Medical Casebook of Doctor Arthur Conan Doyle:
From Practitioner to Sherlock Holmes and Beyond.* Malabar, FL: Krieger, 1984.

Rogers, Philip. "Fraudulent Closure in *Villette's* 'Faubourg Clotilde.'" *Brontë Studies*
30 (2005): 125–30.

Rosenberg, Charles E., and Janet Golden, eds. *Framing Disease: Studies in Cultural
History.* New Brunswick, NJ: Rutgers University Press, 1992.

Rothfield, Lawrence. *Vital Signs: Medical Realism in Nineteenth-Century Fiction.* Princeton:
Princeton University Press, 1992.

198   Ruth, Jennifer. *Novel Professions: Interested Disinterest and the Making of the Professional in the Victorian Novel*. Columbus: Ohio State University Press, 2006.

Sadoff, Dianne F. *Monsters of Affection: Dickens, Eliot, and Brontë on Fatherhood*. Baltimore, MD: Johns Hopkins University Press, 1982.

Scarry, Elaine. *The Body in Pain: The Making and Unmaking of the World*. Oxford: Oxford University Press, 1985.

Schiappa, Edward. *Defining Reality: Definitions and the Politics of Meaning*. Carbondale: Southern Illinois University Press, 2003.

Schwarzbach, F. S. "*Bleak House*: The Social Pathology of English Life." *Literature and Medicine* 9 (1990): 93–104.

Sebeok, Thomas A., and Jean Umiker-Sebeok. "'You Know My Method': A Juxtaposition of Charles S. Peirce and Sherlock Holmes." In *The Sign of Three: Dupin, Holmes, Peirce*, edited by Umberto Eco and Thomas A. Sebeok, 11–54. Bloomington: Indiana University Press, 1983.

Self-Respect. "Social Position of the Profession." *Lancet*, October 2, 1858, 365.

Sharpe's London Magazine of Entertainment and Instruction. "Popular Poisons." November 1864, 257–60.

Shaw, Margaret L. "Narrative Surveillance and Social Control in *Villette*." *SEL* 34, no. 4 (1994): 813–33.

Shelley, Mary. *Frankenstein*. Edited with notes by Johanna M. Smith. 2nd ed. Boston: Bedford/St. Martin's, 2000. First published 1831.

Shultz, Suzanne M. *Body Snatching: The Robbing of Graves for the Education of Physicians*. Jefferson, NC: McFarland, 1992.

Shuttleton, David E. *Smallpox and the Literary Imagination, 1660–1820*. Cambridge: Cambridge University Press, 2007.

Shuttleworth, Sally. "'The Surveillance of the Sleepless Eye': The Constitution of Neurosis in *Villette*." In *One Culture: Essays in Science and Literature*, edited by George Levine, 313–35. Madison: University of Wisconsin Press, 1987.

Smiles, Samuel. *Self-Help, with Illustrations of Character, Conduct, and Perseverance*. Edited by Peter W. Sinnema. Oxford: World's Classics, 2002. First published 1859.

Smith, Crosbie. "*Frankenstein* and Natural Magic." In *Frankenstein, Creation, and Monstrosity*, edited by Stephen Bann, 39–59. London: Reaktion, 1994.

Smith, Johanna M. "'Cooped Up' with 'Sad Trash': Domesticity and the Sciences in *Frankenstein*." In *Frankenstein*, edited by Johanna M. Smith, 313–33. 2nd ed. Boston: Bedford/St. Martin, 2000.

Sontag, Susan. *Illness as Metaphor*. New York: Farrar, Straus, Giroux, 1978.

Stallybrass, Peter, and Allon White. *The Politics and Poetics of Transgression*. Ithaca, NY: Cornell University Press, 1986.

Stashower, Daniel. *Teller of Tales: The Life of Arthur Conan Doyle*. New York: Holt, 1999.

Stern, Rebecca. *Home Economics: Domestic Fraud in Victorian England*. Columbus: Ohio State University Press, 2008.

Sutherland, John. Introduction to *Armadale*, by Wilkie Collins, vii–xxvi. London: Penguin Classics, 2004.   199

Swenson, Kristine. *Medical Women and Victorian Fiction*. Columbia: University of Missouri Press, 2005.

Tambling, Jeremy. Introduction to *Bleak House: Charles Dickens*, 1–28. Edited by Jeremy Tambling. New York: St. Martin's, 1998.

Taylor-Ide, Jesse Oak. "Ritual and the Liminality of Sherlock Holmes and *The Sign of Four*." *ELT: English Literature in Transition*. 48, no. 1 (2005): 55–70.

Toumey, Christopher P. "The Moral Character of Mad Scientists: A Cultural Critique of Science." *Science, Technology and Human Values* 17, no. 4 (1992): 411–37.

Twice a Week: An Illustrated London Journal of Entertaining Literature and Useful Information. "Alcohol a Poison." May 1862, 64.

Vasbinder, Samuel Holmes. *Scientific Attitudes in Mary Shelley's* Frankenstein. Ann Arbor, MI: UMI Research Press, 1984.

Vernon Galbray; or, The Empiric: The History of a Quack Dentist. London, 1875.

Vrettos, Athena. "From Neurosis to Narrative: The Private Life of the Nerves in *Villette* and *Daniel Deronda*." *Victorian Studies* 33, no. 4 (1990): 551–79.

Walkowitz, Judith R. *City of Dreadful Delight: Narratives of Sexual Danger in Late-Victorian London*. Chicago: University of Chicago Press, 1992.

Weisz, George. *Divide and Conquer: A Comparative History of Medical Specialization*. Oxford: Oxford University Press, 2006.

Wells, Susan. *Out of the Dead House: Nineteenth-Century Women Physicians and the Writing of Medicine*. Madison: University of Wisconsin Press, 2001.

Welsh, Alexander. *George Eliot and Blackmail*. Cambridge, MA: Harvard University Press, 1985.

Westminster Review. "Anatomy." January 1829, 116–44.

———. "Regulation of Anatomy." April 1832, 482–96.

"What Is Our Land Come To?" In *Burke and Hare: The Resurrection Men*, edited by Jacques Barzun, 345. Metuchen, NJ: Scarecrow, 1974.

Whitlock, Tammy A. "'Taint upon Them': The Madame Rachel Case, Fraud, and Retail Trade in Nineteenth-Century England." *Victorian Review* 24 (1998): 29–51.

"William Burke." In MacGregor, *History of Burke and Hare*, 291.

Williams, Raymond. *Marxism and Literature*. Oxford: Oxford University Press, 1977.

Wood, J. G. "Inner Life of a Hospital." *Cornhill*, April 1862, 462–77.

Young-Zook, Monica M. "Wilkie Collins's Gwilt-y Conscience: Gender and Colonialism in *Armadale*." In *Victorian Sensations: Essays on a Scandalous Genre*, edited by Kimberley Harrison and Richard Fantina, 234–46. Columbus: Ohio State University Press, 2006.

Index